X Marks the Spot

Praise for X Marks the Spot

'X Marks the Spot is a fascinating book; both as a greatest hits compendium of archaeological breakthroughs, and as a subtle examination of how 'discovery' has evolved. In tracing Archaeology's journey – from imperialist scholars, polyglot geniuses, and marauding adventurers, up to the modern-day collaboration of multi-decade projects – Professor Michael Scott shows that 'discovery' often required more than just courage, persistence, and talent, but also geopolitical pressure, local knowledge, dubious ethical choices, and pure blind luck!'

Greg Jenner, historian, author and host of
You're Dead to Me podcast

'If you love Indiana Jones, this is the real thing. Michael Scott celebrates the fusion of scholarship and adventure in a book full of both.'

Dan Snow, historian, author and host of *History Hit* podcast

'Through eight of history's most audacious acts of discovery, Michael Scott tells us the story of archaeology itself. This is a thrilling investigation of humankind's obsession with the physical remains of its past.'

Suzannah Lipscomb, historian, broadcaster and author

'An essential read for anyone with even a fleeting interest in exploring the past. Michael weaves a world around each discovery, which tells us as much about modern attitudes as it does about the ancient civilisations unearthed. I couldn't put it down!'

Janina Ramirez, historian, broadcaster and author

'Do you wish you knew more about some of the most fascinating archaeological discoveries made around the world? Then pick up Michael Scott's fabulous, learned, smart and never-dusty new book immediately. It's wonderful.'

Natalie Haynes, classicist, broadcaster and author

'With his fedora and bullwhip, one of the most famous heroes in popular culture is an archaeologist: Indiana Jones. Now here are some of the larger-than-life stories that lie behind the films, comics, novels and video games: Hiram Bingham on the heights of Machu Picchu, Aurel Stein in Kashgar, Mary Leakey at Olduvai Gorge and many more. These are the tales of some of the most extraordinary discoveries in archaeology, in deserts, jungles, and even under water. Michael Scott tells these stories in an affable, scholarly and accessible way with an expert eye, giving us incisive portraits of the fascinating, often difficult and driven characters who expanded the frontiers of knowledge, whilst also examining their actions in light of our modern values and debates about restitution, display and ongoing scholarly investigation.'

Michael Wood, historian, broadcaster and author

'Vivid, pacey and full of fascinating detail, X Marks the Spot is a riveting adventure through time, propelled by Michael Scott's excellent scholarship and accessible writing style.'

Alice Loxton, historian, author and presenter at History Hit TV

'A masterful storyteller. These days, serious archaeology sometimes shies away from tales of exploration and adventure. The colonial overtones and sensational headlines are too much of a risk, and too raw for a discipline steeped in difficult imperial origins. In *X Marks The Spot*, Michael Scott manages to pull off an inspired feat – to capture the excitement and wonder of discovery, but to situate these astonishing tales in their complex, messy historical realities. *X Marks the Spot* takes us around the world and through deep prehistory, but always leads us back to the pressing questions of our time. Whose history is it? And who should tell the stories of these ancient times? It's a page-turner and eye-opener. It will inspire you to wonder more at the world and its people – both present and past.'

Mary-Ann Ochota, anthropologist, broadcaster and author

'Who knew that the Uluburun shipwreck's finds include 32 land snails? Or that there may be a further 6,000 suits of armour yet to uncover in addition to the Chinese imperial Terracotta Warriors already unearthed? Or that Kenya's Olduvai Gorge preserves footprints proving that the featherless biped – us – walked on two feet far earlier than previously imagined? Or that the Rosetta Stone contains not three, but four inscribed texts? All that and much, much more is known and beautifully related here by the indefatigable Michael Scott, famous both as an archaeological scholar and as a communicator, an Indiana Jones *de nos jours* and for our time. *X Marks the Spot* hits the spot.'

Paul Cartledge, historian and author

'Michael Scott deftly captures the trials and triumphs of archaeology, from the privations of life on a dig to the thrill of discovery. Wide-ranging in time and space, *X Marks the Spot* is a fascinating mix of history, biography and – above all – adventure.'

Toby Wilkinson, Egyptologist and author

'I am thoroughly absorbed by Michael Scott's wonderful new book – a generous, warm retelling of eight world-changing archaeological finds, from the Rosetta Stone to the Altai Princess via Machu Picchu. It's a tour de force of scholarship and an unputdownable read.'

Katherine Schofield, historian

'Scott's new book certainly hits the spot. It tells the fascinating story of how archaeological digs are never simply fact-finding missions but are driven by the same present-day concerns that we find in any other human activity. An impressive piece, with an incisive analysis of a broad sweep of examples, all written in an engaging and lively style.'

Jerry Toner, classicist

'Scott's highly personal and passionate account of eight very different discoveries delves deep into two centuries and more of archaeology. As he explores the wonder and excitement of our love affair with the past, unearthing extraordinary lost cultures, and celebrating those determined men and women who work in often gruelling conditions to help bring them to light, the common thread that binds humanity across space and time becomes increasingly apparent. Scott's enthusiasm is palpable, and his compelling, charismatic book will undoubtedly inspire a whole new generation of future archaeologists. Who knows what they will find?'

David Stuttard, classicist, theatre director and author

'Stylish, witty, and informed by wide ranging scholarship, X Marks the Spot tells intensely exciting stories, while illuminating the profound links between the past and the present. An absolute joy to read.'

Harry Sidebottom, historian and author

'A gripping account of some of history's most extraordinary archaeological discoveries. Filled with larger than life figures that give Indiana Jones a run for his money. A triumph of a book!'

Tristan Hughes, author, producer of History Hit podcast, and host of *The Ancients* podcast

'Michael Scott meticulously explores eight different discoveries from the Rosetta Stone in Egypt to the unravelling of the Keros Enigma. He explains how the discovery of the past is always creating a shifting appreciation of who we are across the background of the rich tapestry of human history. I much enjoyed and learned a great deal from this book.'

Charles Freeman, historian and author

X Marks the Spot

The Story of Archaeology in Eight Extraordinary Discoveries

MICHAEL SCOTT

HODDER &
STOUGHTON

First published in Great Britain in 2023 by Hodder & Stoughton
An Hachette UK company

2

Copyright © Michael Scott 2023
Maps © Mike Parson/Barking Dog Art 2023

Epigraph quote from *Indiana Jones and the Last Crusade* (1989),
directed by Steven Spielberg, screenplay by Jeffrey Boam

The right of Michael Scott to be identified as the Author of the Work has been
asserted by him in accordance with the Copyright, Designs and Patents Act 1988.

A CIP catalogue record for this title is available from the British Library

Hardback ISBN 9781529367768
Trade Paperback ISBN 9781529367775
eBook ISBN 9781529367782

Typeset in Sabon by Hewer Text UK Ltd, Edinburgh
Printed and bound in Great Britain by Clays Ltd, Elcograf S.p.A.

Hodder & Stoughton policy is to use papers that are natural, renewable
and recyclable products and made from wood grown in sustainable
forests. The logging and manufacturing processes are expected to
conform to the environmental regulations of the country of origin.

Hodder & Stoughton Ltd
Carmelite House
50 Victoria Embankment
London EC4Y 0DZ

www.hodder.co.uk

This book is dedicated to my wife, Cassie,
who has helped me discover the sunshine again.
With all my love and deepest thanks
MWNLCC

*'So forget any ideas you've got about lost cities,
exotic travel, and digging up the world.
We do not follow maps to buried treasure,
and "X" never, ever, marks the spot.'*

Indiana Jones, speaking to his
class of archaeology students
Indiana Jones and the Last Crusade, 1989

Contents

Introduction
Who Cares About the Past?

The first Roman Emperor, Augustus, soon after winning sole control of the Roman world in 30 BCE, was in the city of Alexandria in Egypt. While there, he requested to visit the grave of the man who had given the city its name: King Alexander the Great, who had conquered all in his sway between Greece and India some three hundred years earlier. Augustus was shown into the tomb and stood in front of Alexander's decayed body. In one set of ancient sources, he is respectful and careful: laying a golden crown on Alexander's mummified head and pouring flowers on his remains.[1] In another, he runs his hands gleefully and clumsily over the ancient flesh of the man he sought now to outdo, and in doing so, broke off Alexander's nose.[2] Ancient seekers of the past, it seems, may have been no more careful than the modern archaeologist Hollywood character Indiana Jones, who also managed to destroy nearly every archaeological site he walked into.[3]

Augustus was not alone in wanting to see, touch, honour and compare himself to the great heroes of the past. Alexander the Great himself, during his lifetime, had visited the temple of Athena at the city of Troy and is said to have taken armour left there from the time of the epic Trojan war a millennium before. Having left some of his own armour in its place (seemingly feeling it was an equitable exchange), Alexander had soldiers carry these ancient pieces of armour into battle before him as symbols of his impending victory and glory.[4]

1

But the ancient Greek and Roman interest in the past was, thankfully, about far more than providing PR opportunities and symbolic trinkets for their latest would-be conquerors. The past – and its physical remnants scattered around them – anchored the ancients' very sense of how the world had come into being. Herodotus, the fifth-century-BCE historian, used the presence of marine shell fossils in the mountains of Egypt to argue that once upon a time that area of land had been under water.[5] The fossilised bones of dinosaurs and mammoths, discovered by the Greeks across the Mediterranean world, were interpreted as physical evidence for the heroes, giants and monsters who had lived before the age of man and become the stuff of Greek myth and legend.[6] As their literary greats outlined the genealogy of the world and its gods since the time it emerged from primeval Chaos, the objects the Greeks discovered around them thus provided evidence for the reality of these stories. Not for nothing did the Greeks, as a result, worship many of the relics they found and build temples in the ancient ruins that littered their landscape as a link between their present and their past, between their mortality and the divine and powerful that had shaped and ruled their world. The Romans were no different. The past, while to be sure a place where they may have done things differently, was no foreign country. It was a critical element of who the Greeks and Romans were in the present.

The Greeks called the stories they told and the search for the objects they found and worshipped 'archaiologia' – the 'logos' being the 'account, reckoning, explanation, discussion' of the 'archaios', the 'primordial, the long ago, the past, the old, the ancient'. Archaiologia included, as described in one of Plato's fourth-century-BCE dialogues, 'the genealogies of heroes and of ordinary men, and stories of the foundations of cities'.[7] Nor was this archaiologia the preserve of intellectuals and scholars. Pausanias, the second-century-CE tour-guide writer, recalls how he witnessed workmen at the sanctuary of Olympia, while preparing the ground for a new victory monument for some Roman bigwig, excavate ancient fragments of armour and horse-riding gear.[8] Virgil, the great Roman epic poet, speaking of one of Rome's early battles, reflects that one day it will be a farmer who, while in the middle of ploughing his fields, will find the 'spears corroded by foul rust', or, with his hoe, 'hit upon empty helmets', 'gaping at the heroic bones he has disturbed'.[9] Anyone could – and would – be interested in, and have the chance to come face to face with, the physical objects of the past. The ancients came across them in every part of their landscape.[10] They used, honoured, worshipped, studied and wrote about them.[11] They even dreamt about them.[12]

No human civilisation or community has not similarly been fascinated by the physical relics of those who came before them. We have always related ourselves to the past. The past creates the storyboard on which we play out our lives, and we are lost if we move forward without it. To quote a well-known phrase: 'the past is never dead, it's not even past'.[13] It is that thirst for relating and anchoring ourselves to the past that makes *archaiologia* an innate part of what it is to be human. The irony is that it has only fairly recently (in historical terms) been once again called that. The Romans translated *archaiologia* into Latin as *antiquitates*, which echoed through into English and other European languages.[14] As a result, for many centuries students of the physical relics of the past were *antiquaries* and *antiquarians* rather than archaeologists.[15] Indeed, it is only really since the late eighteenth century that archaeology has been (re)born as a term and a recognised discipline, developing at a rapid pace ever since.[16]

This book is dedicated to this quintessentially human itch to find out about, and relate ourselves to, the physical remnants of our pasts. It focuses on the period over the last two hundred or so years during which archaeology has once again been taken up as the battle cry for this endeavour, and has developed its own character, methods and self-awareness. In each of the following eight stories, which speak of beguiling discoveries from different ancient cultures made in different parts of the world by different individuals and groups during that time period, we will investigate how

3

and why the discoverer(s) came to look for what they did. We will follow their footsteps in the extraordinary moments of discovery. We will sweat alongside them, and sometimes the generations that followed, in their efforts to recover, study and understand what was found. We will pursue the evolution of that understanding through to the modern day, and we will ask finally what the discovery now adds to our picture of the past. And through these eight stories I want not only to underline how much searching for our past is an innate part of what it is to be human, but to make three crucial points about what is at stake in the study of the past.

The first is that what we look for, find and subsequently study is always an active choice. How could it be otherwise? We simply cannot look for, excavate and study everything – there isn't the time or indeed the money. So, of course, a choice and prioritisation about what pasts to look into, where to look for them, what kind of evidence to prioritise and how to interpret it is inevitable. But at the same time, that active choice is actually guided by a series of bigger shifting tectonic forces that govern what we choose to look for in our pasts at different times. As we shall see in each of our stories of discovery, world events, geopolitical forces, political and cultural values, as well as shifting academic fascinations and foibles, which swirled around our discoverers at the time they were formulating their thoughts and plans, have played a major role in influencing what has been looked for and when it has been discovered – and indeed by whom. This is not to take away from the complex fascinating characters of our discoverers, nor from their often epic and gruelling adventures and achievements. But they worked and explored within a powerful context that often shaped them, primed them and guided them towards the great discoveries they made. As such we must remember that the past we look for is all too often the product of our present.

The second key point running through these eight stories of discovery is that the way we search for the past has changed beyond all recognition, particularly during the last 200 years in which archaeology has been reborn and developed as a discipline.

Part of the spur to the rebirth of archaeology was the quantum leap forward in the early nineteenth century in our understanding of how to study the ground underneath our feet. For it was then that pioneering geologists and proto-archaeologists developed for the first time an understanding of stratigraphy: the ability to read and date different levels of the soil as they dug, and thus to provide an accurate timeline for the pasts they were uncovering. This crucial skill turned the previously potted search for bits of our past into a scientific map of the antiquity of the human race and paved the way for the mid-nineteenth-century birth of a timeline of human societal evolution based around the materials mankind had worked with: the 'Stone' Age, the 'Bronze' Age and the 'Iron' Age. Combined with simultaneous revolutions in our understanding of the evolution of the human species itself, symbolised by Charles Darwin's publication of *On the Origin of Species* in 1859, these great leaps forward propelled archaeology on a trajectory of rapid and exciting discovery and growth.

Such development was not of course – and still is not – without its growing pains. Each of our eight stories of discovery situates our discoverers in a particular era of archaeology's evolution. These men and women, as they strain to make their breakthroughs, are often simultaneously both exemplars of the standard practice in the field at the time and also leaders in the development of new techniques, mindsets and, at least in more recent decades, ethics. Their stories are thus the stuff of legend but are also full of attitudes and actions from which we may recoil today. In particular, the early chapters of this book delve into stories of discoveries that were, at the time, removed from their place of origin and discovery to become the property of the discoverer (and most often the nation backing them). In some cases this happened within the context of warfare, in others as part of official permissions given at the time for excavation, and in others still as part of much more unofficial negotiations dressed up as efforts to preserve the past.[17] We will follow the stories of these discoveries through to the modern day to understand how, in some of these cases, an understanding and resolution has now been reached about how, where and by whom such discoveries should be handled, and how, in others, the sores caused by these past actions have yet to be healed. At the same time, in our later chapters, we will see how, particularly over the last seventy years, archaeological practice has evolved to consider afresh the question of ownership, care and display, alongside a much wider set of ethical questions about what can and should be excavated and studied in the first place. As a result, while in many ways we have made substantial progress, we shall see also how complex and delicate the balancing act of discovery has become.[18]

The third – and perhaps the most crucial – point this book makes is that what we do with the pasts we discover is just as important as the initial discovery and interpretation itself. In each of these eight stories, we see the discoverers making initial sense of their discoveries and publicising their version of that past to the world. That initial breakthrough on the value and meaning of the discovery sometimes came quickly and sometimes took decades. But either way the story by no means ends there. In many cases the academic study of these discoveries has never stopped, thanks to new technologies and questions that open fresh avenues and possibilities for investigation, revealing deeper truths about the discovery or indeed demanding revisions to (and in some cases scrapping of) our previous understanding. What a discovery can tell us about the past is never a finished story.

Alongside this ongoing academic discussion, it is crucial also to remember that the continually evolving meanings of the discoveries do not remain the property of the discoverers, or indeed of the generations of scholars who come to study them. Like children, the discoveries grow up and leave the nest to become part of the wider world. They, in tandem with the evolving understanding of them provided by scholars, become stories that are told and retold over time by individuals, groups, communities and nations, and as such are also refashioned, re-presented and remodelled according to the needs of those groups and their times. That ability to be changed and reshaped is, of course, one of the reasons why the past is of such value to the present, but it also makes it a challenging customer indeed. As another of my favourite sayings goes: 'Only the future is certain, the past just keeps on changing.' While archaeology as a discipline has attempted to evolve as a science that provides us with the best possible factual record and interpretation of the past (one that is always evolving as new evidence and insights come to light), its shifting image of the past stands alongside other overlapping and shifting versions of what the past means within the wider world. Indeed, an important part of archaeology's most recent development as a discipline has been in response to the need for it to continue to be part of the public debate, long after the discovery itself has been announced.

Over the course of the next eight chapters, we will cross millions of years from some of our earliest human ancestors to the remains of more recent civilisations. We will travel from the jungles of South America to the plains of Africa, from the islands of the Mediterranean to the barren deserts and frozen highlands of Central Asia and on to the vast expanse of China. We will follow military invasions accompanied by teams of academics. We will trek with individuals who headed out into the perilous unknown to search for new worlds, and with foreign adventurers who capitalised by bringing global public attention to treasures locals had long known about. We will fight alongside scholars who pushed through the many obstacles in their path to uncover the earliest moments of humankind. We will lament with those whose accidental discoveries benefited the world, but not them. We will empathise with communities who feel their heritage and history has been taken from them. We will hold our breath as artefacts are slowly persuaded to give up their secrets, thanks to evolving technologies and the herculean efforts of global networks of scholars working over decades. And we will be challenged by the past not just in terms of understanding what happened, but in terms of what should happen next. In short, in contrast to what Indiana Jones told his students archaeology was about, we *will* be discovering lost cities, engaging in exotic travel, digging up the world and even, on occasion, following a treasure map. But the one thing we can all agree on is that X, never, ever, marks the spot.

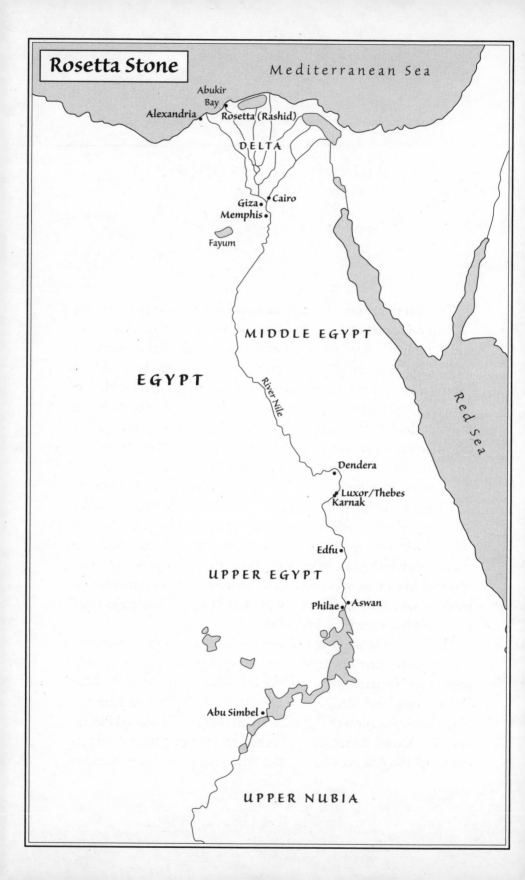

1

Making Stones Speak

The first time I saw the Rosetta Stone, it was taller than me. Set up on a pedestal, incarcerated within a pristine glass box, and lit sympathetically by the soft glow of gallery lights, its sharp broken top edge pierced the empty air above like the peaks of Everest. I was on my first trip to the British Museum in London at the age of eight. I remember the tour guide's melodic voice cycling through the key facts about this stone. But, pressing up against the stone's glass prison, all I could focus on were the thousands of tiny symbols and letters dancing across it, making the front of this otherwise unmoveable slab of dark grey granodiorite come to life. It wasn't an Egyptian mummy – which to be honest was what we all as eight-years-olds were most interested in seeing – but the stone made an impression on me. In my mind I was picturing the people who had stood in front of the stone thousands of years ago, just like I now was, who had inscribed all those symbols and letters I was now gazing at. Who were they? What were their names? What were their lives like?

The Rosetta Stone was discovered a little short of two hundred years before I first saw it, near the Egyptian port city of Rashid (known to Westerners as Rosetta), on the western end of the Nile Delta facing the Mediterranean. On 15 July 1799, during the Napoleonic invasion of Egypt, a French lieutenant named Pierre-François Xavier Bouchard had been commanding his soldiers to build up the defences of an old dilapidated fort near Rashid.

11

Toiling in the fierce dry Egyptian summer heat to excavate material they could use to bolster the fort, his men had unearthed an
unusual block of stone from the scalding shimmering sand. The
stone was a hefty 1.1 metres in length, 75 centimetres wide and 28
centimetres thick, about half the height of a standard door, and
Lieutenant Bouchard was immediately captivated by the very
same thing I was two hundred years later: it was covered in
writing.

Following standard military procedure Bouchard informed his
superior, Michel Ange Lancret. Unlike Bouchard, Lancret was not
simply a soldier: he was also a member of the Institut d'Égypte.
The Institut had recently been set up by Napoleon Bonaparte to
study Egypt's geography, environment, culture and history, as
part of his (not to mention France's and more widely Europe's)
recent development of an interest in, and desire to be associated
with, ancient Egypt. Lancret recognised that the writing on the
stone was partly in ancient Greek, partly in Egyptian hieroglyphs
and partly in an unknown script. With his knowledge of ancient
Greek, he was able to work out that the last lines in Greek recorded
the decision to write out this text not only in Greek but also in
'sacred' and 'native' characters: in other words, this was the same
text, translated into three different languages. And one of those
languages was Egyptian hieroglyphics – a language that no one
on earth could translate at the time. It seems incredible now to
think that no one could read Egyptian hieroglyphs in 1799, but
any understanding of the language had been entirely lost from
human civilisation after the adoption of Christianity by the
Roman Empire in the fourth century CE and the abandonment of
'pagan' worship, which included the Egyptian temples and the
hieroglyphic 'sacred' language used in Egyptian religion. In the
intervening centuries – when there had been little interest in
ancient Egypt – this inability to read hieroglyphs had not been a
problem. But now that everyone was interested in ancient Egypt
again, reading ancient Egyptian texts had become a top priority.
And if – as Lancret realised standing in the sweltering Egyptian

heat – this stone had two identical texts in Greek and hieroglyphs, it might be possible to break the hieroglyphic code by comparing the two.

Lancret swiftly entrusted the stone back to Bouchard, who was to escort it to the Institut d'Égypte in Cairo for further study. He sent this message back to the scholars at the Institut, his enthusiasm and excitement for the discovery just about breaking through the understated academic tone expected in that era: 'citizen Bouchard, has discovered in the town of Rosetta some inscriptions whose examination may offer much interest'.[1] The news of the discovery – and the possibilities it offered – spread fast. By 29 July 1799, the *Courier de l'Égypte*, the official journal of the Napoleonic expedition to Egypt, reported the find by saying: 'this stone offers great interest for the study of hieroglyphic characters; perhaps it will give us the key at last'.[2] It was soon being referred to as 'the Rosetta Stone' – the key to unlocking the writing and thus the world of the ancient Egyptians.[3]

*

Soldiers rarely stop for stones, especially when fighting a campaign as arduous as Napoleon's in Egypt. But this was no simplistic land grab – the French conquest of Egypt had much loftier ambitions and ideals. In March 1798, just over a year before the Rosetta Stone was first discovered, the Directorate (*le Directoire* in French) – the group of five governing committee members who held executive power in France following the seismic revolution of 1789 – had authorised a French expedition to Egypt. After losing out to Britain in the race for control and influence in India, French authorities saw the military conquest of Egypt as a crucial riposte to France's weakening stance on the world stage.

But the other equally important purpose of the expedition was to position France as the inheritors of Egypt's rich and enticing ancient history and cultural heritage. Egypt had been part of the Ottoman Empire since the early sixteenth century, and before that it had been part of the Arab world since the seventh century. It had therefore been largely out of bounds to the West for centuries. But during the period of the European Enlightenment in the seventeenth and eighteenth centuries, the history of ancient Egypt had become an important element of Western thinking – for Western powers, Egypt provided the fundamental context for biblical narratives and, conversely, it was a source of esoteric knowledge, mystical insight and magic.[4] For instance, to copy Egyptian architecture in this period, because it was so different in style to everything in Europe at the time, was to signal that you were a free thinker, open to new and radical ideas.

The problem was that very little was actually known in Europe about ancient Egypt, its buildings, culture and history (beyond the general shape of the Pyramids of Giza, which were only just being recognised as funeral monuments rather than as the granaries of Joseph from biblical narratives), because it was so difficult and dangerous to visit. There are only fifty first-hand accounts of Western visits to Egypt between 1650 and 1800 (which compares favourably to just six in the period 1500 to 1650).[5] But twenty-seven of these accounts were by French explorers. France was quickly developing a particular affinity with ancient Egypt, not because of its biblical connotations, but because of its symbolic value as something radically different from current tradition. And as France tipped into revolution – the ultimate radical thought – in 1789, that feeling of comradeship only grew stronger.

At the same time, the other model for the French Revolution – that of the birth of the Roman Republic in which Rome had abolished its monarchy just like France had done – gave French authorities another reason to be interested in Egypt. For it was the Roman Republic (or at least the very final phase of the Republic before it collapsed into an empire under the Emperor Augustus) that had conquered Egypt in antiquity – the era of Julius Caesar and Mark Antony falling under the spell of Cleopatra. In setting its sights on Egypt, France was not only rebalancing the geopolitical map to counter modern British influence in India, but also asserting its cultural identity both as the inheritor of ancient

Egypt's mystical and radical thinking *and* as the next Roman Republic, (re)creating an empire. And best of all, in turning to Egypt, Revolutionary France could also portray itself as a liberator, freeing Egypt from the Ottoman Empire. Thus, unlike the Romans who had conquered purely for territorial gain (and, indeed, unlike the recent British conquest of India), the French could claim to be conquering Egypt in the pursuit of *liberté*. To square the irony of seeking to liberate Egypt in order to place it within its own empire, the French argued that they were ensuring Egyptian prosperity. As the French Foreign Minister Talleyrand put it in 1798:

> Egypt was a province of the Roman Republic; she must become a province of the French Republic. Roman rule saw the decadence of this beautiful country; French rule will bring it prosperity. The Romans wrested Egypt from kings distinguished in arts and science; the French will lift it from the hands of the most appalling tyrants who have ever existed.[6]

Napoleon was by this time a stunningly successful general in the French army. Born in Corsica in 1769, he had originally entered the army in 1785, just before the Revolution. By 1796, he was leading the army to dramatic victories over the Austrian forces in Italy. He was also quite a thorn in the side of the Directorate, who, concerned for their own grip on power, felt that he was becoming too popular. Packing Napoleon off to Egypt in charge of the expedition enabled the Directorate to remove Napoleon from political influence in Paris. For Napoleon, however, it was exactly what he wanted. Not only did it allow him to avoid his Revolutionary reputation being tarnished with possible involvement in the multiple plots against the Directorate that were fomenting in Paris, but it also allowed him the opportunity to cloak himself in the military success of conquest and the powerful cultural meaning of ancient Egypt. As he planned the expedition, his ancient exemplars were not the Roman Republic, but Rome's first Emperor, Augustus, who had conquered Egypt (and forced the suicide of Cleopatra and Mark Antony), and, centuries before that, Alexander the Great, who had carved out an empire that stretched from the Mediterranean to India.

Napoleon's expedition set off from Toulon on 19 May 1798. There were 17,000 soldiers and mariners, 1,000 pieces of artillery and 700 horses (Napoleon hoped to source camels when in Egypt). Joined by further ships from different ports, it became the largest expeditionary force to sail for Egypt since that of ancient Rome in the first century BCE.[7] This was no ordinary military expedition though. Given the need not only to conquer Egypt, but also to study it and become the inheritors of its ancient culture, among the soldiers was also a group known simply as *'les savants'*, 'the wise ones'.[8] One hundred and fifty-one men had been chosen from across all branches of knowledge and enquiry: surveyors, civil engineers, mechanics, mining engineers, mathematicians, naturalists, astronomers, artists, printers. Featuring some of the most knowledgeable men in France at the time, including Nicolas-Jacques Conté, the inventor of the graphite pencil, *les savants* were led by the scientist Jean-Baptiste Joseph Fourier.[9] And accompanying them was a copy of every book on Egypt available in France at that time, as well as endless pieces of scientific and measuring equipment. So worried was Napoleon about what the consequences for France would be if their intellectual *crème de la crème* were killed or captured by the British as the flotilla sailed from France to Egypt that, in order to mitigate any potential losses, *les savants* were equally spread out across the seventeen French warships. Even more cautiously, each specialist group (of surveyors, astronomers and so forth) were split across different ships to ensure that even if some ships were captured, there would be at least some specialists in each discipline arriving in Egypt – not unlike the old tradition in which direct heirs to the British throne were not allowed to travel together, to ensure the survival of the line in case of catastrophic accident in transit.

But before this group could do their work, the grislier business of conquering Egypt had to be accomplished. Napoleon arrived on the shores of Egypt near Alexandria on 1 July 1798. He wasted no time: immediately setting off towards Alexandria before the whole army had even disembarked from the ships. Alexandria was a port and trading city, garrisoned by Mamluk troops. The Mamluks, who had originally been slave armies in the Muslim world, had grown in power to create their own dynasty and had ruled Egypt and Syria from the thirteenth to the sixteenth century. They had then been conquered by, and formally made part of, the Ottoman Empire, but had been left in day-to-day charge of Egypt. By the 1790s, the Ottoman Empire was, however, in steep decline and the Mamluks were once again in effective control of Egypt and the only ones left to defend it. Their military might, however, was limited. Alexandria fell to Napoleon in just three hours on 2 July 1798, with the final elements of his army only disembarking on 3 July.

Five days after taking Alexandria, Napoleon set off with his army to take Cairo, the stronghold of the Mamluk forces. It was a punishing 200-kilometre march through Egyptian desert in the baking summer heat. The French army, in their heavy hot uniforms, were ludicrously ill equipped – many soldiers didn't even carry a water flask. The Mamluks had sabotaged most of the wells en route, leaving many of the French soldiers to die of thirst and heat exhaustion. Many committed suicide rather than face the gruelling conditions any longer. However, despite arriving in Cairo exhausted, diminished in number and low on morale, Napoleon's forces managed to defeat the Mamluk rulers of Egypt in what became known as the Battle of the Pyramids. Napoleon entered Cairo as the country's conqueror on 25 July 1798, less than a month after landing on its shores.

But Napoleon's success was short-lived. Just six days later, on 1 August 1798, the British admiral Horatio Nelson, by this time with only one eye and one arm, having lost the others in previous battles, sailed into Abukir Bay on Egypt's Mediterranean coast. His orders were to disrupt French attempts to add Egypt to their empire and generally cause them as much damage as he could. Arriving where the French fleet was moored, with most of their army hundreds of kilometres away near Cairo, Nelson decided that the smartest thing to do was not to land and try to find Napoleon's army but to inflict maximum damage on French ability to rule the seas. He promptly managed to destroy all but two of the French warships. In recognition of this stunning achievement, he was later made Lord Nelson, and in fact the coffin that he was eventually buried in was made from wood that came from the main mast of the French flagship destroyed that day.[10]

Napoleon had enough transport ships to get his troops home, but no warships to guard them. They would be sitting ducks on the open sea for the British fleet to pick off. He was therefore, suddenly, stuck in Egypt – conqueror of a land he could not now safely leave. Equally, however, the British, at this point, did not have the necessary soldiers to fight Napoleon on land, and so had to content themselves with control of the seas. Faced with this stand-off in which he could not be challenged on land but also could not leave, Napoleon turned his attention instead to the second priority of the Egyptian expedition: discovery.

He swiftly set up the Institut d'Égypte as the intellectual epicentre of *les savants* and their quest to uncover the mysteries of Egypt. Fourier, the leader of *les savants*, was made the permanent secretary of the Institut and its four branches of enquiry: maths, physical sciences, political economy, and arts and letters. The headquarters was a former Mamluk palace on the outskirts of Cairo, where the members of the Institut had their formal meetings in the rooms that used to house the harem of the Mamluk ruler.[11] It was here, just under a year later in 1799, that the first official report about the Rosetta Stone, sent by Michel Ange Lancret along with the stone to Cairo, would be read, and where many other (now infamous) insights into the Egyptian environment, culture and history would be delivered.[12]

Napoleon himself visited the Great Pyramid at Giza to see the initial work of the Institut, which had overseen the clearing of the inner chambers and maze of internal passages within the pyramid, following in the footsteps (and no doubt litter) of many who had found their way into the pyramid over the centuries to loot or just explore. French engineers estimated that there was enough stone in the Pyramids at Giza to build a wall half a metre thick and 3 metres high all the way around France.[13] Napoleon is said in some sources to have asked to be left alone in the king's chamber at the heart of the Great Pyramid, perhaps contemplating the great triumphs and creations of these ancient rulers, comparing them with what he hoped himself to achieve.

Members of the Institut were inundated with work – however, they weren't sifting through ancient treasures and artefacts, as you might imagine. Instead, their work was mostly related to understanding Egypt's terrain and how best to make use of it, as the army sought to strengthen its position in case the British did decide to land forces, as well as to improve communication and travel between major cities. In terms of ancient monuments to study in Alexandria and Cairo – bar the Pyramids and Sphinx (which was gradually being dug out of the sand) – there was relatively little of the same gigantic scale to amaze and excite. This only changed when the army, accompanied by a small group of *savants*, set out to explore Upper Egypt.[14] This southern area of Egypt was altogether totally unexplored by Western travellers and traders, for whom it had simply been too dangerous and remote to venture into. Napoleon's forces, however, moving steadily south through the late autumn and winter of 1798, were dumbstruck at the ancient gigantic wonders they saw. Huge temple complexes at Dendera, complete with ornate buildings and sculptures, took their breath away, and they were said to have burst into spontaneous applause when they saw the towering remains of the ancient city of Thebes (in modern-day Luxor) for the first time.[15] The lead *savant* of the expedition to Upper Egypt, Dominique-Vivant Denon, madly sketched out the buildings they witnessed: giant statues towering over the landscape, sky-tall temples butted up against shifting sand-dunes; ornate and beautiful buildings often half filled with sand. He later recounted that no other labour of human hand could show humanity in such splendour. As he walked in the ruins of Dendera, the Egyptians appeared to him as giants. The main problem for *les savants* as a whole, it seems, was running out of pencils with which to fervently record their observations, even when their inventor, Conté, as one of *les savants* based in Egypt, was tasked with making more. Many, including those like Denon working far from Cairo, took to melting down lead bullets to make their own.[16]

Meanwhile, in February 1799 Napoleon himself had to head to Syria to counter a renewed threat from the Ottoman Empire, which was seeking to retake Egypt. Hearing that the Ottomans were planning a two-pronged invasion – by sea (aided by the British fleet in the Mediterranean, which took the view that the enemy of their enemy was their friend and thus they were happy to help the Ottomans defeat the French and save them the job of doing so) and by land (approaching Egypt through Syria) – Napoleon marched his troops into Syria to head off the Ottoman army. He was partially successful in slowing their advance, but could not stop it entirely. By July, he was back in Alexandria, leading his troops against the Ottoman/British seaborne invasion, during which Ottoman troops were landed in Abukir Bay, where Nelson had previously destroyed the French fleet. This time Napoleon was successful in halting the Ottoman advance – but he knew this was temporary and that it was only a matter of time before Egypt was reconquered and the French ousted for good.

Dispatches coming from France also told Napoleon that plots against the Directorate had now ripened to fruition. Suddenly, Egypt was not where the action was for Napoleon – he needed to be on the ground in France if there was going to be a governing void to be filled (and filled preferably by him). In complete secrecy, in late August 1799, Napoleon, accompanied by *le savant* Dominique-Vivant Denon and a few others, boarded a ship and slipped past the British fleet back to France, leaving the French army and the majority of *les savants* in Egypt. Napoleon had instructed them to carry on with their work of making a systematic inventory and documentation of Egypt's antiquities, and he had put General Kléber in charge of the army (but failed to inform Kléber that he himself was leaving Egypt). By October, Napoleon was back in Paris, spinning stories of his (limited) successes in Egypt (before any real news of the vulnerable position he had left the army in could become common knowledge). Having timed it perfectly and buoyed by the glory of his recent 'victories', he propelled himself to a leading role in the *coup d'état* that ousted the Directorate on 9 November 1799, and took for himself the role of lead 'consul' of the Triumvirate (the three key men) that now ruled France. He would go on to crown himself sole Emperor in 1804.

*

It was during this heady month, between mid-July and mid-August 1799 when Napoleon was plotting his return to France, that the Rosetta Stone was first discovered and sent to the Institut d'Égypte in Cairo. Given everything that was going on at this time (the Battle of Abukir Bay against the Ottomans; Napoleon's hasty and secret departure; the abandonment of the French army and *les savants*), it is testament to how important a discovery this was that it still attracted such immediate attention.[17] However, because of the timing, we are still to this day not sure whether Napoleon ever had the chance to see the stone for himself before he left Egypt. No doubt he would have been told about it – he was passionate about the work of the Institut – but given that he was in Alexandria in those weeks after the stone was discovered and sent to Cairo, it is possible that the two passed like ships in the night. The great expeditionary leader may never have actually seen what would become the expedition's greatest discovery.

In fact, as the French army and *les savants* came to terms with their abandonment in Egypt, the Rosetta Stone became even more the focus of their attention. While General Kléber promptly started negotiations with the British to surrender, *les savants* started to make printed copies of the inscriptions on the stone, by covering it in printer's ink, laying thick paper over it and then running India-rubber rollers over the paper until a good impression was inked onto the paper.[18] Their immediate goal was not so much to understand the text itself – they already knew the gist of what it said because they could easily read the ancient Greek section of the stone. And the contents were not earth-shattering – it was a document dated to 196 BCE relating to tax rebates allowed for Egyptian priests during the reign of Ptolemy V. No – instead, what excited Lancret and *les savants* was what the stone could unlock beyond this one piece of text. The Greek writing on the stone specified that the same text was also inscribed in a 'sacred' letter (meaning hieroglyphics) and what the stone called 'native' characters – a language that no one had even heard of up to this point. The magic of the Rosetta Stone was that it could provide the key to finally translating hieroglyphics. And if they could do that, then *les savants* would be able to read a language that no one had been able to decipher for roughly 1,400 years (as well as perhaps go on to read the 'native' language, whatever that turned out to be).

Les savants were only too well aware of how eye-opening it would be to be able to read Egyptian hieroglyphics. Their initial discoveries across Egypt in 1798–9 had shown them the wealth and richness not only of Egyptian art and architecture, but also of their writings. Temple walls were covered in hieroglyphic texts, as were statues and other stones just like the Rosetta Stone. If scholars of the day – and particularly French scholars – wanted to tap into the wealth of mystical knowledge, insight and 'free-thinking' that ancient Egypt represented, and claim themselves as inheritors of its cultural achievements, nothing was more important than being able to read Egypt's official 'sacred' language of hieroglyphics.

And perhaps nothing was more galling than the knowledge that humanity had, of course, once been able to do so – but that the skill had been lost in the mists of time. The ability to read hieroglyphics had continued well beyond the years of building of the Pyramids (c.2500 BCE) – as the Rosetta Stone proved, the Egyptians were still writing in hieroglyphs in 196 BCE. In fact, the last hieroglyphic inscription we know of was written on 24 August 394 CE, etched into the stone on a temple gateway on the island of Philae near Aswan in Upper Egypt.[19] But with the growing popularity of Christianity within the Roman world during the first centuries CE, and its adoption as Rome's official religion from the late fourth century CE, hieroglyphic writing – as symbolic of Egypt's divine worship of multiple gods – had been rejected as a symbol of paganism. Communities shied away from its use and understanding as if it were a plague victim, fearful of worldly persecution and divine damnation. Humanity collectively chose to forget how to read and write the language of one of its principal ancient civilisations.

Now, though, there was a chance to regain that knowledge once more. And whoever did so (not to mention their nation), could claim to be the rightful inheritor of ancient Egyptian achievement. The race to decipher the Rosetta Stone had begun, and it would occupy some of the greatest minds in Europe for the next quarter of a century.

The Rosetta Stone itself, however, still had a turbulent future ahead of it. General Kléber had begun surrender negotiations with the British immediately after hearing of Napoleon's secret departure. These were progressing smoothly through the autumn and winter of 1799, and on 27 March 1800, *les savants* and the stone boarded a ship in Alexandria hoping to make it back to France. But the ship was refused final permission to leave while the British government in London reflected on the peace terms hammered out on the ground in Egypt. *Les savants* remained on board for a month with their precious Rosetta Stone, hoping that each day might bring the news they could leave.[20] But the permission never came. Instead, the British government rejected the treaty and demanded unconditional surrender. The war was back on, and *les savants* – along with the Rosetta Stone – returned to the Institut d'Égypte.

The faltering French cause was not helped when General Kléber was assassinated by a native Egyptian on 18 June, with General

Menou taking his place.[21] The French struggled on for months, with the last recorded meeting of the Institut d'Égypte on 22 March 1801.[22] That month, the British landed troops in Abukir Bay, and General Menou was compelled to lead his remaining forces (and *les savants* with their precious Rosetta Stone) to confront them. Defeated in battle, Menou and the tattered remains of the army retreated to Alexandria, where they were besieged by the British until Menou officially offered unconditional surrender on 30 August 1801.

The British, however, now wanted the spoils of war – and that included the Rosetta Stone. But how had knowledge of this particular stone spread to Britain? In steep contrast to the bitter rivalry between the French and British on the Egyptian battlefield, *les savants* had sent their early print copies of the Rosetta Stone inscriptions back to Paris soon after they were made. Academics in Paris had then circulated copies to their colleagues across Europe, allowing scholars of many different nations to start working on the problem of decipherment.[23] This effort to involve all the greatest minds in the quest (and competition) to solve the greatest historical problem of the age meant that by the time of the unconditional French surrender in Egypt in 1801, the British were only too well aware of the Rosetta Stone and its importance. Moreover, the British harboured now their own desire to establish themselves more widely as the inheritors of ancient Egypt's great creations. As a result the British demanded not only the unconditional surrender of the French army, but also the handing over of *every* object discovered during the expedition. At first Menou refused, arguing that these objects were the property of the Institut. The British retaliated by saying they wouldn't lift their siege of Alexandria until the French complied. In a threat that echoed the now famous burning of the ancient Library of Alexandria, destroying the sum of world knowledge it housed in antiquity, *les savants* said they would rather burn everything in the Institut than hand it over to the British. A compromise was offered in which certain kinds of objects would be considered the personal property of *les savants* and not part of the surrender agreement. General Menou – in whose home the Rosetta Stone was now being kept (according to some sources wrapped in some old carpets) – now claimed the stone as his personal possession. But the British were having none of it. It was forcibly taken from Menou's house and carried on a British gun carriage to the port, where it was put on a ship – a captured French ship no less – renamed, with no small irony, HMS *l'Égyptienne*.[24]

The Rosetta Stone, along with other Egyptian artefacts secured in the surrender agreement, was triumphantly escorted back to Britain, arriving in Portsmouth in February 1802.[25] And it was now that a fourth inscription (and indeed fourth language) was added to the Rosetta Stone, just under 2,000 years since its initial inscriptions in Greek, 'sacred' hieroglyphs and 'native' characters had been carved. On the side of the stone, the painted words in English can still be seen: 'Captured by the British Army in 1801. Presented to King George III.'[26] The stone was now the official property of King George III, who had suffered several bouts of the mental illness that would incapacitate him as king from 1810 onwards and cause him to be remembered as Mad King George. But in early 1802, the king was sufficiently in charge of his faculties to gift, among other things brought back to Britain from Egypt, the Rosetta Stone to the British Museum. London's *Gentleman's Magazine*, an erudite monthly publication that had begun back in 1731, summed up Britain's achievement in 1802 thus: 'The conquest of Egypt, independent of its political consequences, has enriched our country with a number of rare and ancient monuments.'[27] The stone was placed, after a brief sojourn in the library of the Society of Antiquaries, in a temporary structure in the British Museum's grounds (because the floors of the building itself were not strong enough to bear its weight.[28]

*

The stone was now settled in Britain, but how did the great think-
ers of the day go about trying to crack the code? While the Rosetta
Stone itself was being sent back and forth between Cairo and
Alexandria, hidden in old carpets, transported across the
Mediterranean to Britain, and between the Society of Antiquaries'
library and the British Museum, copies of the inscriptions on it
were being sent even further afield. Interest in the stone was fierce,
as scholars around the world realised the possibility that it offered
the key to finally solving a problem that many had considered
impossible to solve. In the period 1800–3, scholars from Britain,
France and Germany all offered full translations (into English,
French and Latin) of the Greek text, which, while generally under-
standable, was full of little-understood technical terminology
relating to Egyptian priesthoods and their tax rebates. There was
also a portion of the Greek text missing because a corner of the
stone had been broken off, long before Bouchard's soldiers found
it in the sand.

In their attempt to decipher the 'sacred' hieroglyphics and the
'native' text written on the stone, scholars focused first not on the
hieroglyphs, but instead on the unknown 'native' characters. This
was for two reasons. First, because the Rosetta Stone was in fact
only surviving in part: much of the stone's upper half (containing
the majority of the hieroglyphic version of the text) had broken
off (again before Bouchard's discovery). Scholars thus had much
more of the 'native'-character-language text to compare to the
Greek text than they did of the hieroglyphic one. And second,
because scholars had realised that lots of other examples of this
'native' language were appearing in newly discovered papyrus
fragments from across Egypt, so there was an ever-larger pool of
material to work with.

Where do you start when trying to use one language you can
read to translate another you can't? You have to find a single
phrase, or word, that you can reliably identify in both languages
as being the same, and use that as the key to start deciphering the
meaning, or 'value', of the individual letters of the word in the

language you don't know. This gives you a secure base from which to expand to other words and their constituent letters until you have assigned a value to every letter or symbol used in that unknown language. For the scholars working on the Rosetta Stone, that key starting word was the name of the Egyptian king: Ptolemy. The word Ptolemy was repeated eleven times in the Greek text and so should be identifiable as a repeated set of symbols in the other language.

That may make it sound like they were already well on their way to deciphering the whole text. However, it would actually take the greatest minds of the age another twenty years to crack the Rosetta code. Collaboration between French and Swedish academics in 1801–2 got as far as identifying the names of Ptolemy, as well as 'Alexander', 'Alexandria', 'Arsinoe' (Ptolemy's wife) as well as *Epiphanes* (Ptolemy's official title as ruler) in the 'native' language. Using these as a basis, they produced an alphabet of twenty-nine 'native'-language characters with their corresponding Greek ones. At the same time, this 'native' language was now being called 'cursive' as it was thought to be the 'day to day' language of the Egyptians (with 'sacred' hieroglyphs as their more formal language).[29] The general international public interest in these early attempts to decipher the Rosetta Stone is underlined by the fact that the *Gentleman's Magazine* in London had a new article covering the latest linguistic arguments and ideas in nearly every edition from this period: this was no stodgy dry academic debate; it was an unfolding quest of discovery gripping the reading rooms and front parlours of the world, equivalent in our times perhaps to the interest shown in the scientific process of experimentation and development behind the creation of the Covid-19 vaccine.[30]

We now know that only about half of these twenty-nine characters identified in the cursive script by 1802 were actually correct. Because there was an additional problem: no one knew whether the symbols of the cursive script were 'phonetic' (each symbol/letter representing a sound – like Spanish or German today), or 'ideographic' (each symbol representing an idea/thing, as in ancient Sumerian) – or perhaps even a mixture of both (as in, for example, Chinese). Without knowing what kind of language they were looking at, scholars were really shooting in the dark.

Early steps forward, then, quickly gave way to a frustrated stalemate, with scholars from across the world failing to progress any further in deciphering the 'native' text. Their failure to make further headway was only more deeply underlined as the interest in ancient Egypt mushroomed during the first decades of the nineteenth century. In 1809/10 the first volume of the *Description d'Égypte* appeared in print as Napoleon's authorised account of the intellectual discoveries made there during *his* expedition. A total of eight volumes of text, accompanied by nine volumes of images, would be published as lasting testament not only to the wonders of Egypt, but to France's claim to be the inheritor of that ancient cultural prowess.[31] At the same time, Britain and France in particular invested huge amounts of money, diplomacy and time in securing further ancient Egyptian cultural relics for their respective countries (and subsequently transporting them there). Egyptomania had officially started.[32]

In 1802, just as efforts to translate the languages of the Rosetta Stone were hitting a brick wall, Napoleon, now as First Consul and just two years away from declaring himself Emperor, had given a lecture in Paris about his Egyptian adventures. In the audience sat an Englishman by the name of Thomas Young.[33] He *was* young, only in his twenties, and yet was already phenomenally accomplished. By the age of fourteen, he could read French, Italian, Latin, Greek, Hebrew, Syriac, Arabic, Persian, Turkish and Ethiopic among other languages, and had deduced (before anyone else) that a whole swathe of ancient and modern European languages had all derived from the same 'Indo-European' root. He was a trained doctor and would also go on to discover the wave theory of light, which Einstein would claim was second only to Newton's discoveries.[34] Inspired by Napoleon's lecture, he eventually found a gap in his schedule and in the 1810s he turned his attention to the mystery of the Rosetta Stone.

What prompted Young, a decade after hearing Napoleon speak, to focus full-time on the Rosetta Stone was an idea from the French Oriental scholar Antoine-Isaac Silvestre de Sacy, who had been at the forefront of the initial attempts to crack the 'cursive'/'native' language. Facing scholars were two problems: how to identify key words in each script, and then how to know whether or not the cursive and hieroglyphic scripts were representing sounds (as phonetic symbols) or ideas/words (as ideograms). De Sacy, as an Oriental scholar, understood that when translating a foreign name into the Chinese language, Chinese always used a phonetic approach. That is to say, they pick the Chinese language symbols that sound most like the different sounds within the name they are trying to transliterate into their language and write it like that. The cursive/native and hieroglyphic writing on the Rosetta Stone effectively had to do the same thing with the name Ptolemy: it was, after all, a Greek name rather than an Egyptian one (the original Ptolemy who had come to rule Egypt had been a Macedonian general of Alexander the Great). As such, De Sacy argued, it was a decent bet that the cursive *and* hieroglyphic texts employed a phonetic approach to translate the constituent sounds of Ptolemy's name into cursive/hieroglyphic.

Scholars had already identified the words in the cursive text that translated Ptolemy's name, but had struggled to do so in the hieroglyphic one. Around this time, however, it was collectively agreed by the scholarly community that the names of important royals – like Ptolemy – in the hieroglyphic script were always encircled (in what is known as a 'cartouche').[35] And it just so happened that in the surviving piece of the hieroglyphic text on the broken Rosetta Stone was a name in a cartouche, occurring in about the right place at the end of the text where scholars knew (in the Greek version) Ptolemy's name occurred.

De Sacy – in a generous academic gesture of what we today would call 'open access': the free sharing of knowledge – made these suggestions to Young and told him to try them out. We should not underemphasise how extraordinary this was, particularly at the time. De Sacy was a proud French academic, Young a British one. Britain and France had been at war since 1803 as Britain wrestled to hold on to its geopolitical power in the face of Napoleon's efforts to expand his (and France's) own. Against this background of acrimonious conflict there was also a camaraderie of academic scholarly investigation that transcended those boundaries – at least for now.

Across the next few years, between 1814 and 1819, Young published a series of articles, eventually summing up the entirety of his work in his anonymous entry on Egypt for the *Encyclopaedia Britannica*, published in 1819.[36] Beginning from ascribing phonetic sounds to the symbols used to transliterate Ptolemy's name in both the cursive and hieroglyphic texts, he had then looked for these same symbols in other names and words, ascribed the same phonetic values to them and then sought to understand the phonetic value of the remaining symbols in those new words. It was a painstaking process, with Young needing to constantly cross-check any phonetic values he ascribed to one symbol against where that symbol appeared in another word to ensure it made sense there too. In this way, by 1819, he was able to offer his translation of about two hundred words in the 'cursive' language (which Young preferred to call 'enchoric', denoting a writing coming from a particular country) and another two hundred words in the hieroglyphic text, as well as about eighty suggested correlations between cursive and hieroglyphic signs. While others previously had thought hieroglyphics and the cursive text were two unrelated languages, Young argued that cursive was in fact an evolved form of hieroglyphics. Once again, we now know that Young's translations in his 1819 article were actually largely incorrect. But the method he had hit upon at De Sacy's suggestion to focus on the phonetic value of transliterated foreign names and work outwards from there, as well as the idea that cursive and hieroglyphs were linked, was right.

Young corresponded freely with many academics across Europe in this period – however, he had been warned not to communicate with a certain infamous Jean-François Champollion.[37] Champollion was seventeen years Young's junior and had been born in 1790, the year after the French Revolution. In those early Revolutionary years the state education system had crumbled and schools had closed, leaving no option for families but to home-school. Champollion was lucky though; his father was a book-seller and clearly passed on his love of reading to his children. Taught by his father and his elder brother, Jacques Joseph Champollion, and later by a private tutor hired by the family, he received a brilliant and wide-ranging early education, preparing him to be able to excel once the schools reopened after Napoleon became First Consul in late 1799.

Champollion first saw a copy of the Rosetta Stone text in 1804, aged fourteen, and he started learning Coptic the very next year. A language that developed in Egypt in the first centuries CE, Coptic employed a mix of Greek and Egyptian alphabets, gram-mar and vocabulary to translate early Christian biblical texts, and was also spoken by 'Copt' (Christian Egyptian) communities. It eventually died out as a spoken language at the time of the Muslim conquest of Egypt in the seventh century CE, continuing only in written form. By the age of fifteen, Champollion was delivering papers to the Grenoble academic community arguing that the Coptic language was directly related back to ancient Egyptian hieroglyphs.[38] That same year, he declared that he would devote his life to developing the knowledge and understanding of ancient Egypt. This ambition was unlike that of other academics at the time, like Young, who had turned to work on the Rosetta Stone translation as one of a number of varied academic interests rather than as an all-consuming speciality. By 1818, the year before Young published the anonymous summation of his work in the

Encyclopaedia Britannica, Champollion was in Grenoble in a permanent teaching position, devoting every spare second he had to his Egyptian studies.[39]

However, just as French politics had prevented Champollion attending regular schooling when he was a boy, now again French politics intervened in Champollion's career. In 1815, Napoleon had finally surrendered to the British following the Battle of Waterloo and had been exiled to the island of Saint Helena in the south Atlantic. The Bourbon monarchy had been restored in France. Champollion – understandably as someone who had felt the benefits of the French education system come back into operation under Napoleon – had grown up to become a committed Republican. So when, in 1821, a group of Bonapartists staged a rebellion in Grenoble, Champollion was accused of being the ringleader. He was, thanks to his academic contacts, eventually acquitted of all charges, but had to surrender his job and leave Grenoble. In the summer of 1821, Champollion arrived in Paris – jobless and without his own home – to live with his elder brother, Jacques Joseph, who was, in contrast, a well-respected academic working at the revered Académie Royale des Inscriptions et Belles Lettres, the epicentre of Parisian academic enquiry. Jean-François settled down in his brother's home and buried himself in his brother's library, returning full-time to the question of the Rosetta Stone.[40]

Little did he know at the time that crucial additional clues, which would provide the key to unlocking the Rosetta Stone text, were about to fall into place. In Egypt, a power vacuum had developed following the French defeat of the Mamluks, France's own military capitulation in 1801–2, the inability and reticence of the British to commit the manpower that would be required to rule Egypt and the continued crumbling of the Ottoman Empire, which technically did still rule it. That vacuum was filled by a man called Mehmet Ali. Originally born in Macedonia to an Albanian family, Mehmet Ali declared himself viceroy of Egypt in 1805 and would soon be recognised as the 'Pasha' (the Ottoman title for ruler) of Egypt by the Ottoman sultan in Constantinople. It was the start of a dynasty that would rule Egypt for the next 150 years. But Mehmet Ali also realised that he needed to keep the Western powers sweet and so tolerated the French and British embassies, and associated trading networks, that were busy discovering and copying ancient objects from all over Egypt – as well as trying to then take them back to Europe. For example, William John Bankes, a wealthy dilletante, masterminded the successful transport of one complete obelisk, and a large broken part of its partner, from the Temple of Isis on the island of Philae in the middle of the Nile in Upper Egypt, all the way to his stately home at Kingston Lacy in Dorset. The obelisks arrived in London in December 1821 and were the first Egyptian obelisks to arrive into the country. To this day, the unbroken one is still at Kingston Lacy.

What Bankes was interested in, however, was not just the obelisk itself, but the texts carved on it. He had noticed back in 1815 that the complete obelisk now at Kingston Lacy carried a hieroglyphic text on its shaft and a Greek text on its base – perhaps this could be another parallel text like that of the Rosetta Stone?[41]

He had copies of the inscriptions made and circulated them to the wider academic community, which is how both Thomas Young and Jean-François Champollion came across this next set of clues. Young was at the time in Rome looking for other bilingual inscriptions among the Egyptian objects that had been taken to Italy during the time of the Roman Empire. Jean-François Champollion was in his brother's apartment in Paris. A race began to decipher the obelisk inscription. But it later emerged Young had received a copy with an error in it.[42] Champollion was luckier.

The inscription contained crucial Greek royal names (Ptolemy and Cleopatra) that had been translated into hieroglyphic text. Using Young's published work, Champollion was able to identify the phonetic values of the hieroglyphic symbols for the names of both Ptolemy *and* Cleopatra on the Bankes obelisk. It was this additional reference point provided by the Bankes obelisk that, alongside the Rosetta Stone, allowed Champollion to start to

expand and cross-reference his suggested translations of hieroglyphic symbols – and move on to test his workings to read other
foreign ruler names translated into hieroglyphics. The question
was now: could he start to read words that were originally
Egyptian rather than foreign imports translated into hieroglyphics? Could Champollion at last unravel the mystery of the Rosetta
Stone?

*

The summer of 1822 was scorching in Paris. Champollion was
too hot to undertake any concentrated work in his brother's
library. But a let-up in the heat on 14 September allowed Jean-
François the chance to study a copy of a new hieroglyphic inscription that had just emerged from the great temple at Abu Simbel
on the Nile in Upper Egypt, almost at the border with Sudan. By
noon that day, Champollion was tearing the two hundred or so
yards down the street to his brother's office at the Académie
Royale des Inscriptions et Belles Lettres, bursting into the room
and throwing his papers down on his brother's desk: '*Je tiens à
l'affaire!*' he cried – 'I've done it!' He then promptly dropped
unconscious on the floor.[43]

What Champollion had been able to do that morning was link
together the different parts of his knowledge that he had gained
across his lifetime to crack the code. First he had taken his proto-
type system of translation between Greek, cursive (which he
preferred to call 'demotic' and which Young still called enchoric)
and hieroglyphics, born from studying the foreign names on the
Rosetta Stone and Bankes's obelisk. Second, he combined that
with his in-depth knowledge of the Coptic language (which he
had correctly realised was linked to both cursive and hieroglyphics). Third, he added to this his excellent understanding of ancient
Egyptian history and culture. The result was that he was able to
locate and read the Egyptian royal title 'Rameses' amid the hieroglyphics on the Abu Simbel text. He had then gone back to the
Rosetta Stone hieroglyphics and been able to translate the

Egyptian royal title given to Ptolemy. He knew then that he had cracked it.

It is hard to overestimate how much of a momentous intellectual accomplishment Champollion had achieved that morning – a true eureka moment. In part, he was of course lucky: lucky to be working on the problem at the time that multiple bilingual texts were beginning to circulate (and indeed to receive copies of them without errors in). But he was also the only person with all the requisite skills and knowledge in different languages and ancient history. He was also perhaps the only one with sufficient intellectual capability, combined with both a stubborn determination to succeed and an equally strong ability for what we would call today 'blue-sky thinking', to be able to make the breakthrough. The effort it took – even for him – is borne out in the fact that he collapsed with the shock and toll of making the discovery. His brother thought he was dead. It took Jean-François five days of bed convalescence to recover.

Soon after, on Friday 27 September 1822, Champollion read a report to the assembled members of the Académie Royale des Inscriptions et Belles Lettres about his discoveries. The report, formally known as the *Lettre à M. Dacier, relative à l'alphabet des hieroglyphs phonétiques*, was later published and has – rightly – taken its place as one of the most fundamental documents in the history of Egyptology.[44] Thomas Young was in the audience when Champollion delivered his report that day in Paris. Indeed, in recognition of Young's earlier advances in the journey to decipherment of Egyptian hieroglyphics and the cursive language, he was invited to sit next to Champollion as he read out the report. The two were introduced to one another at the end of the session. It was the first time that the two men most responsible for deciphering Egyptian hieroglyphics had actually met.[45]

I can't quite imagine the wealth of emotions – no doubt hidden under the enforced academic *politesse* of the Académie session – going through Thomas Young's mind. Young had been so close to the answer himself. He would never know whether – if he had had the correct copy of the Philae obelisk inscriptions – he too may have been able to crack the code, and sooner than Champollion. And worse still, he had been warned off corresponding with Champollion because of his apparent tendency to not acknowledge the work of others that he incorporated into his own. Sure enough, Champollion's report had not fully referenced Young's contribution thus far. Two days after the report was read to the Académie, Young wrote charitably to an academic colleague that

> Mr Champollion . . . has lately been making some steps in Egyptian literature which really appear to be *gigantic*. It may be said that he has found the key in England which has opened the gate for him . . . But if he did borrow an English key, the lock was so dreadfully rusty that no common arm would have had the strength enough to turn it.[46]

Later, however, he wrote more plainly: 'I did certainly expect to find the chronology of my own researches a little more distinctly stated!'[47]

Young's response was to eschew his anonymity and in 1823 he published his own account, pointedly entitled *An Account of Some Recent Discoveries in Hieroglyphical Literature and Egyptian Antiquities, Including the Author's Original Alphabet, As Extended by Mr Champollion*. In it he shows himself torn between wanting to maintain some kind of academic modesty and wanting recognition for his part in the discovery. While he held back from accusing Champollion of portraying Young's discoveries as if they were his own, he could not help but restate that 'however Mr Champollion may have arrived at his conclusions, I admit them, with the greatest pleasure and gratitude, not by any means as superseding my system, but as fully confirming and extending it'.[48]

Shots had been fired, and Champollion was having none of it. In a letter dated 23 March 1823, he wrote: 'I shall never consent to recognise any other original alphabet than my own . . . and the unanimous opinion of scholars on this point will be more and more confirmed by the public examination of any other claim.'[49] Young, seemingly unable to turn the tide on the view of Champollion as the single-handed hero of the Rosetta Stone, turned his back on the subject and moved on to study other matters.

Champollion, however, was only just getting started. Throughout 1822, he had been feverishly studying as many hieroglyphic texts as he could to test, refine and expand his understanding. He realised that the hieroglyphic symbols were always a mixture of phonetic and ideographic, and that the language rarely represented vowels. This realisation, alongside his in-depth knowledge of Coptic, allowed him to rapidly expand his hieroglyphic vocabulary and by 1824 he had published *Précis du système hiéroglyphique des anciens Egyptiens*, in which he made the famous description of Egyptian hieroglyphs in the following terms (capitalisation was his choice but the translation is mine):

> Hieroglyphic writing is a complex system, a script all at the same time FIGURATIVE, SYMBOLIC, and PHONETIC, in a single text, in a single sentence and, I would say, almost in a single word.[50]

The cracking of the hieroglyphic code in the 1820s only accelerated the Egyptomania sweeping Europe, with different nations even more eager to own a piece of Egyptian antiquity for themselves. At the same time, the field of Egyptology – as an academic subject in its own right – blossomed. Scholars now had the tools they needed to unlock the rich mysterious world of ancient Egyptian writing, and thus delve into the country's culture, history and religion. A golden age of Egyptian discovery was dawning, which would last through to the infamous discovery of the tomb of Tutankhamun by Howard Carter in 1922, exactly 100 years after Champollion's breakthrough.

The Rosetta Stone stood resolute in the British Museum during that time and has continued to be – by and large – the museum's most popular attraction even to this day.[51] Over that time, it has been studied and, as our knowledge and understanding of ancient Egypt has grown, so too have we been able to unlock more insights into the creation and meaning of the stone itself. First, we know now that the Rosetta Stone was not itself a one-off. The text declares not only that the same message should be written in Greek, 'sacred' and 'native' characters on the stone, but also that copies of the trilingual text should be erected in every sizeable temple across Egypt.[52] We think that our Rosetta Stone was originally set up at an Egyptian temple in the town of Sais, on the western Nile Delta.[53] Three other fragmentary copies of the same text have now been discovered at other sites across Egypt – in essence this was a second-century-BCE version of a modern mass-propaganda campaign. Indeed, we know that the Rosetta Stone copied (almost verbatim) a style of announcement that had been used by previous Ptolemaic rulers of Egypt several times through the third century BCE.[54] As such, in many ways, a stone that began life as a unique key to unlocking ancient Egyptian writing has now morphed into an example of something much more common and mass-produced.

At the same time, however, our finer-grain understanding of Egyptian history has allowed us to pick up on some of the nuances of our Rosetta Stone, and the particular circumstances it was responding to. The ruler in whose honour it was set up, Ptolemy V *Epiphanes*, had come to the throne of Egypt in 205 BCE as a very young child at the age of five. By this time, Ptolemaic rulers had held sway in Egypt for over a hundred years, since the first Ptolemy, a Greek general of Alexander the Great, had established his personal rule over the land in the wake of Alexander's death. From this point Egypt now had Greek rulers and an increasingly Greek ruling class, alongside its native Egyptian population. Ptolemaic rulers were therefore in some ways quite two-faced – and had to be – as they sought to project their regal power to two very different cultural groups. One way the Ptolemaic rulers developed to do this was to have two entirely different types of royal statues: one carved in the Greek style with a youthful energetic face and a full head of hair (i.e. looking like Alexander the Great) and another carved in the traditional Egyptian style of the Pharaohs with a much more stylised oblique face carrying all the official headwear of an Egyptian Pharaoh (i.e. looking like the death-mask of Tutankhamun). A second way in which the Ptolemaic rulers catered to their very different subject audiences was, as with the example of the Rosetta Stone, to ensure official decrees went out in multiple languages so that the different constituent parts of their kingdom could read them.

· Yet things become more complicated when you factor in the other major power group in ancient Egyptian politics: the Egyptian priesthood. The priests wielded such power in Egypt because the model of the Egyptian ruler since the time of the Pyramids – the Pharaoh – was always himself a divine being. But a new Pharoah could only have his divinity recognised by the Egyptian priesthood. And as such a Pharoah always needed to keep the priesthood onside to ensure they would endorse him as a god and rightful ruler. This applied just as much – if not more – to the Ptolemies, who sought to be portrayed (to the Egyptian population at least) as Pharaohs, and thus needed the support of the priests. This was particularly true in times of dynastic unrest, countrywide revolution, and weak – or young – rulers coming to the throne.

The problem for Ptolemy V *Epiphanes* was that he had to deal with all three. His father, Ptolemy IV, had been a lazy ruler, more interested in luxurious living than in ruling Egypt, and had even lost part of Upper Egypt to revolution the year before he, along with his wife, had been murdered. The five-year-old boy Ptolemy V was pronounced ruler, but in effect power was held by regents, who may well have themselves been involved in the murder of his parents. Between 205 and 196 BCE, as Ptolemy V grew up, not only were there multiple further revolts leading to the murder of these regents, but their replacements failed to keep Egypt's foreign enemies at bay. The only glimmer of sunshine was the eventual reconquering of the part of Upper Egypt that had been lost to rebels by Ptolemy's father.

In 197 BCE, after the failure of so many regents, the thinking was that Ptolemy V – then only thirteen years old – needed to be seen to personally take control in order to strengthen the image and reputation of Ptolemaic Egyptian rule.[55] To do this, he first needed to be recognised as an adult (via one religious ceremony) and then as a divine Pharoah by another set of religious ceremonies. Both required the co-operation of the Egyptian priesthood. And for that, favours had to be given. And this is where the Rosetta Stone comes in. This piece of propaganda, and its partners, was issued by the council of Egyptian priests in 196 BCE to commemorate the first anniversary since the boy's coronation – it lays out the tax breaks and other favours granted to the Egyptian priests as part of their recognition of Ptolemy V as the rightful divine Pharoah and them giving him a full Pharaonic coronation the year before. A sign of how far Ptolemy V had to go to ensure their co-operation is that, while much of the Rosetta Stone is copied from earlier deals with the Egyptian priesthood, one new concession made by Ptolemy and not seen before is that the priests no longer had to come every year to meet in Alexandria (the traditional seat of Ptolemaic power), but could meet in Memphis (the traditional seat of Egyptian religious authority).[56]

More so than the individual point scoring contained in the Rosetta Stone, however, my favourite insight, which has only come to the fore as our knowledge and understanding of both hieroglyphic and the cursive (now most often called demotic, taking up Champollion's preferred name for it) languages has improved, is that the texts are not exact translations of one another. Hieroglyphics was, at the end of the day, the language of the gods – and of the priesthood. By the second century BCE, it was already a rarefied and specialised language that could be read only by those with the right education and instruction (a bit like the continued use of Latin within the

Catholic Church). Being able to read it was in itself a symbol of power – one that the Egyptian priesthood liked to reserve for themselves. As such, it is notable that where words in the cursive are close to their equivalent in hieroglyphics, the text chooses a synonym in hieroglyphics to ensure that you can't read it unless you know hieroglyphics as well. For example, the words for 'decree' in hieroglyphics and cursive are quite similar, so the Rosetta Stone pointedly uses the word 'memorandum' in the hieroglyphics.[57] I love the irony that while the original creators of this text intended to make it harder for the people at the time to read the hieroglyphics, the Rosetta Stone ended up becoming, 2,000 years later, the key in cracking the hieroglyphic code once again . . .

*

There are many overlaps between the ancient creation and modern discovery of the Rosetta Stone. It was created at a moment of instability in ancient Egypt's history as rebellions, revolts and political intrigue rocked the Ptolemaic throne. It speaks to the desperate political power-wrangling going on between the ruler and the priesthood as Ptolemy V sought to secure his hold over the land, and as the Egyptian priesthood sought to underline their own authority and superiority over the rest of the population. In modern times, of course, the Rosetta Stone was discovered at another moment of instability in Egypt's history as Napoleon sought to wrestle the country from its Ottoman-appointed Mamluk rulers, with his army subsequently surrendering to the British and the power vacuum being filled by a new ruler, who would style himself just like the sole authoritarian Egyptian rulers of old. At the same time, the subsequent race to own the stone – and to translate its hieroglyphics – reflects the wider geopolitical power games being played out between Western powers as they each sought to cloak themselves in the authority and wisdom of ancient Egyptian culture and language, mirroring the ancient political power brokering between the Ptolemaic ruler, his court and the Egyptian priest-hood in the second century BCE.

Ptolemy V himself hung on to power for another fifteen years after the creation of the Rosetta Stone through to 180 BCE, when it seems he was poisoned by his courtiers. Ptolemaic rule more widely would struggle on for another one hundred and fifty years in an ongoing cycle of political power-wrangling between the ruler, his court and the priesthood, until the last Ptolemaic ruler – Queen Cleopatra – was crushed by the might of the man who would become the first Roman Emperor: Augustus. At some point – we will never know precisely when – the Rosetta Stone was taken from its original home at the temple in Sais and used as building material in the nearby town of Rashid, to be dug up again as part of Napoleon's building works in 1799.

Like its ancient protagonists, the stone's modern discoverers and decipherers faced their own fair share of difficulties. Napoleon – who would have loved the kind of divine Pharoah confirmation for himself that Ptolemy V bought with his priestly tax breaks – died in 1821, the year before Champollion cracked the hiero-glyphic code. Not only does it seem that Napoleon may never actually have seen the Rosetta Stone for himself; he certainly never bore witness to its successful decipherment. Moreover, his reputa-tion today, even in France, is a complicated one. President Macron commemorated the two hundredth anniversary of Napoleon's death in 2021 by saying he 'could be both the soul of the world and the devil of Europe'. But he added: 'we love Napoleon because his life gives us a taste of what is possible if we accept the invita-tion to take risks'.

Of the other protagonists in the story, no one fared much better. Lieutenant Bouchard, who originally discovered the stone, was captured and imprisoned several times while fighting for Napoleon in Egypt and the Caribbean, and later died of a long and painful illness in 1822, the same year Champollion cracked the hiero-glyphic code. Thomas Young, who was inspired to take up once again the task of translating his beloved cursive language on the

Rosetta Stone in 1827 after losing out to Champollion, died pen in hand in 1829 while correcting proofs of his book on the subject. Meanwhile, Champollion, following his triumph of translation, was crowned as curator of the Louvre and travelled to Egypt to copy down and translate many hieroglyphic texts unread for centuries. But the harsh conditions of the journey ruined his health and he died of multiple strokes in 1832, aged just forty-one. His last words are reported to have been: 'and now for the afterlife, on to Egypt, on to Thebes!'[58] And Bankes, who had secured the return of the Philae obelisk and circulated its inscription as the second key to unlocking hieroglyphics, found himself facing the threat of execution after he was caught having sex with a soldier in London's Green Park. Forced to flee Britain into exile in 1841, he died in Venice in 1855.[59]

And what of Egypt herself? Napoleon's invasion kick-started European Egyptomania and its more respectable academic brother, the discipline of Egyptology. Each fed the other, leading not only to a much greater understanding of ancient Egyptian culture and history, but also to a steady denuding of Egypt of its ancient treasures, which were (for the most part) bought and officially exported to museums around Europe. It is a sad testament to the colonial approach of the discoverers of this period that no one ever asked whether Egypt was the best place for the Rosetta Stone – or indeed any of the other objects shipped off across Europe in the years after the stone's discovery to become today key pieces in museums and collections around the world. They no doubt inspire – as happened to me when I was eight – new generations of visitors in all those global locations to learn more about ancient Egypt. But in the modern Egyptian town of Rashid where the Rosetta Stone was originally dug up, despite several calls for the return of the stone, there is only a fibre-glass full-size replica standing in one of the busy public squares. I wonder if any eight-year-old has ever looked at it with the same awe I was fortunate enough to experience?

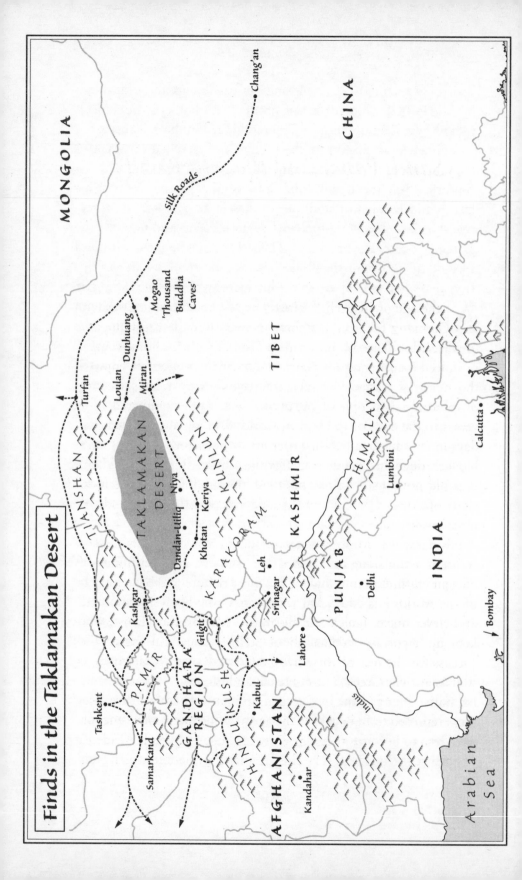

Finds in the Taklamakan Desert

MONGOLIA

CHINA

Chang'an

Silk Roads

Mogao
'Thousand
Buddha
Caves'

Dunhuang

Turfan

Loulan

Miran

TIANSHAN

TAKLAMAKAN DESERT

KUNLUN

Niya

Keriya

Dandān-Uiliq

Khotan

TIBET

Kashgar

KARAKORAM

Leh

Srinagar

KASHMIR

HIMALAYAS

Lumbini

Calcutta

PAMIR

Gilgit

GANDHARA REGION

HINDU KUSH

Kabul

AFGHANISTAN

Kandahar

Tashkent

Samarkand

Lahore

PUNJAB

Delhi

INDIA

Indus

Bombay

Arabian Sea

2

Sand, Paper and the Silk Roads

At the age of just ten the boy was sent to school in Dresden, Germany, far from his home town of Budapest in Hungary, to perfect his German. But instead of pining for his home town – or indeed focusing on his German – what this youngster enjoyed the most was reading the ancient Greek author Arrian's account of the campaigns of Alexander the Great as he conquered eastwards to the ends of the known world. Whiling away his schooldays in Dresden in 1873 (just over fifty years since Champollion's breakthrough in deciphering Egyptian hieroglyphics), this ten-year-old boy dreamt of nothing less than following in the footsteps of Alexander east into the depths of Asia, thousands of miles away.[1]

His name was Marc Aurel Stein and he would one day make a series of astonishing discoveries that spoke to the interlinking of ancient cultures even in one of the most remote and barren parts of the world. His education was overseen by his well-connected and clever uncle, Ignaz, and his much-elder brother, Ernst, who kept up a correspondence about Stein's education, career and success for the rest of their lives.[2] Having learnt his German, as well as ancient Greek, Latin, French and English (to complement his native Hungarian) in Dresden and subsequently in Leipzig, Stein returned to Budapest at the age of fifteen. His uncle encouraged him to become a regular visitor to the newly built Academy of Science in Budapest, very close to the apartment in which Stein had been born.[3] There, among the scholarly tomes, this fifteen-year-old, with his own long-running fascination with Alexander the Great and his conquests east, found himself in lock step with a much wider Hungarian academic fascination with the East. This wider interest stemmed from the belief at the time that the Hungarian people had originally migrated to the Danube from somewhere in Central Asia nine centuries earlier. As a new nation, which had only achieved independence from Austria in 1873, the year Stein had been sent to Dresden, Hungary was dedicating time and energy to the understanding of Hungarian roots, culture and language in order to guide its blossoming national identity.[4] Swept up in this wider fascination with the East, Stein's interest grew from being focused on the campaigns of Alexander the Great to focus equally on the different ancient cultures, languages and histories of the regions Alexander had travelled to. Pursuing his wider interest in the East through his university studies in Vienna followed by stints at the Universities of Leipzig and Tübingen, Stein came to focus on the languages of the East, particularly Sanskrit and Old Persian, alongside the study of comparative languages, as well as the culture and history of Iran and India. By the age of twenty-one, he had his PhD, and moved – not east – but to London.

In the 1880s, if you could not be in India or Central Asia, London was the next best place to immerse yourself in the culture of that part of the world. England's interest and expertise stemmed of course from its long-running presence in India, first under the auspices of the East India Company and, since 1858, through its direct control of vast swathes of the Indian sub-continent in the name of the Crown. London was packed with those who had spent lengthy periods of time in India, and its libraries and institutes – as well as those of Oxford and Cambridge – were replete with material from the region.

Stein now learnt Punjabi at the Oriental Institute in London, and quickly fell in with a group of intellectuals and experienced officials who were equally mad about the region of India and

Central Asia as he was. One of them was Theodore Duka, a fellow Hungarian who had served in the Indian Medical Service and was writing a biography of a Hungarian explorer who had, several decades earlier, headed east to find the origins of the Hungarian people. Another was Henry Yule, who had recently translated Marco Polo's accounts of his journey east all the way to China.[5]

The question was where Stein would settle next. He dearly wanted an academic post in a European university, a place from which to indulge his fascination in the individuals and peoples, languages, ideas and cultures that had travelled both east and west across Central Asia since ancient times, leaving a heady mix of overlapping influences strewn across the area. Instead, thanks to a good word put in by Henry Yule, he was offered a position in India itself: to act simultaneously as Principal of the Oriental College and Registrar of Punjab University in Lahore (in modern-day Pakistan). On 16th November 1887, Stein set off for India.[6]

Lahore in the 1880s was a beautiful and lively city complete with museum, public library, art college and an active British Raj social scene including an ongoing cycle of garden parties, picnics and tennis matches. Stein's uncle Ignaz and his elder brother Ernst, their correspondence reveals, were not altogether thrilled at Stein's decision to take the India job. They commented to one another that – at the age of twenty-six – surely he should not be travelling but, rather, settling down to an occupation. They were both also still unhappy with the insufficiently refined and culti-vated nature of his written German.[7]

Stein worked assiduously in his day job as Principal and Registrar, but never missed an opportunity to demand special conditions of employment, pension, salary and, most impor-tantly, annual leave. By 1898, after a decade in India, he had cajoled, persuaded and fiddled it so that his official job took up less than half the year, leaving him plenty of time to explore the wider region. With that time, he had travelled widely north of Lahore up into the more mountainous region of Kashmir, perfect-ing his skills in camping, mountain climbing and surveying. In doing so he had achieved his boyhood dream of exploring the very limits of where Alexander the Great had managed to venture, and his attention was now caught by accounts of other ancient travellers to the region coming this time not from the West, but from the Far East. Using a seventh-century account of travels to India by the Buddhist Chinese monk Xuanzang, Stein successfully located a forgotten Jain temple in the mountains north-west of Lahore.[8] He also acquired a fox-terrier dog called Dash, who came with him wherever he went. Marc Aurel Stein was swiftly transforming from an academic student of books and languages in dusty libraries to an explorer and adventurer (with trusty canine sidekick) – and he had no plans to turn back. In 1898 he wrote to his brother Ernst: 'I admit that my last year in India has been so good to me that I find it difficult to even think of saying farewell.'[9]

The question now was not where Stein would settle next – he would never settle anywhere again for long for the rest of his life. The question was where he would *explore* next.

*

In the same decade that Stein discovered his Jain temple, other scholars had used the same text – that of the Chinese Buddhist monk Xuanzang – to discover the physical remains of the final unidentified key site from the Buddha's life: his birthplace, in Lumbini (modern-day Nepal).[10] Others again were busy filling in the gaps in the then-current understanding of how Buddhism had itself spread from India to China and become an official religion there in the first centuries CE. And at the same time, scholars were also fascinated by the growing evidence for the interaction in northern India between Indian and Greek cultural and artistic traditions. As Stein had been aware since reading the works of Arrian aged ten, Alexander the Great had conquered to the banks of the River Indus in north-western India (modern-day Pakistan). This conquest in the late fourth century BCE had initiated centuries of Greek interaction with resident communities in the region, leaving traces everywhere of the mixing of cultural ideas, artistic techniques and physical monuments. In Lahore's museum, curated by Lockwood Kipling, father of Rudyard, Stein had seen for himself the early Buddhist sculpture coming from the Gandhara region (in modern-day Pakistan and Afghanistan) which reflected both Greek and Indian styles.[11]

Greek artistic ideas flowing east, Buddhism travelling east, and Chinese Buddhist monks, centuries later, travelling west. The world was waking up to the fact that there had once been an arterial set of super-highways connecting up cultures, empires and worlds from the Mediterranean in the west to China in the east. In 1877, Baron Ferdinand von Richthofen, a German geographer and explorer (and uncle of the First World War-era famed flying ace Baron von Richthofen, aka the 'Red Baron'), had named this set of arterial super-highways along which ideas, goods and peoples had travelled east and west in antiquity '*Seidenstraße*': the 'Silk Roads', after the primary good that had been traded west out of China along its routes.[12]

Stein was in many ways already in the perfect place – at the heart of this connective network in India – to play a role in the developing global understanding of the ancient Silk Roads. Yet exploration and study of cultural and religious interactions in northern India were already, by the 1890s, well underway. He needed a more remote and unknown area of the Silk Roads that he could make his own. And that lay to the north-east.

If you look at a world map, running above modern-day Pakistan, India, Nepal, Bhutan and Bangladesh like a gigantic thick bushy eyebrow are the Himalayan mountains, separating the Indian subcontinent from the Tibetan plateau. This largely impenetrable chain of mountains ends in the west in Central Asia in an enormous clump of mountain ranges centred at the meeting point of modern-day Afghanistan, Pakistan, Kashmir and India. This clump, comprising mountain ranges such as the Hindu Kush, the Karakoram and Pamirs, extends north, roughly along the boundaries of today's Afghanistan, and then swirls eastwards again as a further set of mountain ranges through the modern territories of Tajikistan, Kyrgyzstan and into China. Together, these vast mountain ranges constitute a massive barrier to those attempting to move east or west through Central Asia.

Early studies of the Silk Roads had shown that routes coming from the west through Afghanistan and up from northern India had managed to find passes in the Pamir Mountains through which to navigate the mountain barrier and descend into Kashgar, on the western edge of the modern-day Autonomous Region of Xinjiang in China. From here, ancient traders were faced with an environment in many ways more perilous than the mountains: the Taklamakan Desert. The name's etymology, in the local Uighur dialect, underlines its nature: 'the place of nothingness' and 'the place of no return'. Roughly the size of Germany, the Taklamakan is 85 per cent shifting sand-dunes, making it the second-largest moving sand desert in the world, and its proximity to Siberia and to the Himalayas means that its temperatures shift from minus 20 degrees centigrade in the winter to 40 degrees centigrade and above in the summer. It is one of the most inhospitable places on earth.

The only places where life could survive in the Taklamakan were the small oasis communities formed around water sources that ran down from the mountains surrounding the desert on its north, west and south sides. The ancient Silk Road routes, weaving through the mountains and arriving at Kashgar on the desert's western edge, had thus run around both the northern and southern sides of the desert, moving between oasis communities, until they met again on the eastern side of the Taklamakan at Dunhuang, where the famous Jade Gate symbolised entry to the empire of ancient China. From there, the Silk routes had then spread more easily eastwards to the great markets in the Chinese capital at Chang'an.

This unwelcoming mix of mountains and desert in Central Asia was the chokehold on East–West interaction in antiquity and meant that in Stein's time the area was still one of the most inaccessible and least well-known places on the planet. But the archaeological remains scattered within it also potentially held untold rewards for those determined, brave (and reckless) enough to make their way there.

For Stein, this was an area of scholarly investigation and discovery in which he could make his mark. It also spoke to his Hungarian roots: the Hungarian explorer Csoma de Koros, who had been one of the main proponents of the idea that the Hungarian people had migrated from this part of Central Asia, had died back in 1842 exploring the area. More importantly, the most recent explorers in the region had returned with promising examples of the kinds of archaeological evidence that might be found there. While inhospitable in the extreme, the dry sandy desert conditions were perfect for preserving paper and wood, the sorts of things that had rotted away long ago in most other parts of the Silk Roads. In 1890, for example, Captain Hamilton Bower had returned from the region with the oldest surviving example of a text written on birch-bark.[13] Other finds discovered by French and Swedish expeditions in the mid-1890s, now being examined by scholars, indicated not only surviving texts, but also whole new as yet unknown and undeciphered languages.[14] Marc Aurel Stein was an expert in the languages of Indian and Central Asia. He was a man skilled in, and eager for, mountain climbing and adventurous exploration. In 1898, the day before he wrote to his brother saying how much he loved life in India, he proposed to the authorities of Punjab province, under whom he served in his roles as Registrar and Principal in Lahore, a major expedition to Khotan, one of the ancient oasis communities on the southern side of the Taklamakan Desert.

One of the things Stein mentioned in his application was the need to move fast to beat competing planned expeditions by the Swedes and the Russians. His application also made clear that his would be a British expedition – with funding ultimately from the British government, finds going to the British Museum and himself as lead explorer currently in the process of applying for British citizenship. His casting of this expedition as a British effort to beat others and particularly the Russians to new finds in

Central Asia was well placed, because, for most of the century, Britain had been engaged in what became known as the 'Great Game' – the struggle between Britain and Russia for political and military influence in Central Asia.

British interest in Central Asia stemmed from their desire to defend their control of India. In 1865 the Russians had taken Tashkent and in 1868 Samarkand (both in modern-day Uzbekistan). Russian Central Asian and British Indian front lines were therefore coming ever closer, separated only by Afghanistan and then by the mountainous clump of the Hindu Kush, Pamir and Karakoram mountain ranges that coiled around the Taklamakan Desert (the desert was at that time part of Chinese Turkestan).[15] The British knew well the particular passes through the mountains between Afghanistan and British India's north-western flank – among them the famous Khyber and Bolan Passes – but at this point they did not know much about the Pamir and Karakoram mountain ranges on British India's northern flank. They did not know, for example, where Afghanistan's eastern border actually was in the Pamir Mountains, nor whether a Russian army could in reality make its way through the Pamir and Karakoram mountain ranges to attack British India.[16] The Russians knew no better. The world maps of both sides showed a vast white blank across these mountain ranges and into the area of the Taklamakan, with the locations of oasis towns such as Kashgar only indicated within an approximate area.[17]

In 1868 a British traveller called Robert Shaw became the first Briton to reach Kashgar across the Pamirs. He was followed by George Hayward, who had been sponsored by the Royal Geographic Society to begin to map the different navigable passes in the mountains. Over the next decade, Britain trained a series of Indians as undercover spies known simply as 'the Pundits', who travelled often disguised as Holy Men across the Pamirs, making rough maps of the mountains and in particular trying to fix where exactly the border of Afghanistan was.[18]

By the late 1880s, the geopolitical situation had become even more high stakes: China had reasserted its authority in the Taklamakan Desert and crushed a number of the local rulers whom the British and Russians had been negotiating with either to allow their troops to move towards India or act as a buffer against Russian advance.[19] Now Russia, Britain and China were each secretly exploring the routes through the Pamir Mountains and the potential for expansion and defence of their spheres of influence. For the British, this became even more urgent when their mapping teams and spy networks realised that the agreed boundary of Afghanistan actually left a narrow unclaimed corridor of land high in the Pamirs between Afghanistan and Chinese Turkestan, through which, if the Russians discovered navigable passes, they could move unopposed against British India. In 1891, British troops came face to face with a small Russian force trying to do exactly that and only an intense international outcry encouraged the Russians to withdraw from this 'neutral ground'.[20] Finally, in 1895, Britain and Russia agreed with Afghanistan that it should extend its boundaries to cover the unclaimed corridor of land. Britain had its buffer – but that would not stop Russia if it decided to go on the offensive.[21]

When Stein put in his application to mount an expedition up through the Pamirs and into Chinese Turkestan and to the oasis settlement of Khotan in 1898, he knew he was venturing into still-fraught political and military territory where Russian, Chinese and British interests converged. To do so ahead of a Russian expedition would prove a welcome boost to British morale. He received the go-ahead on New Year's Day 1899.

The slight problem for Stein was that he had, just the month before, also been offered a new job: as Principal of the Calcutta Madrasah over on India's eastern flank. Soon enough, however, he had persuaded his new employers to give him leave from the summer of 1900 to undertake the expedition funded by the Punjab government. He was assiduous in his preparations, ordering specialist garments and supplies from London as well as from the area around Lahore. From Cadbury's in England he ordered a good supply of chocolate, and from Burberry in London a set of clothes in their patented famous 'Gabardine' extra-durable, warm and water-resistant cloth. From Jaeger in London, their woollen underwear and thick woollen blankets, and from his tailor in India he ordered a whole host of different garments, including a coat with fur and one without fur to be fitted to his dog Dash. On 31 May 1900, Stein set out from Srinagar, in the foothills of the vast Pamir and Karakoram mountain ranges, to wind his way through the navigable passes of the mountains first through to Kashgar, and from there, out into the Taklamakan Desert, to Khotan.[22]

*

It is only just over 600 kilometres from Srinagar to Kashgar and today you can drive it fairly easily by taking the Karakoram Highway which runs through the mountains. But in 1900 there were no roads in this part of the world. Stein covered that distance on foot and by pony across rock-strewn uneven ground, climbing up to altitudes of between 16,000 and 20,000 feet in order to pass between the giant mountains gathered around him. With him was his faithful dog Dash in his dashing fur- and non-fur-lined coats, his servant, his cook, an Indian surveyor called Ram Singh, and Ram's servant and cook. Together it took them two months to cover the 600 kilometres to arrive in Kashgar, where Stein intended to rest, regroup, repair his kit and recruit the men, camels and supplies he would need for his expedition into the Taklamakan Desert to Khotan. He also needed to do some serious diplomacy with the Chinese authorities. And for that he needed Britain's man in Kashgar: a half-Scottish and half-Chinese translator-turned-diplomat called George Macartney.

Macartney had come to Kashgar in 1890 as part of the British team sent to negotiate with the Chinese for the opening of a British Consulate there. The Chinese – annoyed at the way that the British had been too friendly and supportive to rebellious local rulers in the region over the past decades (trying to win their support to act as buffers to Russian expansion in the region) – refused the request, but allowed Macartney to stay on living in Kashgar as the unofficial British representative.[23]

It was almost dark when Stein arrived at the outskirts of Kashgar on 29 July 1900. He recorded later in his account of his expedition how the mud-built walls of the city rose up before him, complete with battlements and bastions like some kind of medieval fortress. All was quiet: the gates of the town already shut. But along a poplar-lined avenue outside the city walls, there swung a single lantern to mark the outer gate of the Macartneys' home.[24] He was welcomed into dinner and spent the night camped in their orchard garden.

For five weeks Stein rested in Kashgar and made his preparations, which included multiple visits to the Chinese authorities and a crash course in Chinese diplomatic etiquette from Macartney. It also included innumerable mentions by Stein of his love for his 'patron', the Chinese Buddhist monk Xuanzang, who had made his journey westwards in the seventh century, and in whose footsteps Stein had travelled around northern India, and was now attempting to do so in Chinese Turkestan.[25] On 4 September 1900, with the necessary permissions from the Chinese authorities in hand, Stein was ready to leave for Khotan.[26] The camels he had secured seemed even keener to leave than he was: they wandered off before breakfast and had to be found and brought back to be part of the expedition group photo.[27]

Stein soon came face to face with the heat and fatigue of the desert as his party made their way across the shifting sand-dunes on the southern rim of the Taklamakan. The sand ridges rose 30 to 40 feet high, and every step in their ascent was made more arduous as feet sank deep into the loose sand. Even when they made it to the 'langars', the travellers' shelters built at intermittent stages along the route to Khotan, everything was 'monotonous khaki'. Stein at least managed to take comfort in the fact that the colour of his clothes fitted in with his surroundings.[28] The trek to Khotan took a month, climbing endless sand-dunes and following flattened tracks around the edge of the Taklamakan Desert. But even these flattened tracks bore evidence of the dangers of the environment through which Stein was moving: the tracks themselves were mostly marked simply by the parched carcasses and bleached bones of animals that had died there.[29]

Once arrived in the small desert oasis community of Khotan, some 500 kilometres' journey around the rim of the Taklamakan Desert from Kashgar, and having presented his permissions to the local Chinese governor, the 'Amban' of Khotan, Stein set out to locate sites of interest for him to excavate. By December 1900, he was excavating at the site of Dandān-Uiliq, five days' march north of Khotan. Stein spent Christmas Day 1900 with his dog Dash in a cold tent amid the sand-dunes and surviving remnants of the site. But the hardships were worthwhile. Not only did his team partially excavate from the sand and map over fourteen different previously unknown buildings at the site, but more importantly they proved beyond question what excavation in this inhospitable part of the world could deliver: antiquities that could not survive anywhere else. The team uncovered painted murals on the walls of a Buddhist shrine and monastery building; lacquered and painted wood bowls of Chinese design; painted wood panels; and, most significantly, small panels of wood and paper with writing on them. One scrap of paper folded up into a narrow roll – when recovered, unrolled and read – turned out to be a petition in Chinese for the recovery of a donkey that had been lent on hire to two individuals who, after ten months, had failed to return the animal. It was dated to the sixth day of the second month 781 CE.[30] Other paper scraps revealed writing not in Chinese but in a strange form of cursive Brahmi – an Indo-Iranian dialect – which would later be termed Khotanese after the oasis settlement of Khotan.

By 4 January 1901, with the moveable finds from Dandān-Uiliq secured in travel crates ready for eventual return to Kashgar and then on to the British Museum as promised in his expedition funding application, Stein was on the move again. This time to the east of Khotan, where, having navigated swelling sand-dunes now rising up to 50 feet high and sub-zero temperatures at night, he finally reached the next oasis settlement of Niya. This too was a place that Stein's 'patron saint', Xuanzang, had visited, calling it the 'eastern frontier' of the King of Khotan. Stein had scarcely been at Niya a few hours when the man in charge of his camels introduced to him a local who had in his possession two inscribed wood tablets picked up from ancient ruins in the desert outside of Niya. They were inscribed with a text written in the ancient Kharoshthi language from extreme north-western India.[31] Stein was soon back out into the desert on the trail of the site, pitching camp there at the end of January 1901 to begin a series of excavations. Wooden tablets, all inscribed with the same language as the first two, started pouring out of the sands. Many were wedge-shaped and arranged in pairs, with their writing placed on the inside of the two wedges, which were then held together with string, and the string note secured with a clay seal. Opening these wedge tablets revealed ink 'as fresh as if penned yesterday'.[32] Their language, the Kharoshthi script, was used by the Indo-Scythian kings who had ruled in the region of north-west India and the River Indus in the first three centuries CE.

Many more documents in the Kharoshthi script were to turn up during Stein's excavations across a series of ancient residences in the desert outside of Niya. Some were even found in an ancient refuse heap, whose smell was still 'pungent after so many centuries', leaving Stein and his team to 'swallow liberal doses of antique microbes luckily now dead'.[33] But bearing the smell was worth it. The team found complete documents written not only on wood tablets but on leather in the Kharoshthi script, folded up into neat little rolls and still pliable and readable after centuries in their desert tip.

The languages of north-western India written on wooden tablets and leather rolls in the Taklamakan Desert were conclusive proof of the ways in which cultures, languages, peoples and ideas had moved east and west across vast swathes of the globe in antiquity. But perhaps the greatest surprise for Stein and his team were the clay seals that had been placed over the string tying two wooden inscribed wedges together. For a number were imprinted with images of Greek gods, including Athena and Eros, and heroes like Heracles. And on one particular set of wooden wedge tablets, a double clay seal: one with Chinese characters and the other with an image of Athena.[34] Here, in the barren sands of the Taklamakan Desert, Stein held in his hands the proof that, in the first centuries CE, the worlds of extreme east and west had met.

With the approaching summer heat making work in the desert impossible, Stein took back with him to Kashgar all the finds his camels could carry. From there he – and the finds – made their way not back to India but to Samarkand, and then on to Osh, where he and they boarded a train on the Trans-Caspian railway to head west. His final destination was London and the British Museum, where the finds were deposited and the long business of cataloguing and studying them began. But Dash – Stein's faithful fox-terrier – did not come with him. Dash returned direct to India with the rest of Stein's expedition party, to avoid the mandated four-month quarantine he would have had to endure if he had arrived on British soil!

Stein himself was back in India by October 1901 – to start another new job. He had hated the oppressive humidity of Calcutta where he had briefly worked as Principal of the Calcutta Madrasah in the first part of 1900 before taking off on his expedition, and so, while on expedition, he had applied for a new job back in the Punjab as Inspector of Schools. How many schools he actually inspected is unclear as he seems to have made immediate requests for leave to write and publish the account of his expedition. By May 1902 he was back in Europe, speaking about his expedition and finds at international conferences, and he was based back in England for most of 1903 furiously writing a full-length popular account of his expedition. In the summer of 1903, *Sand Buried Ruins of Khotan* was published and was an instant bestseller, going into a second print run in 1904.[35] The public were enthralled with the evidence for the ideas, beliefs, art and languages mixing together along the Silk Roads in this most barren remote part of the world, and Stein enjoyed the acclaim he received for his daring explorations. This was a heady era of exploration of the least-known parts of the world. In 1901–5, five different European teams set out to explore Antarctica, and a similar number of teams from around the world would set out that decade to explore more of the Taklamakan Desert. These two places – two complete opposites in terms of their terrain and temperature – were the great unknowns. And those who dared to investigate them were celebrities.

Back in India in 1904–5, and having changed job again in the Punjab to become Inspector-General of Education and Superintendent of Archaeology (at least a little more in his ball-park), Stein was busy writing up the formal academic report on his first expedition.[36] But he was also simultaneously seeking funds for another expedition – this one bolder than the first. His superiors in India most certainly grumbled about Stein's apparent inability to stay in one place and do his job, but were finally persuaded. So too were the British Museum and the Royal Geographic Society, who co-sponsored the second expedition alongside the British Government of India. On 20 April 1906, at the age of forty-three, Stein set off from India once again to make his way through the Pamir Mountains to Kashgar on the western edge of the Taklamakan Desert. Along with him was Dash the fox-terrier. Well, in fact this was Dash II (the first Dash had died while his master was away in England in 1902–3). Dash II was an even more canny canine companion than his predecessor. He soon learnt to save his own feet when the going got tough through the mountain passes by jumping up into the stirrup of one of the packhorses and from there leaping up on the saddle, from where he would happily watch the world go by as the horse took the strain, picking its way through the rocky passes. Not for nothing did Dash II become known as 'Dash the Great'.

The horses also carried Stein's treasured supplies from London: two years' supply of Cadbury's chocolate; jars of the newly invented Marmite, of which Stein was an immediate fan; as well as tins of compressed cabbage, carrots, tea, coffee and pea soup. This collection of necessities arrived – along with Dash the Great, Stein and his small retinue – in Kashgar and into the welcoming hospitality of the home of the Macartneys once again. After recruiting the necessary camels and workmen, as well as a man called Jiang Xiaoyuan, who would act as his Chinese-speaking secretary, translator and language teacher, and having spent the required diplomatic time securing permissions from the Chinese authorities, Stein set out on 23 June 1906 along the southern rim of the Taklamakan Desert. But this time he planned to make it all the way to the other side.[37]

Stein's departure from India for Kashgar was noted in *The Times* newspaper on 29 May 1906. At the time, *The Times* had a circulation three times that of the combined circulation of its five closest competitors, and the inclusion of Stein's departure demonstrates not only the national and international interest in his expedition into this still-unknown part of the world, but also the increasingly influential status Stein himself enjoyed in this period.[38] Moreover, this was no single announcement: *The Times* published regular updates on Stein's progress throughout his second expedition, giving increasingly more space on the printed page to each update as excitement and interest continued to build in what Stein was discovering. This increasing interest was not only to do with the nature of the finds. There was also very much a sense of national pride involved, not least as Stein had formally been made a British citizen in 1904. While the 'Great Game' of British–Russian confrontation in the region had eased with the outbreak of war between Russia and Japan in 1904, and subsequently thanks to British concerns about Germany's growing ambitions back in Europe and its new-found desire to keep Russia on side, there was still plenty of national competition in the air in this remote part of the world.[39] *The Times*'s announcement of Stein's departure had ended with a list of other nations making expeditions to the area at the same time – American, Russian, German and French – all of whom were keen to make new discoveries in the desert.[40] The question was who would get there first.

Stein moved quickly, making his way past Khotan and on to Keriya on the southern rim of the Taklamakan Desert by October 1906. He continued to excavate as he moved eastwards, uncovering more and more manuscripts written in Sanskrit, Chinese and 'Khotanese' – the unknown and undeciphered language he had discovered examples of during his first expedition.[41] By February 1907 he was 1,200 miles further east, having moved through and excavated at and around the settlements of Niya, Miran and Loulan on the eastern end of the Taklamakan Desert. *The Times* report, published on 25 May 1907, outlines how Stein continued to find vast hoards of manuscripts in both Chinese and Kharoshthi – indicating that the use of this language from northern India had spread across the entire Taklamakan in antiquity. And at Miran, Stein commented that the art and sculpture decorating the Buddhist temples he had discovered 'are so thoroughly western in conception and treatment that one would expect them rather on the walls of some Roman villa than in Buddhist sanctuaries on the very confines of China'.[42]

None of these reports printed in *The Times* were being sent by radio or telegram. No such thing was possible in the Taklamakan Desert. Stein was himself writing them and sending them back to the Royal Geographic Society in London. After long days of travel and excavation, he would busy himself with examination of the day's finds, writing letters to friends and colleagues and particularly to the secretary of the Royal Geographic Society. These letters would be entrusted to particular members of his team, who then travelled back around the Taklamakan Desert to Kashgar, where they would in turn be handed to a system of '*daks*' – mail runners – who travelled across the Pamir and Karakoram mountain ranges through to Gilgit, where the mail could be sent on to British India and then by boat to London. The secretary of the Royal Geographic Society, on receiving one of Stein's updates, would then produce a condensed version for publication in *The Times*. But the postal system also worked both ways. Letters for Stein could be entrusted to the *daks* to take to Kashgar, where his man would pick up the mail that arrived and then travel back around the Taklamakan to seek Stein out wherever he had moved to in the desert to deliver it. On 24 December 1906, the lucky team member finally caught up with Stein with four months of mail – over a hundred and fifty letters – for him to go through.[43]

On 15 October 1907, *The Times* published the next update on Stein's expedition: an update that Stein had written back on 18 June and that had since been making its way slowly from the eastern end of the Taklamakan Desert back to London. He had been busy, heading to the fabled settlement of Dunhuang on the very eastern edge of the Taklamakan Desert, a place he called the '*limes*' ('the boundaries') of the ancient Chinese Han Empire. Arriving at Dunhuang was like arriving at an eastern version of Kashgar: the endless sand gave way once more to poplar-tree-lined streets and farms, orchards and fields. And just like at Kashgar, Stein, invoking the local rules of hospitality to strangers, simply moved into the garden of one of the houses, setting up his tent and his canvas circular bath for the duration of his stay. But he lost no time in relaxing. Instead, he and his team, in early March 1907, had begun to survey the remains of the Han Chinese fortification walls that ran for almost sixty miles north of Dunhuang, mirroring the Great Wall on China's northern border. In the regular watchtowers and forts set into the wall, he discovered hundreds of Chinese texts written on wooden slips alongside endless examples of everyday life along the wall: combs, mouse-traps, purses and tent hammers, as well as the first surviving examples of another early Aramaic script: the language of the Sogdians, one of the greatest trading communities of antiquity, who had ranged far and wide along the Silk Roads from their base back in present-day Iran. By May 1907, however, the heat was so fierce (not to mention the abundant mosquitoes and scorpions) that he and his team returned to Dunhuang, and it was now that

Stein turned his full attention to another of the prize goals of his expedition (one he knew the competing German, French, American and Russian teams were also keen to explore): the 'Mogao' or 'Thousand Buddha Caves'.

*

Stein had originally been told about the Thousand Buddha Caves by a fellow Hungarian explorer, who had visited back in 1897, and who had described paintings and sculptures there as similar to those of Indian Buddhist art.[44] Inhabited by hermit monks since the fourth century CE, the caves – part natural and part carved, honey-combing a 2-kilometre-long rock face – were a venerated site of Buddhist worship. Over time, Buddhist temples had been constructed within the caves to serve the growing number of monks. In turn, rich donors, following Buddhist practice, had given money to the monks to build and richly decorate individual cave shrines on their behalf, and Chinese Emperors had even paid for the construction of giant Buddha statues out of the natural rock around the caves' entrances. In the millennium spanning the fourth to four-teenth centuries CE, the cave complex had mushroomed into a sprawling collection of a thousand Buddhist temple caves, shrines and ancillary rooms, decorated with half a million square feet of painted murals. Keen to unearth the long reach of ideas, artistic styles and languages going east along the Silk Roads, Stein had thus made the caves an early key goal of his second expedition.

The Times report of 15 October 1907 says nothing about what happened next, except to note – in relation to Stein's time at the caves overall – that 'the materials collected are so ample and varied that they will require prolonged labour on the part of several specialists'.[45] In fact, as Stein would later himself recount in his public account of his second expedition, on first arriving at Dunhuang back in March 1907, he had heard a rumour about a massive collection of manuscripts that had been discovered at the site two years previously and that was now looked after by one of the Buddhist monks resident at the caves.[46] 'It was useless to disguise', he admitted in his later account, that 'what was now drawing me back with the strength of a hidden magnet . . . was that great hidden deposit of ancient manuscripts'.[47] These manuscripts, Stein's Chinese-speaking secretary Jiang Xiaoyuan had ascertained, were stored in a walled-off side cave and the only person who could authorise access was the resident Buddhist monk Wang Yuanlu. Stein later wrote, in relation to the manuscript's guardian, that 'it was clear from the first that he would be a difficult person to handle'.[48]

Stein's first goal was to be allowed to see the whole collection of manuscripts in their original place of deposit in order to 'ascertain the true character and approximate date of the collection'. His Chinese-speaking secretary was dispatched to negotiate with Wang, his 'tactful diplomacy' 'backed up by the promise of a liberal donation for the main shrine'.[49] But all that was initially permitted by Wang was for Stein to see one or two of the manuscripts. The secretary's suggestion that Stein might eventually take some away, on the other hand, was met with 'such perturbation, prompted equally, it seemed by scruples of a religious sort and fear of popular resentment'.[50]

Clearly, however, this was always Stein's ultimate goal. He was pleased to find out that while Wang had reported the manuscript find to the Chinese authorities, they had been content with Wang's statement that the entire collection amounted to 'about seven cartloads', rather than making an official inventory, which would have made things 'from our point of view . . . far more complicated'.[51] Stein now went on a charm offensive, realising 'that to rely on the temptation of money alone as a means of overcoming his scruples was manifestly useless'.[52] He asked to be shown the cave-temple that Wang had lovingly restored himself over the previous years, and promptly waxed lyrical about Wang's efforts. He was, though, clearly impressed by the monk's determination. This was a man, he recounted, with a 'curious mixture of pious zeal, naïve ignorance, and astute tenacity of purpose'.[53] There was only one trump card to play: Stein's 'Chinese patron saint', the seventh-century Buddhist monk-turned-explorer, Xuanzang. Stein told Wang – in his own faltering Chinese – about his devotion to Xuanzang and how he had followed in Xuanzang's path from India back to China. Wang was delighted because he shared Stein's love of Xuanzang, and promptly showed him a series of frescoes Wang had had painted by local artists of the explorer monk's travels. One showed Xuanzang attempting to travel safely across a river with bundles of ancient manuscripts he was hoping to bring back from India to China. A large turtle was swimming towards them to help them across. As Stein noted in his own account, could he use this analogy to persuade the monk to now let him take manuscripts safely back to the spiritual home of Buddhism in India?[54]

Late at night, several days later, Stein's Chinese translator appeared at his tent with a bundle of manuscripts Wang had brought to him in secret. They appeared to be copies of Buddhist sutras (religious texts) brought from India and translated by Xuanzang himself. That these texts were translated by Stein's favoured Chinese monk explorer, whom he and Wang had recently been discussing, must have been a total coincidence – Wang could not have known their authorship when selecting them to hand over. But now this happy coincidence was – in Stein's and his translator's hands – nothing less than a sign of divine approval for the developing relationship between Stein and Wang. And such a characterisation had an immediate effect. Within hours the doorway to the cave of manuscripts had been unblocked. The priest, 'still combating his scruples and nervous apprehensions', 'under the influence of the quasi-divine hint now summoned up courage' to let Stein in.[55] As Stein later recounted 'the sight of the small room . . . was one to make my eyes open wide. Heaped up in layers . . . there appeared in the dim light of the priest's little lamp a solid mass of manuscript bundles rising to a height of nearly ten feet, and filling . . . close on 500 cubic feet.'[56]

Wang was nervous about losing his position – and local patrons – if news spread around the oasis of his allowing Stein free rein with the manuscripts. Instead, he brought a couple out at a time for Stein to study in a room close by. Stein worried whether 'the timorous priest, swayed by his worldly fears and possible spiritual scruples, [would] be moved to close down his shell before I had been able to extract any of the pearls?'[57] But during that day, more and more 'pearls' revealed themselves: a wide variety of Buddhist sutras in Chinese as well as a number of Tibetan texts, and even writing in Indian Brahmi script with which Stein was familiar. Nor was there only writing. Stein was handed rolled paintings on fine gauze-like silk and linen, silk banners painted with figures of Buddhas and Bodhisattvas, and larger silk paintings of up to six feet in size.

Stein guessed that Wang was showing him the paintings in an effort to distract him from being interested in what Wang considered to be the most important documents: the canonical Buddhist texts in Chinese. Stein was happy to take what Wang offered – especially given that such texts often ended up being included by accident in the piles of paintings dragged out of the storeroom.[58]

By the end of the day, Stein had accumulated a neat pile of manuscripts and paintings in the corner of his 'reading room' that, it was suggested to Wang, needed to be removed for 'what our diplomatic convention styled "closer examination"':

> The great question was whether Wang would be willing to brave the risks of this removal, and subsequently to fall in with the true interpretation of our proceeding. It would not have done to breathe to him unholy words of sale and purchase; it was equally clear that any removal would have to be effected in strictest secrecy.[59]

The persuasion game continued into the night – and focused again on Xuanzang. Would it not be, Stein's Chinese translator argued, an 'act of religious merit' to 'render accessible to Western students the literary and other relics in [Wang's] keeping?'[60] Under the cover of darkness that night, the Chinese translator was allowed to bring to Stein everything they had set aside that day, 'on the solemn condition that nobody besides us three was to get the slightest inkling of what was being transacted, and that as long as [Stein] was on Chinese soil the origin of these "finds" was not to be revealed to any living being'.[61] For seven days Stein studied manuscripts brought to him by Wang, and for seven nights his translator brought the day's haul secretly to Stein's tent, with 'judiciously administered doses of silver ... counteracting [Wang's] relapses into timorous contrariness'.[62]

Eventually, the trio reached the large rolls of Chinese texts – the ones Wang seemed to attach the most value to. And it was here that Wang 'came to business', asking for a substantial subscription to his temple before Stein could look at them, and asserting that it would be impossible to take any away.[63] Stein himself admits he could not begrudge Wang's 'scruples' as Wang feared that, were his local patrons, who had given money to the temple previously, to notice the absence of the manuscripts, his reputation would be in tatters and his 'life-task destroyed'. Over the next two days the discussions continued, with, at one point, Wang even overnight moving manuscripts he had brought out for examination back into their cave. But Wang also needed money for his temple. Finally, they struck a deal: fifty well-preserved bundles of Chinese text rolls and five Tibetan ones, as well as everything already in Stein's possession, for four horseshoes of silver.[64] Wang left to visit his local patrons and returned reassured that no one knew of their agreement and that his reputation had not suffered. He allowed Stein to take twenty more bundles of manuscripts in exchange for a further donation to the temple. In all, twelve cases of documents were packed by Stein's team. And before Stein left the region, Wang had let depart with him 'for that "temple of learning" in the distant West' another 230 bundles of documents. Stein left the Thousand Buddha Caves for the West with, in total, twenty-four cases of documents and five more filled with paintings and art relics.[65]

Stein had done what he came to do: to discover and obtain materials to bring back to the British Museum for further study to exemplify the depth and intricacy of cultural and linguistic connections across the Silk Roads in antiquity. But whereas in his excavations at different sites he had obtained the necessary permits and then been left to excavate and retain as he saw fit, here at the Thousand Buddha Caves, he had not excavated as much as persuaded – in all sorts of ways – the local guardian to hand over a huge number of manuscripts from a 'live' ongoing site of religious devotion. It was an act the guardian knew – if the exchange had become widely known – would have caused huge controversy and that was, as a result, carried out at the time in the upmost secrecy. And while Stein had paid a mutually agreed sum (four horseshoes of silver/500 Rupees), it was in reality a pittance (about £130) – much less than he had been prepared to pay.[66] Stein was of course not the only explorer to act in this way. The French team not far behind Stein, led by Paul Pelliot, secured a large number of manuscripts from Wang in the same way (which were taken to the Bibliothèque Nationale in Paris), with the result that the Chinese central authorities became aware of the transaction and insisted that the remaining manuscripts be cleared from the cave and transported to Beijing.[67] It has forever remained a significant thorn in China's side, with Stein and Pelliot cited as two prime examples of the many foreigners who, particularly in this period, robbed China of the bones of their history. In 1930, the Chinese National Commission put it like this:

> Taking advantage of the ignorance and cupidity of the priest in charge, [Stein] persuaded the latter to sell to him at a pittance what he considered to be the pick of the collection which, needless to say, did not in any way belong to the seller. It would be the same if some Chinese traveller pretending to be merely a student of religious history went to Canterbury and bought valuable relics from the cathedral caretaker.[68]

Stein's defence, in his own words, was that 'it was my duty towards research to try my upmost to rescue, if possible, the whole of this precious collection from the risk of slow dispersion and loss with which it was threatened in such keeping'.[69] Of course this is an unprovable argument: the material has remained safe (although not altogether) as a result of Stein's intervention – but who can say if it would have been equally safe if left undisturbed in its cave? What Stein holds back from speaking of is the personal gain to his reputation that came from bringing this windfall to light. That personal gain is manifest in the way *The Times* gave more and more space to his exploits as an explorer in the final phases of his expedition. It recounts him exploring a number of sites in the north-eastern part of the Taklamakan, before making his way across the desert westwards exploring sites and river courses as he went (and almost dying of dehydration in the process), returning to Khotan and making preparations for fifty camels loaded down with materials he had collected to make the journey to India.[70] The paper reports how Stein himself set off to survey another as-yet-unmapped set of passes through the Karakoram Mountains, with the result that he suffered extreme frostbite in his feet. He was carried on the back of a yak, and then a pony, through the passes in the Karakoram Mountains to Leh in Kashmir, where the now-infected toes on his right foot were amputated. Following his recovery, *The Times* announced his arrival in London on 29 January 1909.[71] His dog, Dash II/Dash the Great, totally uninjured despite accompanying his master everywhere on his travels of the previous two years, arrived in London out of quarantine in May (and hit the headlines in the *Daily Mail*).[72]

Marc Aurel Stein was now an official celebrity. Interviews with him went global. On 30 January 1909, the *Illustrated London News* published portrait photos of fifteen explorers entitled 'Lured by the Unknown, Men Who Fill in the Blanks: the Great Explorers of the Moment'. Stein was number one, in advance of people like Shackleton exploring the Antarctic, Mikkelsen the Artic and Stein's Swedish competitor, Sven Hedin, exploring Tibet.[73] In the next months he was showered with honorary degrees and awards, and by 1912, upon the full publication of his adventures, was made a

Knight Commander of the Indian Empire. As Lord Curzon put it: 'even though he left some of his toes behind him, he has brought back a reputation greatly enhanced, and in the cases which he is now unpacking in London, a treasure-store for our museums which will . . . add materially to the knowledge of mankind'.[74]

The huge volume of material Stein had brought back to the British Museum would take decades to catalogue and study (the work still continues to this day). Stein had proved beyond doubt the incredible mixing of cultures, artistic and sculptural influences, languages and peoples along the Silk Roads in antiquity all the way to the very borders of China, alongside 'discovering' a number of rare and early documents, which proved the existence of printing mechanisms far earlier than had been accepted. One of the documents he took possession of at the Thousand Buddha Caves proved to be a copy of the Buddhist Diamond Sutra, one of the most revered texts in Buddhism. While this text was well known before Stein's obtaining of this particular copy, what makes this copy special is that it is dated. It was produced on 11 May 868 CE. And it was printed using a series of woodblocks, each cut to 'print' a particular section of text, with each 'page' then glued together to form a scroll 16 feet in length. This makes it the world's oldest printed book, beating the Gutenberg Bible (and the invention of the printing press) by some seven hundred years.[75] It is also – many argue – the earliest example of universal copyright. Alongside the date is an inscription by the person who commissioned it, which reads: 'Reverently caused to be made for universal free distribution by Wang Jie on behalf of his parents.'[76]

Stein was back in India in 1912, just as his popular account of his second expedition was published. The *Times Literary Supplement* published a review, which, while praising the two volumes and his discoveries, questioned whether Stein had made life much more difficult for the Buddhist monk Wang Yuanlu at the Thousand Buddha Caves by being so open and explicit about their dealings in his book.[77] Indeed, much had changed in China since Stein's last departure. The Imperial dynasty had been overthrown in the

Chinese Revolution of 1911 and the Republic of China was declared on 1 January 1912. That Republic was even more sensitive to foreign intervention and exploration than its Imperial predecessors.

In 1913 Stein set off again for the Taklamakan Desert on his third expedition (accompanied by Dash III, whom he had acquired on his return to India). He headed straight for the eastern end of the Taklamakan, excavating at oasis towns like Miran and Loulan, as well as visiting Dunhuang and his old friend Wang Yuanlu the Buddhist monk. Wang had managed to keep his role and had spent his 'donations' – as he proudly showed Stein – on building new guest quarters and shrines at the site. But he was also bitter about how his remaining manuscripts had now been taken away to Beijing, especially because the compensation promised him by the central government had never materialised.[78]

Stein spent almost three years in the eastern Taklamakan – his longest expedition to date – returning to India in 1916. But his achievements in continuing to excavate under the new regime of the Republic of China were overshadowed by the outbreak of the First World War and all his finds remained in India rather than being sent on to Britain. Back in India, he settled down to write the full academic report of his second expedition, published finally in 1921, by which time he had lost Dash III to a fight with other dogs and acquired Dash IV.[79] Dash IV died in 1925, and Dash V (an Airedale rather than a fox-terrier) died just at the outset of his fourth expedition to the Taklamakan Desert in 1930. Stein was sixty-eight years old and officially retired. He had also now finally run out of luck with the Chinese authorities. Tainted by a lecture-and-fundraising tour in the USA in 1929, and particularly his association with Harvard's Fogg Museum, whose director had not only visited Dunhuang but removed religious statues and fresco paintings from the caves, Stein arrived in Kashgar to find his official permits cancelled and the expedition over before it began. He never visited China again.

But this did not stop him exploring. Equipped with another fox-terrier – Dash VI – on his return to India, Stein's attentions turned back to his boyhood fascination with Alexander the Great and the impact of Alexander's conquest of the Persian Empire. Between 1932 and 1936 – now in his early seventies – he undertook four expeditions in Iran studying Greek influence on Persian culture. In 1938, aged seventy-six, he changed tack again and started undertaking aerial surveys of Roman defensive walls across the deserts of Syria and Iraq. And in 1939, with the outbreak of the Second World War, he filled in a card with the National Service Central Registry, declaring himself ready for military duty.[80] He was not called up (unsurprisingly to everyone except himself), and returned to India where Dash VI was sadly eaten by leopards in the autumn of 1941, replaced by Dash VII in August 1943. But one final journey awaited him. On 31 March of that year, Stein had been invited – for the first time in his life – to visit Afghanistan, home to so many of Alexander the Great's key landmarks (including Alexandria, a city named after himself, which is today Kandahar). Stein arrived in Kabul on 19 October 1943, aged eighty-one, full of plans for archaeological fieldwork, only to die of a stroke a week later. He was buried in the Christian cemetery of Gora Kabur in Kabul, finally parted for ever from his beloved Dash(es).

Marc Aurel Stein is a complex figure in the history of archaeology. He was a formidable intellect, hardy explorer and extraordinarily tenacious in everything he did. He was attracted to seeking out the most inhospitable and unknown environments in the world and committed to proving the intermixing of cultures along the ancient Silk Roads. He excavated and otherwise took possession of many tens of thousands of small, fragile objects and documents, which in many cases revolutionised our understanding of the past.[81] Due to their sheer volume and fiendish complexity, they are still being processed and studied to this day at the different institutions they now reside in: the National Museum in Delhi, the India Office Library, the Victoria and Albert Museum and British Library in London, the Bodleian Library in Oxford and of course the British Museum. Recent scholarly efforts have focused on creating quality digital copies of the manuscripts obtained not only by Stein but also by other explorers of the Taklamakan and particularly Dunhuang in this period (which are now spread out in museums across the world), so that all scholars can have at least equal access to study all the material going forward.

But these efforts will not change the way Stein is seen in China, where he represents to this day a key example of the pillaging of their culture by the 'foreign devils' of the early twentieth century. And in this, especially over the last seventy years as global attitudes have shifted so significantly on the issues of how excavation should occur, and who should own and have responsibility for the material excavated within a country (let alone on how one should not barter/buy/persuade individuals to give up materials from a 'live' religious site), modern evaluations of Marc Aurel Stein have increasingly concurred. As a result, particularly in his dealings with the Buddhist monk Wang Yuanlu at the Thousand Buddha caves, Stein stands today as an example of an approach that no one wishes to see repeated.

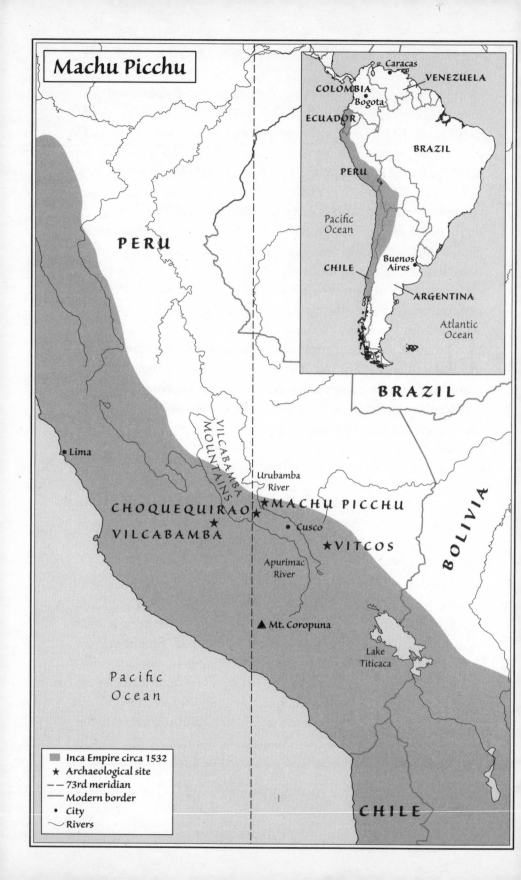

Machu Picchu

PERU

• Lima

VILCABAMBA MOUNTAINS

Urubamba
River

CHOQUEQUIRAO ★★MACHU PICCHU

VILCABAMBA ★

• Cusco

★**VITCOS**

Apurimac
River

▲ Mt. Coropuna

Lake
Titicaca

Pacific
Ocean

BRAZIL

BOLIVIA

CHILE

Caracas
VENEZUELA
COLOMBIA
• Bogota
ECUADOR

BRAZIL

PERU

Pacific
Ocean

CHILE

Buenos
Aires

ARGENTINA

Atlantic
Ocean

▦ Inca Empire circa 1532
★ Archaeological site
--- 73rd meridian
— Modern border
• City
〜 Rivers

3

The Lost City (That Was Not
Lost and Wasn't a City)

Hiram Bingham III was on his hands and knees, clinging to the four slippery wet narrow tree trunks tied together with vines that served as a bridge across the roaring churning waters of the Urubamba River, racing past just inches below him. One false move, one slip, a broken vine tie or rotten tree trunk, and he would be consumed by the rapids. But he would not turn back. Behind him was the dirt track they had followed from their morning camp – on the way they'd passed a dead venomous snake, a reminder of the predators in the thick jungle they had fought through to arrive at the river bank.[1] He knew what was behind him. But he did not know what was in front of him – and that was what always drove him on.

If this all sounds a bit like a scene from an Indiana Jones film, that's because the character of the swashbuckling fictional professor of archaeology is indeed thought to have been in part inspired by accounts of this real-life adventurer. Bingham, too, was a professor with wide-ranging knowledge of ancient civilisations, as well as an intrepid traveller across some of the more unknown parts of South America. Born in 1875 in Hawaii to a missionary family whose ancestors were famous for having led the island's conversion to Christianity, Bingham was caught between a strict (and financially limited) family upbringing and a strong desire for success. His way out was to work hard and marry well – both of which were helped by his handsome looks and athletic build. In 1900, at the age of twenty-five, he married Alfreda Mitchell, part of the Tiffany jewellery family, and left Hawaii behind for good.[2]

Despite the improvement in his financial situation, Bingham's restlessness meant he was still looking for challenges and adventure. These needs were answered in Bingham's decision to focus, in his postgraduate study, on the history of South America. It was a topic little studied at the time among Ivy League universities, an indication of North America's long-held sense of superiority over its southern sister. Yet, by the early 1900s, the relationship between the continents – both in political and economic terms – had deepened significantly, creating a new need for academic study and understanding of South America. Here was an intrepid research field in which Bingham could position himself as a leader.

Bingham undertook a PhD in South American studies at Harvard between 1902 and 1905. While studying for his PhD, Bingham created a post for himself at Harvard as 'Curator of the Harvard Library's South American Collection' – a collection that did not exist. So he had then set about curating it – and as a result he came across the papers of Simón Bolívar, the man responsible for freeing what was to become Gran Colombia from Spanish rule in 1819. Rather than simply writing a biography, Bingham decided in 1906 that he needed to walk in the footsteps of Bolívar and retrace his arduous 700-mile military march from Caracas to Bogotá, which had been compared with Hannibal's journey across the Alps and Napoleon's march into Russia. This was a relatively untouched era of history coupled with the chance for exploration and adventure – the perfect combination for Bingham. Returning from his adventures, he quickly published an account of his personal experience of Bolívar's march.[3]

With first-hand experience of South American history through his Bolívar pilgrimage, Bingham landed a permanent job in 1907 as Lecturer in South American History at Yale University – the first permanent position dedicated to South American history at any university in North America. In 1907 he presented a paper entitled 'Possibilities of South American History and Politics as a Field of Research' to the American Political Science Association in Washington DC. In it he claimed that the 'international friendship' between North and South America, 'for it to be permanent, must rest on a basis of intelligent appreciation. And to secure an intelligent appreciation of South America, we need to have in English many more trustworthy books on her history and politics.'[4]

The prestige of his new role at Yale, combined with the international interest generated by his 1907 paper (and his Bolívar adventures), led to him being invited as an official delegate of the United States government to the First Pan-American Scientific Congress held in Chile in December–January 1908–9. Typically, of course, Bingham did not just attend the conference – he squeezed it in between travels by foot, train and mule along large parts of the 'most historic highway' in South America, the old trade route between Lima in Peru, Potosí in Bolivia and Buenos Aires in Argentina.[5]

By 1909 Bingham had published a second fuller account of his adventures retracing Bolívar's footsteps, and by 1911 he had also published an account of his journey across the historic highway of South America.[6] He had a lot to learn as an explorer – as one reviewer of his work noted: 'for reasons only known to themselves, the travellers did not carry a tent . . .'[7] However, it was on his somewhat wild travels in 1908–9 that Bingham first visited a site related to the Incas, the great empire that had dominated large parts of South America in the fourteenth to the sixteenth centuries up to the time of the Spanish conquest. Bingham had not intended to visit the Inca site – he had been almost entirely focused on much more recent periods of South American history – but he was persuaded by a local Peruvian governor to go to the Inca fortress site of Choquequirao.

Bingham would, much later in his life, cast this as a pivotal moment, in which the call of unexplored Inca ruins within the mountainous Vilcabamba region of Peru hit him hard while standing in the ruins of Choquequirao looking out over the Vilcabamba mountains.[8] But in reality, he was up for any kind of adventure he could get. Back at Yale, he sought funding for new adventures in Mexico to study the remains of the Maya Empire, as well as for an expedition in the Ecuadorian jungle to find the source of the Napo River, and even to find a new route through the Amazon jungle – all without success.[9]

What did, however, eventually raise money – from Yale alumni – was a plan to climb Mount Coropuna in Peru, thought to be the highest mountain in South America. Alongside climbing the mountain, the plan was also to map, for the first time, nearby parts of Peru lying along the seventy-third Meridian line of longitude, as well as, for good measure, to undertake a search for unknown Inca ruins in the vicinity (which happened to be the same area Bingham had looked out over from the Inca fortress of Choquequirao on his last visit to Peru in 1908–9).[10]

The team, formally known as the 'Yale Peruvian Expedition', consisted of an explorer (as Bingham always labelled himself in his *Who's Who* entry throughout his career), a topographer (who was actually Denmark's royal chief surveyor), a mountain climber, a chemistry professor with a love of butterflies, a geographer and a doctor. This varied crew set off from New York for Peru in early summer 1911. Learning from past mistakes, this time the team remembered to bring tents, as well as twenty boxes of crushed oats, coffee, canned meats and chocolate.[11] For Bingham, the most important aspect of this expedition was not discovering new Inca ruins, or mapping the seventy-third Meridian, but climbing the mountain and as a result being able to claim the honour of having climbed the highest peak in South America. He even changed his travel arrangements to Peru in order to be on the same boat as the famous female climber, Annie Peck. She was herself in transit to Peru in order to climb the same mountain and Bingham was keen to weigh up his opposition.[12] The Yale team met up again in Lima, before taking another ship to travel south down the Peruvian coast, to then take a slow four-day train ride into the interior of Peru, finally arriving at the town of Cusco, which would be the base of their operations, in early July 1911.[13]

Bingham had described Cusco, after his first visit there during his 1908–9 South American tour, not in flattering terms: it had 'in fact, long been notorious as one of the dirtiest cities in America; and it justifies that reputation'.[14] He was not being particularly unkind either – but rather echoing the standard sentiment of the day about the town. Cusco was over 500 kilometres away from Lima, Peru's economic and political capital, and the railroad had only reached Cusco in 1908, just before Bingham's first visit to the area (the town would not have permanent electricity until 1914). The inhabitants of the city and its surrounding region were mostly farmers, harvesting their crops of potatoes, barley and quinoa, or looking after llamas, alpacas and sheep, struggling to make a living faced with heavy taxes and the often-brutal demands of the region's few elites who ruled from grand rural 'hacienda' estates. By the time Bingham returned with the Yale Peruvian Expedition in 1911, the city of Cusco was home to fewer than 20,000 people – half of whom were illiterate.[15] And yet Cusco had a past – a glorious past in which it had been the epicentre of the mighty Inca Empire, the greatest civilisation in South American history.

*

While there had been a number of kingdoms that had risen and died away in the area of modern-day Peru in the centuries before the Incas, like that of the Moche and the Huari, the Inca Empire spread the furthest: covering 2 million square kilometres at its height.[16] Despite its size, the Incas left no written records of their own, and as such, most of what we know about them comes from archaeological discovery (which was only just beginning at the time that Bingham was travelling to Peru in the early twentieth century) and from what the Spanish, whose arrival in Peru led to the demise of the Inca Empire in the mid-late sixteenth century, wrote about them in their extensive chronicles. From these works, which often not only detail Spanish observance of Inca practices but also include notes on the oral histories that the Incas passed down across the generations, we learn that the Incas believed their people's history had begun when the god Tici Viracocha emerged from Lake Titicaca (to the south-east of Cusco on the modern Peru–Bolivia border). Tici Viracocha is said to have killed the previous inhabitants of the area, created the sun and the moon and fashioned new beings and installed them in Cusco.[17]

Once in the Cusco region, according to the Inca legends preserved in the Spanish chronicles, the first Inca ruler, Manco Cápac, slowly cemented his hold on power, not least by ensuring his brothers turned into stones. By the time of the sixth Inca ruler, Inca Roca, the Incas controlled the whole Cusco region, with their centre of power in Cusco itself now a thriving settlement. The eighth Inca ruler, Viracocha, not only strengthened the Incas' hold over the Cusco region but pushed their borders beyond it for the first time, creating the beginnings of the Inca Empire. His son, Pachacuti, as a result, spent much of his reign locked in battle with more substantial rival tribes that the Incas now rubbed up against.

It is Pachacuti who is also credited with transforming Cusco from a thriving settlement into a resplendent capital, home of the Inca ruler, his nobles and their full-time servants, the 'yanakuna'. One of the Spanish chroniclers from the sixteenth century, Garcilaso de la Vega, described Cusco as a 'sacred thing' for the Incas, 'one of their principal idols'.[18] Pachacuti was said to have canalised two rivers in order to create a space for the city, which he shaped like a panther with the combined rivers as its tail. The city itself was divided into 'upper' and 'lower' regions, and while the Inca ruler's palace was always built in 'upper' Cusco, the 'lower' part was dedicated to religious worship. Here, grand temples were built, with walls covered in gold and thatched roofs.[19] Temples were dedicated to the three principal Inca deities: the Sun (Inti), the Thunderer/Rain-giver (Illapa) and the ruler himself (known simply as 'Inca'), who was seen as the offspring of the Sun.

The ruler was considered so sacred that everything he touched had to be reduced to ashes and thrown into the air so that no one else could touch it. Equally, even his spit could not be allowed to touch the ground but instead had to be collected in the hands of female servants.[20] His dignity was at all times of paramount importance. To ensure it, he had to travel as slowly as possible, never covering more than twelve miles a day. And almost no one got to see him face to face: he took most of his meetings from behind a screen. When he died, his favourite women were expected to accompany him to the afterlife and were strangled to death. His fortune went to a special group called the *'panaca'*, who were then responsible for embalming his body and looking after it for eternity, feeding it regularly, and bringing it out on display alongside the bodies of other former rulers at key festivals.[21]

By the time of Pachacuti's death (and the deaths of his favourite women) in 1471 the Incas controlled a vast – and still expanding – empire.[22] Over the next few decades, Túpac Yupanqui, the tenth Inca ruler, took up the challenge of expanding the Inca realm even further, turning it into a vast domain, which stretched from modern-day northern Ecuador through to central Chile and contained 10 to 12 million subjects – just under half the size of the contemporary Ottoman Empire in Asia.[23]

What is remarkable about the Incas is that, despite their ferocious empire building, they simultaneously acquired a reputation for being 'kindly despots' thanks to the ingenious ways they chose to govern their vast realm, ensuring both Inca control and a tolerable life for local communities.[24] Pachacuti, for example, is credited with creating a category of Inca citizenship called 'Inca by

Privilege', which served both to extend Inca protection to newly conquered communities and to enlarge the workforce the Incas could then call on. Pachacuti is also said to have established the Inca system of '*mitimaes*', in which large groups of people were arbitrarily transposed from their home region to newly conquered parts of the Inca Empire. This was done in part to help speed up the adoption of Inca practices in the newly conquered region, but also often to improve the agricultural outputs of low-population areas. Nor were the Incas shy of using local systems of power, employing conquered previous rulers in local administrative roles (known as '*curacas*'). The sons of these conquered rulers, however, were always sent to be resident at the Inca royal court in Cusco from the age of fourteen onwards in order to indoctrinate them into the Inca way of life, after which they were returned to their local communities to act as Inca-approved local governors.

The Inca army, the exchange '*mitimae*' population groups and the sons of conquered rulers could move easily around the empire thanks to a well-developed road network. The Incas poured huge resources into creating their road system, some of which still survives today.[25] They used stone and even fibre suspension bridges to ensure that their roads could cross the difficult mix of high mountains and deep valleys their empire ruled over. Each major road had lodges built a day's walk apart along them for travellers to stay in, as well as a complex system of relay posts where runners could verbally repeat messages to one another to take information across the empire.

When not conquering or building roads, Túpac Yupanqui spent his time building great palaces and fortresses around the Inca Empire: the archaeological remains of thirty-seven forts have now been found in the northern Ecuadorian Andes alone. The achievements of the eleventh Inca ruler, Huayna Capa, seem modest by comparison, with much of his time spent maintaining the vast empire created by his predecessor, and on his death, there was a power struggle between rival contenders for the throne (Huayna had both legitimate and illegitimate sons, each of whom wanted to rule). The result was a civil war within the Inca realm, which significantly weakened the kingdom. Just as a victor emerged, Atahualpa (the illegitimate son), who was crowned the twelfth Inca ruler, the Spanish conquistadors arrived in Peru in September 1532.[26] By later that autumn, the Spanish had kidnapped Atahualpa and on 26 July 1533, having tried to bribe the Spanish with the offer of gold in exchange for his release, the Inca ruler was strangled to death (though only after he had converted to Christianity, to avoid death by fire as a pagan).[27]

The Spanish subsequently sought to take charge of the Inca realm and even captured the capital city of Cusco. But they also allowed the Incas to continue their way of life, including allowing the coronation of a new puppet Inca ruler, Túpac Huallpa. He died after only a few months as ruler, to be replaced by Manco Cápac, who was crowned in November 1533. However, Manco escaped his Spanish handlers, and in May 1536 he led a full-scale rebellion against the Spanish. The Incas attacked their own capital city, Cusco, as it was now the epicentre of Spanish control, burning it to the ground. But the Spanish doggedly held on and fought back, with the result that Manco Cápac was eventually forced to take refuge in the mountainous Vilcabamba region to the north of Cusco, where Bingham would later lead the Yale expedition. From there Manco held on to control of a much smaller Inca realm, establishing a key ceremonial centre at Vitcos and a palace capital at a settlement called Vilcabamba, after which the region took its name. This neo-Inca kingdom continued through to Manco's death in 1545 and beyond, with his sons continuing in his stead to rule for several decades.[28] But in 1572, the last Inca ruler, Túpac Amaru, was captured by the Spanish and put to death, bringing a final end to the Incas.

The Spanish Empire held sway in Peru until the Battle of Ayacucho in 1824, when they lost to Simón Bolívar's army, at last paving the way for Peruvian independence.[29] Not surprisingly by this time, Cusco, despite its grand Inca history, was in a sorry state: its great palaces and temples had been stripped, burnt and much of the Inca stonework pillaged for re-use elsewhere. Indeed, since Peru's liberation, the new Peruvian government had pointedly ignored Cusco and its important role as the epicentre of the Inca Empire, in favour of a new national narrative and identity focused around the country's new capital city of Lima on the coast. Peru's identity and future, they felt, should not be based around an inland burnt-out wreck of a former indigenous capital, but around a new thriving coastal city that could trade with the world. Cusco was thus left to its local farming community.

Cusco's fall from grace, from the centre of a great empire to a forgotten mountain town, was thus nothing short of spectacular. Its rich history remained unexplored and its ruins left to slip from sight.

*

Almost immediately after arriving in Cusco, Bingham and the Yale team struck seemingly historical gold. On 9 July 1911, they investigated some bones they found on a gravel riverbank, initially concluding that they might be 30,000 years old, proving that *Homo sapiens* had been present in South America far earlier than the current thinking at the time (that *Homo sapiens* had been present only 10,000 years before).[30] Having already potentially turned on its head the history of South America, Bingham now promptly moved on to his next stated challenges. The planned ascent of Mount Coropuna had to be delayed for now, due to weather conditions, so in the meantime Bingham dispatched some of his team to map the seventy-third Meridian, while he and the professor of chemistry (and lover of butterflies) Harry Foote went to look for Inca ruins. As Bingham later wrote in 1913 for *Harper's Monthly*, the goal in searching for Inca ruins was to find the ceremonial and capital cities of the neo-Inca realm at Vitcos and Vilcabamba that had been established by Manco Cápac after having escaped from the Spanish in 1536. They were hunting for the fabled 'lost and last cities of the Incas', and Bingham's way to do that was, as he put it: '[to go about] asking everyone if they knew of any such [ruins]'.[31]

One of those people was the Rector of Cusco University, Albert Giesecke, who told him about a recent trip he had undertaken on horseback along a relatively new dirt-track road that traced the Urubamba River as it wound its way through the Vilcabamba mountains. This new road had been punched through the jungle in order to facilitate the easier export of farming produce in this otherwise inaccessible area.[32] Giesecke mentioned to Bingham that a tavern owner along the track had told him about some Inca ruins, known locally as 'Machu Picchu', perched near him on cliffs overlooking the river.[33] Based on this anecdotal information, on 19 July 1911, Bingham, Foote and a soldier called Sergeant Carrasco (who had been sent by the President of Peru – whom Bingham knew – to support his expedition) set off along the dirt track. By 23 July, they arrived at the tavern Giesecke had mentioned – though in reality what they found was more of a grass-thatched hut than a tavern – and the team chose to camp on a sandy river-bank nearby. Through their military escort and interpreter Carrasco, Bingham asked the tavern owner, Melchor Arteaga, about the ruins in the area, who in turn described the ruins at 'Machu Picchu'.[34]

Bingham did not want to waste a single day. But the following morning it was raining and Arteaga, reluctant to head out in such weather, had to be persuaded with additional financial compensation by Bingham and Carrasco to show them the way to the ruins (Harry Foote remained behind to study butterflies). After fighting their way through the jungle to the riverbank, the group were faced with the perilous task of crossing the roaring river by means of the rackety and slippery tree-trunk bridge – a real-life Indiana Jones moment.[35] Arteaga and Carrasco took off their shoes to give them better grip, while Bingham crawled across on all fours. Their successful crossing was met with a stiff ninety-minute uphill climb, which Bingham admitted later in *Harper's Monthly* he did mostly again on all fours, sweating in the 'excessive' heat. A little after noon, they reached a hut high up the mountainside where a local Quechua family lived, renting land to farm from Arteaga. They gave their visitors cool water to drink and sweet potatoes to eat, and offered for their young son, Pablito Richarte, to show the group the way to the ruins nearby.[36] Arteaga stayed behind to rest with the family, leaving Bingham and Carrasco to go it alone with the small boy.

They were an odd trio: Pablito dressed in a decorated poncho and large hat, the sergeant in his military uniform and Bingham in his American-made khaki explorer's outfit. As Bingham wrote later: 'suddenly we found ourselves in the midst of a jungle-covered maze of small and large walls, the ruins of buildings made of blocks of white granite . . . surprise followed surprise until there came the realisation that we were in the midst of as wonderful ruins as any ever found in Peru'.[37] Bingham marvelled that they had remained 'so long undescribed and comparatively unknown', especially since he found 'rude scrawls' on one of the temple buildings by a man called Lizzarraga, who had apparently visited nearly a decade earlier in 1902.[38] Partly, he reasoned, the fact that this site had not been properly explored may have been because the Spanish chroniclers had themselves never mentioned it, and partly because it was in what had been – up until the recent construction of the dirt track along the Urubamba River bank – a very inaccessible location.

Bingham only had a couple of hours at the site: they had to descend the mountain and get back across the river to their camp before dark. But in that initial visit, he was able not only to follow a number of grand stone staircases and identify a central plaza area and several temple-like structures, but also even to sketch a brief plan of the site as it could be made out from under its jungle covering. What really amazed him was the quality of the masonry. Single blocks of stone, taller than a man, carved and lifted into place on the summit of the mountainside. Small stones cut and fitted together with the same accuracy 'as a glass stopper is fitted to a bottle'.[39]

By nightfall the group were back at their camp, having made it once more across the perilous tree-trunk bridge. But Bingham and his team did not return the next day, as you might expect. In fact, despite having come across the wonders of Machu Picchu, the team left the area the next morning to continue their search elsewhere. This seems astonishing now, but the decision shows how strong Bingham's focus was on finding the 'lost and last' capitals of the last Inca rulers, Vitcos and Vilcabamba (and ultimately to climb Mount Coropuna). Machu Picchu, while intriguing, simply did not match the Spanish descriptions of the last Inca strongholds Bingham was after. And so he and his team moved on, leaving the little Pablito with Machu Picchu as his playground.

Their search continued for another month, during which time Bingham, Foote and Carrasco traversed numerous valleys, followed several local tips on the locations of ruins, and succeeded in finding two new major sets of ruins, which Bingham was convinced were those of Vitcos and Vilcabamba.[40] Both these sites were even more thickly covered by vegetation than Machu Picchu, preventing Bingham from exploring them any further on each occasion. Thus, in September 1911, Bingham made contact with the rest of the expedition group, asking part of the team who had been surveying the seventy-third Meridian to head to Machu Picchu to make a proper map of the site (given that it was the only one he had found so far that was visible enough for immediate further study). But Bingham himself did not return. For him, the important thing now was to climb a mountain.

Bingham returned to Cusco to prepare to climb Mount Coropuna, which he did with a small party in October 1911, leaving US and Yale flags on the top of the western summit of the mountain as he believed it to be higher than the eastern peaks climbed by Annie Peck a month or so before. The team arrived home in the US just before Christmas. Bingham is said to have dressed up as Santa for his children, who thought it was the real Santa because they simply didn't recognise their father, whom they had not seen since June.[41]

But Bingham was not at home for long. In January 1912, he gave a talk to the National Geographic Society in Washington about his expedition.[42] They offered to co-fund a second venture with Yale in order both to discover further ruins and to continue excavations of the sites found in 1911, with finds brought back to Yale for further study. In spring 1912, Bingham put together a new team and had left again for Peru by May 1912. Once back in Cusco, the team headed not for the lost sites of Vitcos or Vilcabamba that Bingham had been so focused on finding in the first expedition, but straight for Machu Picchu. This volte-face was thanks to a smart assessment by Bingham of effort versus reward. Machu Picchu was practically easier to access and study than Vitcos and Vilcabamba in the time they had available on this expedition. But, in addition, Bingham had reflected on the superior quality of the masonry at Machu Picchu compared to Vitcos and Vilcabamba and had begun to recognise that Machu Picchu, while not one of the fabled last cities of the Inca, could well prove a more impressive discovery to put his name to. It was perhaps the smartest decision he ever made.

Assisted by a local workforce of almost forty people, Bingham's expedition team began the task not only of creating reliable resilient access to the site (including a proper bridge across the river, and a clear zigzag trail up the mountainside), but also of clearing the ruins themselves of vegetation. As the site was gradually exposed, the team began not just to study the surviving buildings in more detail, but also to excavate around them and across the wider site, discovering both Inca pottery and burial assemblages and skeletons. However, Bingham himself only remained with the team for the first two weeks, before heading off to undertake the other work requested by the National Geographic Society: the discovery of further Inca ruins. Accompanied this time just by a local mule driver, and reliant again on local tip-offs, Bingham explored the wilderness between the Urubamba and Apurimac rivers. In the process, he not only discovered several further small sets of ruins, but was, at one point, abandoned by his guides, and almost lost for ever in the depths of a jungle valley.[43]

Once Bingham did make his way back to Cusco he ran into problems. His funding was dependent on him bringing his finds back to the USA. In his first expedition to Peru, he had obtained personal permission from the Peruvian president to take his finds home with him. But now he found that the Peruvian government was no longer planning to allow him to take back finds from Machu Picchu to Yale.[44] Bingham resorted to a second personal – and lengthy – plea to the President of Peru, who eventually gave him permission to take home objects so far excavated, but the president banned any new excavation and stipulated that the team's work at Machu Picchu should finish by 10 December 1912.[45]

By this time, the Yale team at Machu Picchu had been working for four months to uncover and study the site. In that period, the ruins had emerged from the surrounding jungle to become a resplendent collection of shining stone buildings cradled by mountain peaks against a jaw-dropping background of clouds, deep dark valleys and rugged stone peaks that pierced the sky. The team had been able to recognise groups of houses, clear over a hundred stone staircases connecting different parts of the site, and follow parts of the complex stone-channel irrigation, drainage and aqueduct system built by the Incas to simultaneously provide drinking water, enable the growth of crops, and ensure the site did not become waterlogged and get washed away in the rainy season. As such, not only was the site now a thing of beauty to look at; it was also a marvel of human technological skill and achievement: the creation of a sustainable habitat for humankind in a place you might think beyond our reach.

On 1 December 1912, Bingham sailed back to America from

Lima with over a hundred cases of artefacts from Machu Picchu. But he was not entirely a happy man: he felt he had failed to discover any further new exciting ruins and worried about his continuing reputation as an explorer (particularly after a New Haven newspaper got hold of and ran with the story of how he had got lost in the jungle).[46] But he need not have worried. In April 1913, in a *National Geographic* article entitled 'In the Wonderland of Peru', Bingham introduced the world to Machu Picchu.[47] And thanks to the fact that the expedition had also been sponsored by Kodak, Bingham had the very best photographic evidence of his discovery that the technology of the day could enable.[48] The world *saw* Machu Picchu as well as read about it. The *National Geographic* edition broke all circulation records. In May 1913, the *New York Times* put Bingham on the front page with the headline: 'Prof Hiram Bingham of Yale makes the greatest archaeological discovery of the age by locating and excavating the ruins of Machu Picchu on a peak of the Andes mountains'.[49] The fact that Bingham had 'discovered' ruins he had been directed to by locals who already knew of their existence (which Bingham was very open about in his *Harper's Monthly* article detailing the initial discovery, published in the second half of 1913 after the *New York Times* had already labelled his achievement 'the greatest archaeological discovery of the age') did not seem to matter. What mattered was that the rest of the world had not known about the site or indeed much about the culture and civilisation that had created it – and Bingham was the one who had brought both it and them to their attention. Bingham had opened the eyes of the world to the mysterious land of the Incas.

The key question now on everyone's lips, however, as they marvelled at Bingham's discovery and the images of Machu Picchu was simple: what was it? A city? A religious sanctuary? A hilltop fort? There were no descriptions of the site from the Spanish chroniclers to help. The only route to finding an answer lay in the interpretation of the stones and objects from the site itself. Bingham, in his 1913 *Harper's Monthly* article, offered an answer: not the last cities of the Incas, which he had initially set out to find (and indeed found at Vitcos and Vilcabamba), but in fact their first. Bingham argued that Machu Picchu was the lost city of Tampu Tocco – the original stronghold from which the Incas emerged (as part of the myth of the original Inca rulers being created by the god Tici Viracocha). Bingham offered this identification in 1913 because, he argued, Machu Picchu had a key architectural hallmark that connected it to the legend of Tampu Tocco as a place in which 'out of a hill with three openings or windows there came three tribes . . . [which eventually] founded the Inca empire'.[50] Machu Picchu, he pointed out, was a hilltop settlement containing a temple-like structure with three windows in it, which had not been found in any other known Inca site of the period. He concluded his *Harper's Monthly* article with a challenge: 'I may be wholly mistaken in this, and I shall await with interest the discovery of any other place that fits so well the description of Tampu Tocco, whence came the Incas.'[51]

Almost a decade later, Bingham published a full-length book account of his initial 1911 expedition, entitled *Inca Land: Explorations in the Highlands of Peru*. The book begins with an account of himself as the mountain climber extraordinaire (and Bingham lists his membership of the American Alpine Club directly after his Directorship of the Yale Peruvian Expedition in the title page). Chapters on the history of the Incas are followed by his account of how he found the lost and last cities of the Incas at Vitcos and Vilcabamba.[52] It is only in the final chapters of the book that he turns to the jewel in his discovery tale: Machu Picchu. He first recounts the legends of Tampu Tocco, then regales us (once again!) with the story of his discovery of Machu Picchu, before ending the book with a whole chapter on tying the two together and explaining what he thinks Machu Picchu is.[53]

Bingham was still sure in 1922 that Machu Picchu was

Tampu Tocco, the first city of the Incas. But at the same time, he also now recognised that study of many of Machu Picchu's architectural structures had shown them to be from a later period in Inca history. As such, he now claimed that Machu Picchu was not only the first city of the Incas but that it was also given a second life as an important location in the history of the last Incas: not as a fortress or a royal residence, but as 'Vilcabamba Viejo', a city in the province where the last Inca rulers had established the home of the Virgins of the Temple of the Sun. These were the chosen daughters of the Inca, who lived and spent their lives in honour and worship of the Sun, not unlike, as Bingham himself claimed, the Vestal Virgins of Rome.[54]

Despite heaping praise on Bingham for his discovery, and underlining Machu Picchu as a crucial site for better understanding of the Incas, reviewers of the book reacted suspiciously to Bingham's idea of Machu Picchu as either Tampu Tocco or the home of the Virgins of the Temple of the Sun (nor did they comment on his mountain-climbing exploits).[55] Undeterred, in 1930 Bingham published another book – this time focused exclusively on Machu Picchu: *Machu Picchu: A Citadel of the Incas*.[56] In it he covered once more his discovery of the site, the work conducted during the subsequent excavation seasons at the site, as well as, once again, his theory that Machu Picchu was both Tampu Tocco and the home of the Virgins of the Temple of the Sun. His theory though had not aged well. In 1931, the journal *Antiquity* published a review that on the one hand praised the publication of the material finds from the site, but on the other savagely poured scorn on Bingham's reasserted theories, describing them as 'bizarre speculations'.[57]

Bingham, however, held true to his theory throughout his life. In 1948, he published his final book, which would be his most famous: *Lost City of the Incas*. It once again covered the history of the Inca Empire and his search for Vitcos and Vilcabamba, focusing, in the final part of the book, on his 'discovery' in 1911 of the 'lost' Machu Picchu, his excavation and study of the site in subsequent seasons, and ending with the same claim: that Machu Picchu was first Tampu Tocco and later the home of the Virgins of the Sun. As such, he concludes in the book, Machu Picchu was a site that existed from the beginning to the end of the Incan civilisation, a fitting emblem of all their achievements.[58]

Few believed Bingham's theories – but neither did his critics have a more credible suggestion for what Machu Picchu was. This emblem of Inca civilisation, lost in the clouds, continued to taunt the world with its mystery for decades to come.

*

Bingham's writings on Machu Picchu – his initial articles in 1913, then his books in 1922, 1930 and 1948, were so spread out in part because he continued to have the most eventful career that took him in a number of different directions. Following the successful clearing of Machu Picchu in his second excavation season there in 1912, it was only natural that *National Geographic* and Yale wanted Bingham to return to Machu Picchu, which he did in late 1914. But while he was the heroic explorer and discoverer in the US, a very different reception awaited him in Peru, where the government had now tightened up their policies and laws on the excavation of their cultural heritage and had sent Peruvian excavation teams into Machu Picchu after Bingham's 1912 departure. As a result, far from being allowed to look for ruins as he pleased and to work independently at Machu Picchu as he had been on previous expeditions, he now was required to follow Peruvian cultural heritage law to the letter and have his work overseen by local inspectors. Soon enough, he had been formally accused by a local archaeologist of not following Peruvian policy for the preservation of artefacts – in essence, of trying to remove objects from the site without permission. Though he managed to escape prosecution, Bingham was forced to leave Peru soon after, along with his team.[59] He would not return to Peru for over three decades, thanks to the ongoing anger and resentment felt at his removal of artefacts from Machu Picchu in 1911–12 and attempts to do so in 1914. In 1926, the University of Cusco, which had once done so much to encourage Bingham to the region and whose Rector had been instrumental in suggesting Bingham look for ruins in the region of Machu Picchu back in 1911, rescinded Bingham's honorary degree.[60]

Bingham did not have a lot of time to dwell on his swiftly changing reception in Peru. In 1917, America entered the First World War and he felt the call for another new type of adventure. He learnt to fly aeroplanes (although he was technically past enlistment age), and subsequently commanded a crucial flying school for pilots in war-torn France. At the end of the war, he swapped flying planes for another kind of adventure and entered politics, where his tall stature, 'explorer' reputation and strong war record made him a popular choice for the Republican Party. Always aware of the opportunities for self-promotion, in 1920 he published a book about his war-time experiences that deftly reinforced his public image, entitled *An Explorer in the Air Service*. A meteoric rise saw him become a Senator by 1925, but he soon lost his seat in the aftermath of the Great Depression of 1929 and the Democratic election landslide that followed in 1932, a loss that was accompanied by a fraught separation from his wife, with whom he had now had seven children. By this time aged almost sixty, Bingham began a quieter life in semi-retirement, acting as an occasional lecturer and undertaking different civic commissions.

What finally brought him back to Peru and to Machu Picchu was the culmination of a series of tectonic shifts both within Peru and between North and South America. The Cusco academic community, which had cut ties with Bingham after his last departure from Peru in 1914 and rescinded his honorary degree in 1926, had simultaneously sought to capitalise on the discovery of Machu Picchu to put Cusco back on the Peruvian and global map. Cusco had once been the capital of the Inca Empire but had long slipped into decline. Now, they reckoned, was its time to shine again. Despite initially receiving very little support from the Peruvian government, which still preferred to see Peruvian national identity centred around the modern bustling capital city of Lima, the Rector of Cusco University published in 1921 an article claiming Cusco as the 'Rome of South America' – a great historic capital with still much to say for itself in the modern world, and as part of Peru's modern identity.[61]

A subsequent sustained international campaign to revive Cusco's fortunes as a tourist mecca paid off, especially when US President Roosevelt initiated the 'Good Neighbour' policy in 1933: a diplomatic commitment to non-intervention and to co-operation between North and South America. Tourism was a key tool of the policy and the US began to encourage and facilitate mass tourism to South America (as well as encourage further academic study of its southern sister). Cusco's calls to be recognised as the Rome of South America and as a tourism mecca for those keen to understand the long history of Peru fitted well with the US's good neighbour intentions and through the 1930s interest in Machu Picchu began to soar. In 1934, the *New York Times* ran an article praising the work of the local Cusco community in restoring the work of their glorious forebears.[62] Throughout the rest of the 1930s the Cusco community continued to use its new tourism revenues to invest both in the tourism infrastructure of the town and crucially in the curation of their key archaeological sites, including Machu Picchu. What set them back of course was the Second World War, when global attention was directed towards Europe and Japan, international tourism fell into decline and North America had little time for its Good Neighbour policy with the South.

Bingham spent the Second World War lecturing in Naval training schools, and when the war ended, despite now being seventy years old, he became a late and unlikely beneficiary of attempts to revive Roosevelt's Good Neighbour policy. The policy, it was felt, now needed heroes – identifiable figures who embodied the spirit of co-operation between North and South America. Bingham was, despite his fall from political power and his poor reputation in Peru itself, still very popular in the US thanks to his books recounting his adventures, and he had the credentials of being an early leader of North and South American interaction. His work at Machu Picchu – conducted well over thirty years before – could be a powerful symbol of North/South American co-operation in the past, present and future. That is, if the Peruvian government and the Cusco community could be convinced to welcome him back.

With huge amounts of potential tourist dollars on the line, both saw the value in burying the hatchet. In 1948, the same Rector who had initially welcomed Bingham in 1911, rescinded his honorary degree, and pushed for Cusco to be recognised as the Rome of South America, now persuaded the Peruvian government to name the new highway they had built to improve access for tourists to Machu Picchu the 'Hiram Bingham III' highway. So it was that thirty-three years after he had last set foot in the country (and indeed had been asked to leave it by the Peruvian authorities), on 17 October 1948, at the age of seventy-three, Bingham returned to Peru to cut the ribbon, inaugurate the highway and unveil a plaque describing him as the 'scientific discoverer of Machu Picchu'.[63]

As a newly reshaped American hero of North–South American mutual co-operation, Bingham naturally required an updated narrative tale. In the same year that he cut the ribbon on his eponymous new highway in Peru, he published his final book: *Lost City of the Incas*. In it he sculpts his story as an explorer drawn to the Inca realm from the very first time he was introduced to the Inca site of Choquequirao in 1909 through to his discovery of Machu Picchu in 1911 and subsequent explorations of it, ending the book, as we have seen, with his still-firm belief that the site was both the early Inca origin-site of Tampu Tocco and a later home for the chosen Virgins of the Sun.

Lost City is a tour de force of explorer narrative, portraying Bingham as a wholesome and courageous explorer (and leaving out his fall from grace in Peru and his subsequent career highs and lows in the US). It echoes – even in its title – Conan Doyle's epic novel *Lost World*, which was published in the same year Bingham first visited Machu Picchu, and it deliberately marketed itself to a public keen to read gripping and dangerous adventure stories. In *Lost City*, rivers are always 'roaring', 'tearing their way through gigantic mountains of granite'.[64] The landscapes are epic, the jungle dense and humid. Danger is around every corner and nothing is certain. Yet Bingham presses on, resolute in his desire for discovery, and what he finds 'takes his breath away', leaves him 'spellbound' and 'scarcely able to believe his senses'.[65] His duty becomes nothing less than to uncover and understand Machu Picchu – which seems to have grown in significance over his career, even changing from being described as a mere 'citadel' to a full-blown city.[66] And while Bingham does not entirely eradicate the fact that others knew about Machu Picchu before him, and had even been there before him (as he had acknowledged multiple times in his earlier publications), his role as the discoverer of Machu Picchu is emphasised throughout, especially in the title of the book. After all, a 'lost' city requires someone to find it.[67]

Lost City of the Incas was a bestseller. Even the likes of Che Guevara read and reviewed it. In fact, Che perhaps understood the book – its aims both for Bingham and for the wider re-sketching of North–South American interaction – better than many. He said simply: 'Machu Picchu was to Hiram Bingham the crowning of all his purest dreams as an adult child.'[68] It was the ultimate explorer narrative for the man who always wanted to be known as an explorer. Within five years of publication of Bingham's bestseller, Charlton Heston was starring in a film *Secret of the Incas*, which was inspired by Bingham's adventures and even had the Rector of Cusco University as its technical advisor. In turn,

Heston's costume in that film – fedora hat, leather jacket and white shirt – has been acknowledged as an inspiration for the costume of Indiana Jones in his first film outing *Raiders of the Lost Ark*, which premiered in 1981.[69]

Bingham himself may possibly have seen Charlton Heston grace American movie theatres in 1953, but he died in 1956, long before Indiana Jones would burst onto our screens. He did, however, live long enough to see his Machu Picchu disappear once again from the international stage. Just ten days after Bingham had been in Peru to cut the ribbon on his new highway in 1948, a military coup ousted the Peruvian government and the new regime eliminated all state-sponsored tourism initiatives. The coup was followed a couple of years later by a catastrophic earthquake in Cusco in May 1950, which all but devastated the town and region for a decade. It wasn't until February 1960 that Peru saw the first international Boeing 707 land in Lima, bringing with it tourism once again.

After a turbulent period, by 1968 there were domestic air services between Lima and Cusco, paving the way for tourists to arrive quickly at Machu Picchu. The problem for the region in the 1960s became not attracting tourists, but the tourists themselves. While Cusco had always sought to market itself to an elite and upper-middle-class traveller, now the era of mass tourism was beginning and bringing with it a different type of visitor. Backpackers took to sleeping in the ruins of Machu Picchu and left rubbish (and much else) across the site.[70] The situation was not helped by the continuing instability of the Peruvian state, with bomb attacks on tourist hotels and another military coup in 1968, which increasingly put off the wealthier visitors. As the 1970s dawned, Machu Picchu became a mecca for those spurning modernity and innovation and wanting instead a connection to the mysticism of alternative earlier cultures. In a region that thought international tourism would allow it to prove its worth as part of a modern Peru, Cusco and Machu Picchu now found themselves overwhelmed by those who wanted nothing but to dispense with modernity and, as one of the Peruvian newspapers of the time put it, 'share the life of the Quecha Indian'.[71]

Tourism to Machu Picchu was cut off more or less overnight when, on 25 June 1986, a bomb exploded on the tourist train up to Machu Picchu, killing seven tourists and injuring many others. For some years afterwards, the US State Department issued a warning against travel to Peru and particularly travelling to Machu Picchu.[72]

The irony is that the 1980s also saw the beginning of a new – and much brighter – future for Machu Picchu. This was in part thanks to the decline in tourism – a multitude of hotels that had been planned for the area in the 1970s never got built. But the survival of Machu Picchu is also due to the ongoing hard work of the local Cusco government. In 1981, the same year Indiana Jones took to our screens for the first time, the local government moved to have a 'Historical Sanctuary' area declared around the site to protect it from further development. This enabled Machu Picchu to apply for UNESCO World Heritage Site status, which it was granted in 1983, along with access to funding for a series of restoration projects at the site.[73] Machu Picchu would continue to be a tourism mecca – but at least one in which now the preservation of the site itself took priority.

*

But whatever became of all the artefacts that Bingham shipped back to the US? It seems that, until the 1980s, they had been largely left to gather dust at Yale. At the same time, the question of what Machu Picchu was still remained unsettled. Bingham's theories about Machu Picchu being Tampu Tocco and the home of the Virgins of the Sun had never been accepted, but neither had another convincing explanation been offered. In the twentieth century, scholarly interest in the history of South America had been largely focused on understanding the different civilisations that had lived in the region before the Inca. All this was about to change, and Machu Picchu was soon to have its time in the sun.

The first great breakthrough came in 1987, when the scholar John Howland Rowe published his work on documents from the era of the Spanish conquest that were held in the Cusco archives. Rowe discovered that Machu Picchu was in fact mentioned as being part of a 'royal estate' established in the 1450s to 60s by the ninth Inca ruler, Pachacuti, following his conquest of the region.[74] Since that point, our understanding of what Machu Picchu was has grown enormously. It does not date from the earliest era of the Incas at all and is definitely not Tampu Tocco. Moreover, it was never a city – or indeed a citadel – but instead a small community home to a maximum of perhaps seven hundred and fifty people.[75] Nor was it fully occupied all year round. Royal estates were places to which the Inca ruler could escape from Cusco with his elite close retinue – a kind of Incan Camp David. Except such estates belonged to the ruler who built them and did not pass on to the next Inca ruler. So, following Pachacuti's death, Machu Picchu, alongside his other royal estates, continued to serve the '*panaca*' – the group responsible for caring for and honouring Pachacuti's body ever after. The significance of Machu Picchu therefore was multiple: it was a place for Pachacuti to relax away from his capital; it was a strategic marker in the landscape of his conquests and achievements; and it was a source of ongoing revenue to ensure his body and memory was cherished for ever.

The temporary occupation of Machu Picchu by the crème de la crème of Inca society helps us understand the unusual architecture at the site itself. In the north-east sector of the site sits a collection of elite houses, organised into traditional groupings known as '*kancha*'. Each *kancha*, made up of a walled compound enclosing a number of houses situated around an open-air patio, would have been home to a single elite family group. The entrance to each *kancha* was marked by a monumental doorway, which was barred to stop unauthorised access. Studies have also shown that each of the *kancha* at Machu Picchu is architecturally different to one another, perhaps reflecting individual elite family preferences. One of the *kancha*, named by Bingham and his team when they first uncovered them in 1912 as the 'Ingenuity Kin group', contained eleven different houses that could accommodate up to sixty people, and had a view out over the central plaza of the site, where the Temple of the Sun and the Temple with Bingham's famous three windows were located.[76] Just outside each *kancha* compound was a series of much lower-grade housing, home to the full-time servants (*yanakuna*) who moved with their elite family employer as they travelled around.

The residence of the Inca ruler himself at Machu Picchu is set apart from all other buildings. It sits in the south-west sector of the site and as a result it enjoys a uniquely high level of privacy compared to the elite *kancha*, and even has its own individual walled garden. The royal house itself is not larger than the dwellings of the other elite *kancha* (although the stonework is yet more exquisite), but the boundary of the royal enclosure was more monumental: visitors had to pass through two sets of enormous doorways, with lintels twice the size of those used anywhere else in the site. Moreover, the ruler's residence was the only one at Machu Picchu with a private toilet – the ultimate symbol of power.[77]

The water for that toilet, and also for the ruler's private bath and drinking fountains, has been shown by recent study at Machu Picchu to have been delivered through an ingenious system of gravity-driven channels that link back to a perennial spring on the north slopes of the nearby mountain peak. Once at Machu Picchu, the water flows into a descending system of sixteen fountains, the first of which served the Inca ruler's residence. The Inca ruler got his water before anyone else could touch it, crucial for a man whose spit was not even allowed to touch the ground.[78]

Thirty or so of the other main structures within Machu Picchu are dedicated to ceremonial and religious activities, including a Temple of the Sun and a massive carved-stone sundial, underlining how important religious observance was for the Inca ruler and his elites even when on their royal estate getaway.[79] But what is fascinating is that no elite burials have been found at Machu Picchu. This was after all just a holiday getaway, and the elite families and ruler would soon pack up and move with their close retinue back to Cusco. Instead, the burials that have been found at Machu Picchu are those of the permanent resident workforce that farmed the agricultural lands belonging to the estate and kept the place ticking over. As the most recent archaeological surveys of the area around Machu Picchu have shown, agricultural cultivation actually extended far beyond the now-visible and famous stone-constructed terraces that tumble down the mountainsides immediately around the central built area of Machu Picchu. We now know that there were six different agricultural zones stretching out around Machu Picchu that today have been reclaimed by the jungle but at the height of Pachacuti's reign were all connected to water supplies and were all accessible by a series of built staircases, which in turn were linked to a major (and gated) road that descended back to the Urubamba River and joined up with the larger Inca road system.[80] There is also evidence for extensive textile production, stone carving and bronze tool making at Machu Picchu, with the raw metals being brought to the site from royal-controlled deposits up to 150 miles away.[81]

The permanent workforce of Machu Picchu had communal halls to gather in to eat, built outside of the main elite residential areas, alongside large storage buildings for surplus agricultural produce. The burials reveal a diverse population of men, women, children and elderly – the vast majority of whom seem to have come from several different parts of the Inca Empire, which fits with the Inca tradition of moving people around their realm to help with productivity and defuse the potential for rebellion.[82]

Our understanding of Machu Picchu has been transformed since Bingham's initial 'discovery' – we now view it as an example of the extraordinary wealth, power, engineering ingenuity, religious dedication and architectural sophistication of the Inca at the height of their empire and particularly of one of their most powerful rulers. And it is no surprise that as our understanding of the incredible nature of Machu Picchu has grown, so too has the demand to see it – tourism has gradually come back, aided by improvements in the stability of the government of Peru and a decrease in crime and domestic terrorism. In 2011, on the centenary of Bingham's first expedition, tourist numbers to the site surpassed 1 million for the first time.[83]

Cusco has clearly won its battle to make itself and its nearby archaeological sites part of modern Peruvian identity: the Peruvian president in 2011 declared the site 'the synthesis of all things Peruvian'.[84] But national government backing and interest brings with it new challenges. Since Cusco's creation of the Historical Sanctuary around Machu Picchu and its declaration as a UNESCO World Heritage Site in the 1980s, the desire of the local Cusco authorities has been to minimise development immediately around the site and thus retain its natural character. In contrast, the national government has on occasion sought to maximise its tourist potential. For example, government plans to install a cable-car system taking people directly to the site in 1999 led to the first general strike in Cusco's history, undertaken expressly to protect its archaeological heritage. The plans were shelved and both sides moved into the new millennium in agreement that the site should not be meddled with.[85]

Instead, the government found a new target: Yale and its collection of artefacts shipped back by Bingham to its Peabody Museum. Having elected to take his oath of presidency at Machu Picchu in 2000, the Peruvian president Alejandro Toledo publicly called on Yale to return the objects taken by Bingham in his 1911–12 expeditions, arguing that they had only ever been 'on loan' from Peru.[86] After a decade of wrangling, in 2011, as part of the centenary of Bingham's 'discovery', Yale finally agreed to return the collection, which is now on display in Cusco.

Machu Picchu is today as famously recognisable as the Pyramids of Egypt and the Great Wall of China. This tiny royal estate, home to a maximum of just seven hundred and fifty people, occupied for only parts of the year for a fairly brief window of time several centuries ago, has been propelled to such superstardom by a complex mix of drivers. It is of course first and foremost a visually and architecturally stunning site set in a mesmeric location in the clouds. Yet it has – until fairly recently – also been *both* shrouded in mystery as to its purpose and history, *and* emblematic of the great civilisation of the Incas, who themselves, as they did not leave any written sources, are also cloaked in mystery. As such, Machu Picchu has attracted world attention and interest equally for what it reveals and for the secrets it holds.

Machu Picchu, in offering such an enticing mix of revelation and mystery, became an ideal emblem around which Hiram Bingham could develop his reputation as an explorer. For Bingham, it was, as Che Guevara put it, his 'adult dream' – his ticket, as he eventually came to realise, to explorer glory. He came across it thanks to the directions of others at a time when the tectonic plates of geopolitics had aligned to encourage and enable interest in South America. It was not he who first found it, but it was he who both uncovered the site and brought it to the attention of the world, after he had realised its potential (something captured in the plaque at Machu Picchu that Bingham was invited to unveil in 1948 describing him as the site's 'scientific discoverer' rather than simply 'discoverer'). That story of himself as the explorer and discoverer extraordinaire was, however, one that he, by the end of his life, had learnt to milk to perfection. And as such, Bingham is an indissoluble part of the story of Machu Picchu, even if he was ultimately wrong in his beliefs about it being the fabled first city of the Incas, or indeed home to their later chosen Virgins of the Sun.

Machu Picchu has, however, not only been a vehicle for (and beneficiary of) Bingham's journey to explorer-renown. Since its discovery, it has also been an emblem in Peru's, at times fierce, national debate about its identity, as well as a symbol of the wider collaboration sought at different moments between North and South America, and of course a beacon for a whole host of changing global lifestyles, movements and fashions. Ultimately, therefore, Machu Picchu has become so world famous as much because of what it has represented and been able to do for others as due to what it actually is in and of itself. As such, it is, perhaps more than any other site in the world, a clear example of the way in which we so often re-make the past as a mirror of our present: our needs, desires and fixations.

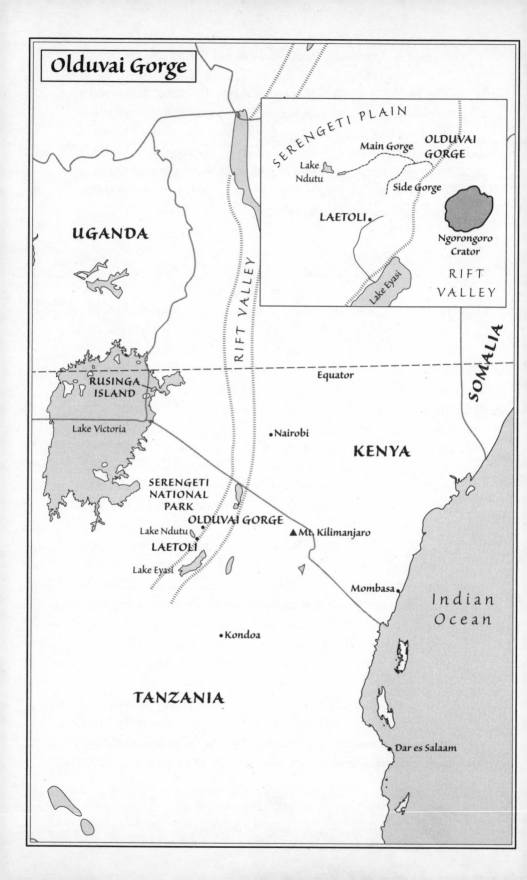

4

Origins of Us

The ash fell like snowflakes, covering the area around the volcano in a layer of soft grey snow just a few millimetres thick. After a few hours, the volcano returned to a state of rumbling slumber, the ash-fall replaced by a light drizzle, which turned the ash blanket lying on the ground into a damp sticky gelatinous mess. A rhinoceros took advantage of the break in the ash-fall to move across the landscape, its thick hooves sinking into the grey ooze beneath it, leaving a clear imprint of its path as it moved. It was followed by a multitude of animals that lived in the vicinity: each going their own way across the grey sticky floor beneath them, each leaving their footprints behind: birds, elephants, even insects.

They did not have long. The volcano, Sadiman, erupted from its slumber once again to spew more ash into the air, leaving a new fine layer of hot dry ash covering the ground, which, in turn, dried out the ooze beneath it until it hardened like cement. At the next break in the ash-fall, the rains came, creating a new layer atop the hardened one that similarly captured the imprints of the animals that moved across it, and even the impressions of raindrops.[1]

Another creature appeared – walking on two legs – placing one foot confidently in front of the other across this grey sticky ground, no doubt keeping a watchful eye on the once-again-slumbering Sadiman. The creature was not alone; two more walked alongside, also on two legs but with smaller steps, suggesting they were of smaller stature. One of the smaller creatures was following the taller one, deliberately putting their feet into the footprints left in the grey ooze by their taller companion, like a child playing a game of 'follow the leader'. At some point a three-toed horse accompanied by its foal crossed the tracks the group had left behind, leaving their own trail.[2]

Eruption of dry hot ash followed eruption of more dry hot ash, interspersed by rains, across a period of just a few weeks, each layer capturing the imprints of those who moved across it. But Sadiman was only clearing its throat. After a few weeks, the big eruption came, bringing down a thick solid layer of ash that not only buried the layers of footprints, but probably extinguished the lives of their makers.[3]

Three and a half million years later, on 15 September 1976, in the very same area, which is today part of Tanzania, a group of geologists, biologists and anthropologists were doing something you might never expect a serious group of researchers to do: throwing elephant dung at one another as part of a game of tag during a break from their work. Elephant dung makes the very best kind of – readily available – ammunition to throw at one another in this part of the world: its texture is solid enough to maintain its shape as it flies through the air and the occasional thorn concealed within it adds just a little spice to the game. One of the biologists knelt down behind a rock to protect himself from the onslaught and came face to face with the hardened footprint of an ancient rhinoceros.[4]

This became Site A of the so-called 'footprint tuff' – with 'tuff' being the technical name for the multitude of thin ash layers laid down in those weeks of gentle eruptions before Sadiman's main eruption 3.5 million years before. In that long expanse of time, the thick layer of solid ash from Sadiman's massive eruption, and subsequent layers of earth, had – in places – been washed and worn away to expose brief pockets of the footprint tuff to the naked eye. Site A – between 1976 and 1979 – became the first of eighteen sites discovered where the footprint tuff could be seen back once again at surface level.

The woman in charge of the team who had been playing elephant-dung tag was Mary Leakey.[5] An experienced and already well-known anthropologist and archaeologist, she was sixty-two years old when, in 1975, she had come with her team to the area of the ancient Sadiman volcano – now called Laetoli near the modern Tanzania–Kenya border. There was no good water source for ten miles in any direction. Temperatures were baking in the middle of the day and freezing at night. The team had only a temporary camp and rudimentary facilities to protect them from the charging buffalo that on occasion rampaged through the area, the plentiful poisonous puff adders that swarmed around them, the covering of ticks that attached themselves to every part of their bodies, not to mention the herds of elephants that still liked to move through the area pulling down trees, stealing plastic sheeting from excavation areas as well as the occasional tent or two.[6]

Despite these difficulties – and her own personal health problems including recovering from a hysterectomy and a broken ankle – in their subsequent excavation seasons between 1976 and 1979, Mary Leakey led the team of African and international experts that discovered thousands of footprints across the eighteen areas in which the footprint tuff was now exposed.[7] In Site A alone, they recorded 18,400 footprints of everything from an insect to an elephant. Each was studied, photographed, drawn and a mould made of it using latex and silicon rubber. The first footprints of the creatures walking on two legs were found in 1976, and across the next three years, the team slowly dug to uncover more of the footprint tuff layer in that area, following the footprints, until they had uncovered a trail eighty feet long of these three creatures walking and playing 'follow the leader' together. The trails were so well preserved in the cement-like ash that they looked, as Mary later wrote for *National Geographic* magazine, 'like they have been left this morning'.[8]

Mary's team had discovered an extraordinary window through which to view our distant ancient past: the entire Footprint tuff layer corresponded to just a few weeks of time, and each individual layer of ash within it just a few hours – a few hours from over 3.5 million years ago. And what made it all the more remarkable was that the date was no hyperbole or interpretation to be argued this way and that. The team had been able to conclusively date the footprint tuff layer, thanks to scientific analysis of the ash itself and the soil and rocks that covered it. And that made the clear and indisputable footprints of those three creatures walking upright – perhaps playing games as they did so – even more precious. Because it proved beyond any doubt that man's ancestors were walking on two legs far earlier than anyone had realised.[9] Mary's discovery fundamentally changed our understanding of the nature of our human story. It was, as she herself later recounted, 'the most significant of the discoveries for which I have been responsible'.[10]

*

Fifty-three years earlier, at the age of just ten, Mary was exploring with her father, Erskine Nicol, in the countryside around the French villages of Domme and Les Eyzies, between Bordeaux and Toulouse in south-western France. She was – by her own admission – always happiest in her father's company. He was an artist, and would dress, she later recalled, 'in the oldest and untidiest clothes that my mother would let him get away with'.[11] Mary's life since the end of the First World War in 1918 had consisted of winters and springs spent abroad in Switzerland, Italy and France with her parents so that her father could paint the beautiful landscapes around them, and summers back in London while the paintings were sold, during which time Mary was spoilt by her three aunts who lived in Chelsea. But it was France – and particularly the countryside around Les Eyzies – that had the biggest impact on Mary. For it was here that she first saw for herself the remains of earliest man. This region of France was littered with prehistoric caves decorated by early humans, and at the local museum this little girl was welcomed by the curator to examine their collections of early man's stone tools. She was hooked.

When her father was not painting, he and Mary would walk out to join the excavations of the museum curator. He would allow them to sift through the heaps of earth he had discarded and it was there that Mary discovered what she called 'the sheer instinctive joy of collecting, or indeed one could say of treasure hunting!'[12] Perhaps it was in her blood. Her father, prior to the First World War, had lived in Egypt in a houseboat on the Nile, and was fascinated by Egyptian mummies and their royal burials (he was good friends with Howard Carter – then just a junior employee of the Egypt Exploration Society – who would go on to discover the tomb of Tutankhamun in 1922. And on her mother's side, Mary's great-great-grandfather was John Frere, who is credited with being one of the first people to ever identify, study and publish detailed drawings of early man's stone tools, which he discovered in Suffolk.[13]

Mary was not content with simply collecting finds from the excavation spoil heaps: she started to classify her finds into different categories of shape, style and use. Her dedication on site was not matched, however, by her attention in the classroom. Her father had hired a governess to teach Mary History and Latin, but the lady soon left, exasperated by Mary's inattention and her tendency to call her 'the uncooked dumpling' because she was – in Mary's words – 'comprehensively ugly and gawky'. The local parish priest did better in the nearby town of Cabrerets, which the family visited in 1925. He took Mary to recently discovered cave-art sites like that at Pech Merle and taught her to dig for fossils and artefacts. Looking back, Mary realised that, from that point on, she never wanted to do anything else. As she put it at the end of her life, she 'was impelled by curiosity'.[14]

In 1926, at the age of just thirteen, Mary lost her father to cancer. Her world turned upside down, she and her mother, Cecilia, returned to London and to a very different way of life. Mary went from having the freedom of the French countryside to the austere routine of convent schools. She hated every second of it – and was expelled from two of them. During this time, Mary and her mother lived in Wimbledon, and Mary's main joy was learning to ride at the Wimbledon Common riding stables. I too grew up there and learnt to ride at those same stables and I think about Mary riding across Wimbledon Common rightfully angry at the joy and companionship she had lost and the bleaker landscape Wimbledon offered compared to that of south-western France. But what England (if not Wimbledon) did have was archaeology. Mary's uncle took her on her first visit to Stonehenge and then to Avebury Stone Circle, where Mary met for the first time the pioneering self-taught female archaeologist Dorothy Liddell. It was at this point she realised 'that a career in archaeology was open to women'.[15]

But Mary had not a single school qualification. Her mother went to plead Mary's case to a Professor of Geology called William Sollas at Oxford, but she was politely refused. Instead, the pair moved to Fulham, so Mary, still only seventeen, could attend as many public lectures in archaeology and geology at London's universities as possible. And when she was not listening to lectures, she was learning to fly glider planes. Mary was the only unmarried female member of the London Gliding Club. I learnt to fly gliders when I was a university student and remember the thrill of the quiet as the glider slid through the air, supported only by the winds, the whole world seemingly laid out below you. For Mary, it must have been another taste of the freedom she had had as a child back in France – a freedom she would crave her entire life.

Her diligence attending university lectures – and writing persistently to archaeologists to request a place on their excavations – paid off. The first, when Mary was just eighteen, was under Sir Mortimer Wheeler at St Albans, and the second at

Hembury in Devon under Dorothy Liddell. Mary was mentored by Dorothy and later by one of the other pioneering female archaeologists of the day, Dr Gertrude Caton Thompson, who worked in Egypt and across the Middle East. Gertrude in particular was one of, as Mary would later recount, 'a remarkable breed of English ladies who for archaeology's sake would go out alone into harsh desert environments and by determination, skill, expertise and endurance achieve discoveries of major and permanent importance'.[16] Mary might as well have been describing her own future.

That future was about to be indelibly intertwined with a country and a person. In 1933, at the age of just twenty, Mary was introduced by Gertrude to Louis Leakey, who had grown up the son of a missionary family in Kenya, even being initiated into the Kenyan Kikuyu tribe. He, like Mary, had fallen in love with the study of the past, having spent the happiest moments in his early life outdoors uncovering the material remains and tools of early man. Unlike Mary, he had been accepted to study at Cambridge and eventually came to work closely with an anthropologist called Alfred Haddon. Anthropology is the study of humankind – its behaviours, biology, linguistics and, of course, its evolution. Up until the early nineteenth century the question of human evolution was most often answered through religious belief. But during the first half of the nineteenth century a flurry of discovery, including the first remains of 'Neanderthal Man' in Europe, and resultant scientific enquiry culminated in Charles Darwin's publication of *On the Origins of Species* on 24 November 1859. It sold out on the day it was published. Darwin's picture of the gradual evolution of all species, including man, powered by his concept of natural selection, now showed that mankind had been on its own journey of evolution. When – and perhaps even more importantly where – did humans evolve was now the ultimate conundrum.

Darwin had suggested that Africa could be the place that humanity began its own journey of evolution as a species, as Africa is also the home of apes and chimps – recognised as some of our closest relatives within the animal kingdom. But in the 1930s few in the Western world were ready to see Africa as the font of all humankind, preferring instead to argue that, because people looked so different in different parts of the world, perhaps each group had evolved independently from one another.[17]

Louis Leakey was convinced that the origins of humankind were to be found in his home continent of Africa. In the late 1920s and early 1930s he undertook three expeditions to where he had grown up in Kenya to uncover evidence for early man. It was on the back of the discoveries he made during these expeditions that he came to be searching for an illustrator for his book *Adam's Ancestors* and was introduced by Gertrude Caton Thompson to Mary as someone who had great skill in drawing stone tools (something she had become expert at during her time working on Dorothy Liddell's dig at Hembury). Over the course of the next eighteen months their working relationship became a love affair that would lead to Louis separating from his first wife and the brutal censure of a society uncomfortable with Louis and Mary's choices. Louis lost his position at Cambridge and Gertrude turned her back on Mary, as did many of their other colleagues and friends. Even Mary's favourite aunts were against her. In January 1935 Mary and her mother flew to South Africa for an extended holiday. Mary's mother hoped to break Mary's attachment to Louis, but on 17 April 1935 she flew back to England alone – having failed to dissuade her daughter – and Mary flew on to Tanzania to meet Louis and begin work with him on a site they would together make famous in the story of early man.

*

Olduvai Gorge is a unique geological feature in the Serengeti plains that stretch out across the modern Tanzanian and Kenyan border. The gorge itself is like a small-scale Grand Canyon, 50 kilometres long and up to 90 metres deep in places, created when tectonic plate shifts about half a million years ago rendered a tear in the otherwise flat landscape, which was subsequently widened and deepened over thousands of years by torrents of water rushing through it during the rainy seasons. What makes it so special in terms of the opportunities it offers to those searching for earliest man is that the gorge's almost vertical sides cut down through layer after layer of ancient lake beds, where the fossilised remains of the creatures that once roamed the area over the last couple of millions of years were now – once again much more exposed – just waiting to be found.[18]

The gorge's scientific interest had first been recorded in 1911 when the whole area was part of German East Africa. The Kaiser himself had supported an early expedition there in 1913 (the year Mary was born) and the expedition leader, Hans Reck, had found part of a fossilised skeleton that was later proved to be about 17,000 years old (although at the time it was argued to be almost half a million years old).[19] The First World War, and the resultant reallocation of German East Africa to become the British Mandated Territory of Tanganyika (later Tanzania), meant that Hans Reck as a German could not return there to continue his search, at least not on his own. It was Louis Leakey who took him back in 1931 as part of Louis's third expedition to East Africa to search for earliest man. While they found no further skeletons, they did find what Hans Reck and his team had not discovered on their previous visit: early man's stone tools. Louis was convinced that Olduvai had many more secrets to give up.

When Mary arrived in Tanzania in 1935, she and Louis set off straightaway for Olduvai. It was no easy journey. It took them two and a half days to cover just the last sixteen miles, most of which were spent repeatedly digging their car's wheels out of the thick mud caused by recent rainfall. By the time they arrived at the highest point of the final stage of the journey and were able to glimpse the gorge stretching out below them, they were both caked in mud from head to toe.[20] Having finally reached Olduvai, they pitched their tent and lost no time in exploring. Over the next three months they identified thirty sites within the gorge where fossilised remains and stone tools were present. Mary even found the fossilised skull of a *Homo erectus* dating back over 1 million years – at the time thought to be the earliest ancestor of man that walked on two feet (hence its title *erectus*).[21]

They were living in the wild – and Mary loved it. One time she came face to face with a rhinoceros; on another she tripped over a sleeping lioness. To supplement their meagre diet of tinned sardines, jam and rice, Louis shot gazelles, which they roasted on an open fire. The only real shortages Mary found it hard to deal with were of water and cigarettes. She – like Louis – was a dedicated smoker and when their supplies ran low, they would search their campsite for old cigarette stumps, re-roll them in toilet paper and smoke them afresh.[22] When even these recycled cigarettes ran out, all they could do was wait for the next supply truck to visit, no doubt fidgeting increasingly as the nicotine-withdrawal symptoms kicked in. When the supply truck was once a week late, they set off in their car to find it. The car got stuck again – this time in a gully – and Mary and Louis had to dig it out with the only tools they had with them: two kitchen knives and two plates. They were watched the whole time by the area's only other human inhabitants: the Maasai. Mary later recounted that the Maasai were never sure whether she was a man or a woman because she always wore trousers.[23]

Water during the rainy season in Olduvai was in plentiful supply, but in the dry season Louis and Mary suddenly found themselves thirty miles from the closest freshwater source. The only water remaining in the gorge was in small puddles in which the local rhinos liked to urinate. Louis and Mary scooped this up, filtered it through charcoal, boiled it and drank it as tea with lemon. But they could still taste the rhino pee. One time, after a freak rainstorm, they rushed to drink instead the freshwater pools that had collected in the sagging canvas of their tent roofs. It was only after they had liberally satiated themselves that they remembered the canvas was treated with a powerful insecticide to help stave off the mosquitoes and other insects that frequented the gorge. They were both violently ill and returned henceforth to drinking lemon-scented, rhino-pee-flavoured water.[24]

Mary and Louis left Olduvai to return to England in September 1935, their expedition funds spent and the reality of their complicated personal lives needing to be faced. Mary had been in Africa for nine months, and in and around Olduvai living in the wild for almost five. As she herself later said, she 'would never be the same again now that Africa had cast its spell on me'.[25] Indeed, in many ways life in the wild at Olduvai was simpler and easier than back in England. Mary and Louis returned to live together in a small cottage in a village called Nasty in Hertfordshire. Neither had any job or regular income outside of the small advances Louis secured for writing. Their cottage had an outdoor chemical toilet and a tin tub in the kitchen for a bath. They still faced social and professional censure from all their former colleagues because of the way Louis had left his wife for Mary, and Louis's wife, Frida, refused to consent to a divorce until the summer of 1936. When it emerged – as a result of the divorce proceedings – that Mary and Louis were living together unmarried in Hertfordshire, Louis was even chucked out of the local tennis club.[26] On Christmas Eve 1936, as war clouds started to form once again over Europe, Mary and Louis were finally married, with the son of the Kenyan Kikuyu senior tribal chief, who was staying with them in Hertfordshire before heading off to spend a year at Cambridge, as their best man.[27] By January 1937, they had left small-town English life behind to travel back to Africa.

But even life in the wild costs money. There was no way Mary and Louis could finance a proper excavation team at Olduvai without financial backing. Over the next few years, therefore, Louis was occupied with writing a history of the Kikuyu tribe funded by the Rhodes Trust, and Mary – after she recovered from severe pneumonia – participated in a small number of excavations near their home base in Nairobi, becoming better and better acquainted with the variety of stone tools early man in Africa had created and used. With the outbreak of the Second World War in 1939, Louis was drafted into the African Intelligence Service, uncovering sources of anti-British propaganda in the region and supporting resistance fighters over the border in Ethiopia against the invading Italian army, and at the same time acting as curator for the local museum in Nairobi. No salary came with the position but it did give them a house, although that was so full of holes that Sundays were designated as rodent-killing days, with the couple destroying thirty to forty at a time.[28]

Mary gave birth to their first son, Jonathan, in 1940, a daughter Deborah (who died of dysentery at just three months) in 1942, and their second son, Richard, in 1944 – in between returning to work on a number of excavation projects around Nairobi (at one of which Mary shared the excavation work-room with a cobra that had taken up residence in the room's grass roof). They existed in financial terms 'on the smell of an oil rag'.[29] They got back to Olduvai just once, briefly, in 1941, and to London only after the conclusion of the war in December 1945 to care for Mary's dying mother. The city Mary had once lived in had been changed irrevocably by the war and, following the death of her mother, held no attraction for her (although her son Jonathan loved riding the escalators in the department stores and tube stations).[30] In 1946 they returned to Nairobi with the job of organising the first ever Pan-African Congress of Prehistory and Palaeontology, which would be held in the city in January 1947. After a decade of living hand to mouth, Mary and Louis were about to claim the attention of the world.

*

The conference was a success, with most attendees agreeing that the origins of humankind were to be found in Africa (rather

than spread out around the world) and recognising the important nature of many of Mary and Louis's excavations through
the late 1930s and early 1940s.[31] But it was what Mary and Louis
did after the conference that really changed their own personal
fortunes. They took a small group of scholars who had attended
the conference to visit Rusinga Island in the middle of Lake
Victoria, the largest lake in Africa spanning the borders of
modern-day Kenya, Uganda and Tanzania. Mary and Louis had
gone there for the first time in 1942 as part of a family holiday.
But it had soon become clear to them that this site could be
extremely important, because it dated to what is known as the
'Miocene epoch' – a period of time between 23 and 5 million
years ago, when some of the great evolutionary separations are
thought to have happened among primates (the development of
apes, and the splitting of human ancestors from the ancestors of
the chimpanzee), and thus important period in the very early
history of the development of mankind. The journey to Rusinga
Island in 1942 involved a trip across Lake Victoria (which had a
very healthy crocodile population) in a boat swarming with
cockroaches. But the effort was worthwhile: even on their first
visit Mary and Louis found part of the fossilised jaw of an early
ape.[32]

The academics Mary and Louis took to Rusinga Island in
January 1947 following the Pan-African Congress of Prehistory
and Palaeontology agreed on the potential of the site (although
they struggled much more than Mary and Louis with the dangerous and difficult conditions they had to endure to reach it). The
outcome was funding, and the new official British Kenyan Miocene
Expedition set off for Rusinga later in 1947 in a new and more
modern boat named *Maji Moto* (Swahili for 'Hot Water'). The
report of this expedition in *The Times* caught the eye of a rich
philanthropist called Charles Boise, who immediately sent Mary
and Louis a cheque to fund further expeditions. Alongside *Maji
Moto*, Mary and Louis could now afford a mobile truck that they
could live in and work from.[33]

On 2 October 1948, Louis was busy looking at the fossilised remains of an extinct variety of crocodile on Rusinga Island, which did not interest Mary in the slightest. There were enough live crocodiles around to contend with: in fact the only way the family could bathe safely in the waters of Lake Victoria surrounding the island was following Louis shooting his gun into the water to scare away the crocodiles that lurked below the surface (this gave them fifteen clear minutes to swim before the crocs regained their confidence).[34] That day, Mary had chosen to work in a different area of the island – one in fact that she and Louis had explored seven times previously without finding anything of interest.[35] But on that day, suddenly she saw a tooth shining on the sloping surface of a small rise. Swift and delicate investigation around the tooth revealed that it was actually still attached to a jaw. This was followed by several long days of sieving the earth on every side of the find to ensure that they did not miss a single fragment that might help them recreate as much of the skull as possible. Mary ended up with over thirty fragments of skull alongside her tooth and jaw piece – and it was her job now to put them back together.

She spent days in her tent on the island working out where each tiny fragment might fit. It was like an impossible jigsaw puzzle for which you don't have the picture you are trying to recreate (Mary, of course, did not at the time know what the skull should look like): you aren't sure which pieces you have and which you haven't; and you don't even know if the pieces you have come from completely separate parts of the skull (or indeed a different skull entirely). The work required everything Mary had to offer: endless patience and determination, a keen and dedicated eye, and lots of experience of working with fossilised remains – something she had been accumulating since she was ten. At one point she dropped a tiny piece of skull on the tent floor and spent hours searching for it down on her hands and knees in the dust.[36] But the end result was worth it: more than half an entire skull glued back together. And this was not just any skull. It was the skull of *Proconsul africanus*, an ape-like creature that had lived around 20 million years ago. No one in the world had found before this point so much of a complete skull of *Proconsul*. Mary and Louis were as a result, as she later put it: 'the first eyes ever to see a *Proconsul* face'.[37] And what made the find even more important was that, at the time, many thought that *Proconsul*, might well be the missing link in the evolutionary chain between apes and the ancestors of modern man.

Mary and Louis 'celebrated' their find by making love (they often later spoke fondly of how their next child, Philip, had been conceived during those celebrations).[38] By late October 1948, they were back in Nairobi and Mary (pregnant but not yet aware of it) was boarding a plane to take the *Proconsul* skull back to England to have it examined by the foremost expert in primate fossils of the period: Professor Wilfrid Le Gros Clerk. The publicity around the find was huge. She had a police escort to the airport. BOAC airline flew Mary to London for free to claim the publicity of transporting the 'missing link'. Mary never let the skull leave her lap – except when the plane stopped over in Cairo and the captain locked it in his cabin. Wilfrid Le Gros Clerk declared it had both hominid (human) and ape features. The newspapers declared it the 'missing link' in human evolution.[39]

We know today that *Proconsul* is no such thing, in fact scientists don't actually believe any more that there is a single 'missing link' primate. *Proconsul* instead is agreed to be a very early ancestor of chimpanzees, gibbons, orangutans, gorillas and humans, which lived roughly 18 million years ago.[40] But this does not undermine the importance of Mary's find: it was the first *Proconsul* skull to be found in anywhere near a complete state.[41] And it made Mary and Louis world famous.

Mary did not like the press attention anywhere near as much as Louis did. After the birth of Philip in June 1949, further visits to Rusinga Island, some more time in London in 1950 and a visit back to France to the village where she had first discovered her love for the study of earliest man as a child, Mary began work in 1951 on studying the cave art of Late Stone Age people in the

Kondoa region of modern-day Tanzania. She had just added a key piece to the world's understanding of evolution, and yet here she was working harder than ever before: her team copied over sixteen hundred images in just three months (and one day during that time the wind was so strong it blew away all their tracings and they had to start all over again) in order to record the delicate cave art for posterity.[42] Mary loved the work, for, as she put it: 'no amount of stone and bone could yield the kinds of information that the paintings gave so freely'.[43] The images depicted hairstyles, clothing, jewellery, a variety of different activities and animals – including pet dogs. These cave paintings were 'a glimpse of Late Stone Age people themselves'.[44]

Mary loved listening to the stories the ancient world told her through these paintings much more than she enjoyed listening to, and being part of, the modern world's media furore around the search for early man. But she could not divorce herself entirely from them: such attention was, after all, the route to securing the money required to continue the couple's investigations. Charles Boise, who had sponsored their Rusinga operation in the late 1940s, had seen the *Proconsul* skull while Mary was in London and agreed not only to continue his sponsorship but also to visit with Mary and Louis the site they both now wanted to excavate more than any other: Olduvai Gorge. In 1951, they took Charles Boise to Olduvai. He was convinced that the two of them could strike evolutionary gold once again here, and, having witnessed Louis repair the car that had brought them from civilisation to the wilderness of the gorge with only dried goat skin and branches as available tools, he understood just how crucial good funding would be to the operation.[45] Boise agreed to fund their work, alongside financial backing they were now receiving from the Kenyan government, for seven years. Mary and Louis could now at last plan a long-term study at Olduvai – something they had wanted to do since their first visit there together in 1935.

*

Mary and Louis's aim in digging at Olduvai was to try and determine 'when and by what steps our ancestors became human and evolved into *Homo sapiens*'.[46] As they had realised back in 1935, Olduvai offered a unique opportunity to answer these questions because of the way in which the gorge cut straight down through – and thus offered easy access to – multiple layers of earth and sediment that had been laid down over millions of years, like taking a knife and cutting through the middle of a multi-layered sandwich and being able to see all of its contents. At the bottom of the gorge was a thick layer of volcanic ash turned into rock, on top of which were a series of lava flows that could be dated to 1.89 million years ago, thanks to a new technique called potassium/argon dating, which was just being developed in the 1950s and was used in the field for the first time at Olduvai.[47]

Hans Reck, who had first explored Olduvai back in 1913 and then later with Louis Leakey in 1931, had identified five different main levels of deposits above the lava flows, which were known as Olduvai's five 'beds'. Each bed spanned hundreds of thousands of years and was itself made up of multiple smaller layers of deposits. What this meant was that, altogether, Olduvai's five beds held a continuous history of activity in the area dating from 1.89 million years ago through to the present time. Under Mary and Louis's supervision, over the next almost thirty years of study, Olduvai would prove to offer the longest continuous record of early man's activity that had been found anywhere in the world.[48]

Mary and Louis, along with their team of African workmen and fellow excavators, had a daunting task ahead of them. It was impossible of course to excavate the entire gorge, and so they had to judge where best to target their efforts. At the same time, Mary was a tough boss who would not tolerate haphazard workmanship from her team. Because of her experience and knowledge of the tools of early man – gained from when she first started sifting through spoil heaps in France at the age of twelve – she was as interested in the tiniest fragments of tools and remnants of activity or habitation as in finding the fossilised bones of the people who had been using those tools, undertaking those activities or living in the area. She understood the value of all these different pieces of evidence for putting together the fullest and richest picture of the story of the area and of the evolution of early man, and thus insisted that the find-spot of every tool and fossil be carefully studied and recorded so that it could be related to other finds.[49] Such an approach sounds obvious to us today – and is of course now the standard for archaeological excavation – but at the time, Mary was breaking new ground in putting tools and other fragments of human habitation and activity on a par with bones.

Despite the now-secured funding from Charles Boise and the Kenyan government, conditions at Olduvai continued to be spartan. The team lived in tents, which were uncomfortably hot when there was no wind. Conversely, the tent pegs could never be properly secured deep enough into the ground to prevent the tents from being whipped away in high winds. One afternoon in 1953, Louis suffered heat stroke and his hair turned white overnight.[50] In January and February each year wildebeest and zebra migrated through the Olduvai area, bringing with them their natural predators, lions, cheetahs and hyenas, which the camp had to then be on guard against. Compare this to Mary and Louis's new home back on the outskirts of Nairobi in Kenya, which they bought in 1952: a large home set in 5 acres of lush land, to which giraffes were frequent visitors. But Olduvai had one clear advantage (for Mary at least): it was cut off from the world. Mary loved the fact that at Olduvai there was no telephone, no radio and no newspapers. During the 1950s, there was also no human threat there to their lives. Back across the border in Kenya, the 1950s were a period of dark political turmoil thanks to the state of

emergency that was declared following the Mau Mau rebellion. The rebellion sought to throw off the rule of the British,
and Louis was caught up in it thanks to his intimate knowledge
of the Kikuyu tribe and their language, some of whom fought
as part of the Kenyan Land and Freedom Army (also known as
the Mau Mau) and some fought for the British. As a result of
being involved as a translator in the official trial of a Kenyan
Land and Freedom Army fighter, a price was put on Louis's
head by the Mau Mau. Both Louis and Mary had to resort to
carrying pistols with them at all times for self-protection, and
trusted guards were put in place to protect their children. Mary
and Louis were never actually attacked, but an elderly cousin
and his wife were brutally murdered by the Mau Mau during
this time.[51]

All this was not helped by the fact that from 1955 onwards
Louis was also involved in an affair with his secretary, bringing
marital misery to Mary and leading to lots of heated arguments.
Their son Richard then fractured his skull in a fall from his horse
and his life hung in the balance for some time. The only positive
from the accident was that it brought Mary and Louis back
together.[52] And so in July 1959, pretty much at the end of their
seven-year funding agreement with Charles Boise, Mary and
Louis were still together working at Olduvai. They had focused
their attention over the past seven years on 'Bed II', which spanned
a period of 600,000 years from about 1.7 million to 1.1 million
years ago. Their excavations had shown considerable 'hominid'
(early man) presence in the area over that time period, with the
remnants of multiple camping sites, and thousands of human-
made tools. But they had not made the breakthrough discovery
that they knew would guarantee them international attention and
further funding: the fossilised remains of earliest man. So in 1959,
Mary and Louis turned their attention to 'Bed I' – the earliest
level in the gorge, dating from around 1.9 million to 1.7 million
years ago.

On 17 July 1959, Louis was feeling unwell and Mary spent the day in the gorge accompanied by her two Dalmatian dogs, Sally and Victoria. She decided to survey a potential new excavation site in Bed I, where she hoped that recent rainfalls might have helped expose some finds to the surface. She was on the cusp of returning to the campsite for lunch around noon, when one glint of bone, she later recounted, caught her eye because it was not just on the surface, but projecting from beneath.[53] Using her soft camel-hair excavation brush, Mary briefly examined the protruding bone to reveal teeth – hominid teeth. She greeted the sight by crying out 'Oh my dear boy!' Mary had done it again. She raced back to camp, calling out to Louis: 'I've got him, I've got him!' Louis forgot his flu and together they raced back to the site.

The 'Leakey Luck', as it would become known, was extraordinary: not only because the rains had uncovered *those* teeth in *that* particular area within that *huge* gorge that Mary had chosen to search in *that* day, but also because the next day a film crew was scheduled to arrive at Olduvai to make a short documentary on their excavation.[54] Stationing a guard to stand by the find overnight, Mary and Louis waited for the film crew's arrival and were then able to excavate their new find live on camera. With the cameras rolling, Mary and Louis uncovered two teeth still attached to a piece of upper jaw. It was the first time that anything like it had been excavated on film. Over the next nineteen days, they patiently located every scrap of bone in the vicinity of the teeth and then sieved the earth of the nearby area to find many further even smaller pieces. At the end of the process they had 400 pieces of fossilised skull bone to fit together – suddenly the *Proconsul* skull Mary had put together over a decade earlier looked like a child's jumbo jigsaw in comparison. Mary and Louis took the pieces with them that September to the Fourth Pan-African Congress on Prehistory, which was held in Kinshasa in the Belgian Congo, and showed them to a variety of anatomy specialists. But it would take Mary eighteen months of patient eye-bending work to fit all the pieces together. The result was a skull that Mary always referred to by the very first words she had uttered on seeing the teeth: 'Dear Boy'.[55]

Dear Boy has since had a variety of names.[56] Mary's naming avoided the complicated and bitterly contested field of scientific names for the skull, which Louis wanted to plunge right into. Giving the skull a scientific name meant placing it within the scientific community's emerging understanding of the evolutionary map, and, crucially, making a claim to what this skull represented in terms of the scientific race to understand and map the gradual evolution of early man into *Homo sapiens*. Moreover, if the skull represented a hitherto unknown branch of evolution, a new 'genus' of ancient early man in technical terminology, then of course the find would attract even more attention (and controversy) and, potentially, funding.

Louis argued that Dear Boy was a new genus – a new kind – of early man, which he called *Zinjanthropus boisei*. *Zinjanthropus* means 'Man of East Africa'. *Boisei* came from their funder: Charles Boise.[57] The Professor of Anatomy at the University of Witwatersrand in Johannesburg, Phillip Tobias, who was entrusted to undertake the scientific study of the skull, disagreed. He did not believe Dear Boy was a new genus, but thought it a new 'species' (a type) of a genus called *Australopithecus* or 'Southern Ape'. The first example of this genus had been found back in 1924 in South Africa, and, as a result, Tobias named Dear Boy *Australopithecus boisei*, which was officially adopted as the right name for the specimen by the scientific community following the full publication of Tobias's report in 1967.[58] As if Dear Boy did not have enough names at this stage, Tobias's report emphasised the enormous molar and premolar teeth that the creature had, suggesting it had adapted to a coarse tough vegetarian diet rather than one focused on meat. The press picked up on this and immediately adopted the name 'Nutcracker Man'.

Dear Boy/*Australopithecus boisei*/Nutcracker Man was found in Bed I of Olduvai Gorge, dating the creature to having lived between 1.89 and 1.75 million years ago. Tobias's report under-lined that, because of the way the spine and skull met, it was likely that Dear Boy moved about more upright than any living ape today. And while nothing from the surviving fossilised bones could provide evidence for Dear Boy's ability to make tools, the fact that his remains had been found in the same levels (thanks to Mary's careful excavation techniques) as a wide range of elementary tools, led Mary to believe that Dear Boy was able to at least use a range of basic tools. She envisaged Dear Boy 'as a small-brained, robustly-built, stocky creature, mostly bipedal [walking on two legs], but perhaps occasionally resorting to all fours and squatting on his haunches when stationary or feeding'.[59]

While Nutcracker Man was not by any means the 'missing link' between apes and man, or indeed a hitherto undiscovered genus of early man, it was the first time any remains of the *Australopithecus* genus could be so firmly dated, and that early date of at least 1.75 million years ago astounded everyone.[60] It was also, as indicated, the first discovery to be made 'live on camera'. As a result, funding now started to pour in for Mary and Louis. By 1960, *National Geographic* magazine had agreed to pick up the tab for excavations at Olduvai in return for exclusive photo and television rights to future discoveries.[61] Mary and Louis were now set to continue excavations through the next decade. With that money, they were able not only to continue excavating, but to make conditions at Olduvai more comfortable. During the 1960s, they built a workroom with an operating refrigerator, and converted a truck into a secure caravan for Mary and her beloved Dalmatians to sleep in at night. This was not for Mary's comfort but for the security of the dogs, which were ideal prey for leopards at night.

In fact the Olduvai camp became a relative zoo in this period. Mary had developed her love of dogs – and particularly Dalmatians – as a child and was never without several of them throughout her adult life. But in 1963, she also came to adopt a pet monkey called Simon. Simon was fascinated by cosmetics and would raid the handbag of any female visitor to the camp, but he was also intrigued by men's moustaches and would leap onto their shoulders to play with and sniff any substantial facial hair.[62] There was also a tame wildebeest calf called Oliver that followed Mary everywhere, and that would wait outside the bathing tent each night until he could hear the water running, upon which he would charge in and disturb female bathers in particular.[63]

Mary and Louis were not the only ones excavating. Alongside them and their team of African excavators, their sons were now joining them in the search. And it was in November 1960 that their son Jonathan – surveying a different area from where Mary and Louis had found Dear Boy – came across the next great Olduvai Gorge fossilised bone find: Olduvai Hominid 7 (OH7), or as he was affectionally known, 'Jonny's child'. Once again both these names avoided the controversy of trying to place the find within the evolutionary map. And once again Louis sought to do just that, in 1964 naming this find a new species within the genus *Homo*: *Homo habilis* – 'Handy man'.

As might be expected, this identification met with a storm of criticism and fierce debate. But in fact Jonny's child/*Homo habilis* presented a bigger challenge to the world's scientific community than just the problem of naming it, because it had been found in a particular layer of Bed I at Olduvai Gorge, and thus – unquestionably thanks to Mary's exacting excavation standards and the new dating technologies of the day – hailed from a slightly earlier period of time than Dear Boy.[64] And while no one could quite agree on the correct evolutionary map name for the find, it was clear that this creature had more human features than Dear Boy had. This challenged one of the fundamental preconceptions of the scientific community of the day: that evolution happened in a linear format with one species giving way to the next (more complex) species. Jonny's child and Dear Boy from Olduvai Gorge suggested that two species of very early man – with different evolutionary abilities – had lived as potential contemporaries in the same area.[65]

Between 1960 and 1968, Mary and Louis (when he was not away on his frequent lecturing tours and starting off other research projects across Africa or as far away as California) oversaw further excavations and discoveries by the team at Olduvai Gorge that proved beyond doubt the overlap of different species of early man. Further remains of different specimens of *Australopithecus boisei* were found across Bed I *and* the whole of Bed II, showing that this particular species had lived in the area from roughly 1.9 to 1.1 million years ago. At the same time, multiple specimens of *Homo habilis* were found across Bed I and into the first layers of Bed II, showing that *Homo habilis* and *Australopithecus boisei* had lived as contemporaries in the area of the gorge.[66] Alongside these was a third species of early man, *Homo erectus,* the first example of which was discovered by Louis in 1960. But what became clear through the excavations of the 1960s was that *Homo erectus* specimens only occurred in the very latest levels of Bed II and into later Beds III, IV and V. As such, Mary and Louis's work in Olduvai Gorge demonstrated conclusively the overlap of multiple different evolutionary stages of early man. *Australopithecus boisei* had lived as a contemporary of both *Homo habilis* and *Homo erectus*. And yet it had also shown that on occasion overlaps did not occur. *Homo habilis* and *erectus* had not existed as contemporaries, with *habilis* disappearing in the early phases of Bed II and *erectus* only emerging in the last phases of Bed II, which equates to being separated by at least 100,000 years.[67] Mary and Louis had thus demonstrated that the development of early man was far more complex than one kind of early man simply evolving into, and giving way to, another.

Mary continued to work at Olduvai Gorge until 1974. By that stage the evidence she and her team had uncovered provided the most complete record in the world of early man and his tools.[68] She had kept her focus despite a mounting number of difficulties and other calls on her time. The camp at Olduvai was rebuilt again in 1968 and again in 1974. Partly this was to provide more resources, comfort and security for the excavation team, the last of which they hugely appreciated when, in 1973, a pride of eight starving lions entered the gorge over several nights, one of which leapt up and shattered the small glass window of Mary's metal caravan in an attempt to enter and eat one of her Dalmatian dogs. Despite her being very used to living in the wild, the lion's ravenous face at the window gave Mary nightmares for a long time afterwards.[69] But the other factor the camp now had to cater for was visitors. In 1963, 403 people visited the gorge. By 1972 the number was 23,000. A small museum was built there in 1971, and a permanent tourist infrastructure including guides was put in place.[70]

Mary also had to manage huge upheaval. As a result of both personal and professional conflict, by 1968 she and Louis were leading separate lives.[71] In 1972, Louis died of a heart attack in London and Mary – who much preferred working in Olduvai to being the public face of the excavation – now had to be public lecturer, fundraiser *and* excavator. But this did not stop her from following up on the possibility of yet more discovery.

Back in 1935, when she and Louis had first visited Olduvai Gorge together, a man, part Maasai, part Kikuyu, had arrived at their camp to tell them about another place he knew where there were 'bones like stone'. He returned later with some examples and Mary and Louis had gone to visit the site but had not found anything more interesting than what they were already finding at Olduvai. As a result, they put the site to the back of their minds.[72] They returned again briefly in 1959, but this time found no stone tools to interest them and again put the site out of mind. It was only in the years after 1969, when further visits confirmed that the site contained layers older than any at Olduvai, that Mary decided to finally turn her full attention to it. In July 1975, aged sixty-two, Mary brought her excavation team to Laetoli, where she would, over the next few years, confound the world once again with her latest breathtaking discovery: the footprints that proved early man had walked on two feet far earlier than anyone had ever imagined.

Mary herself was the epitome of someone who always walked with both feet firmly on the ground, even when the honorary degrees and awards poured in for her, especially in the aftermath of her Laetoli discoveries. She was the first woman to receive the Swedish Golden Linnaeus Medal in recognition of her contribution to biological sciences, alongside several honorary degrees including one from Oxford – the university which, when her mother had gone to ask if there was any chance for her to study there on their return to England after the death of her father, had said no. In 1981, Mary received her Oxford honorary doctorate, in which, during the Public Orator's speech about her achievements, she was described (in Latin of course) as 'working over the terrain like [the goddess] Diana the huntress with her Dalmatian hounds, searching for traces of early inhabitants'.[73] Mary was certainly a force as powerful as an ancient goddess: through sheer hard work and continued effort, she not only reshaped many of the working practices of archaeology and anthropology of the time but added substantially to our understanding of our early human story. She was also responsive to the changing global attitudes and practices relating to how, where and by whom the finds of a project should be maintained and displayed. She adapted to work within the emerging national legislative frameworks concerning excavation and the ownership of antiquities discovered; ensured that Olduvai itself could properly welcome the tourists who came there to see the site and its finds; and indeed at times provided crucial evidence to support the legal case for the return of previously exported pieces.[74] More impressively, she did all this as a woman within a still overwhelmingly man's world, taking inspiration from the few women who came before her to blaze a trail and ensure that many could and would follow. Nor was it only women she inspired and mentored; she also did much to include local African archaeologists in her team and to champion their voice within the international search for early man. And that is my favourite image of Mary: as someone who had little truck with rules and traditions. At the celebratory dinner in 1981 for her Oxford honorary doctorate, she was appalled when, unlike the men, the women were not offered an alcoholic after-dinner drink and cigar.[75] As befitting a Diana, she insisted on having both.

Terracotta Warriors

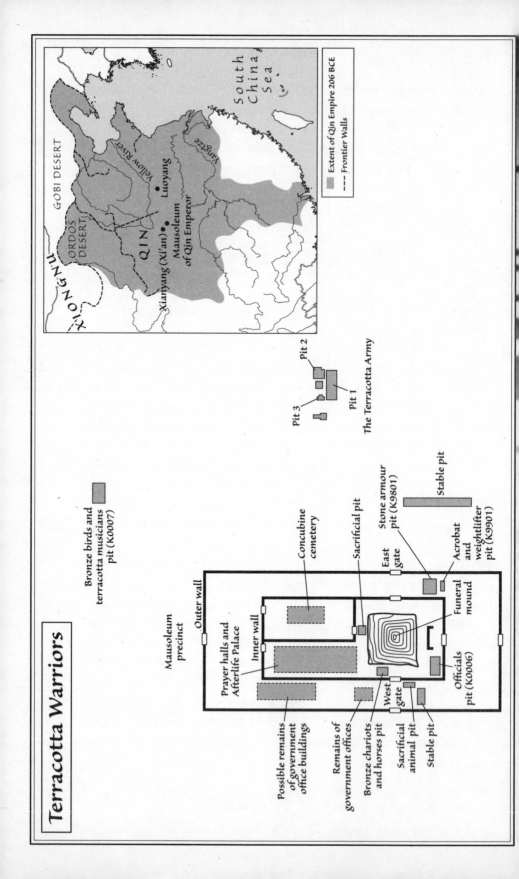

Map (top):

GOBI DESERT

XIONGNU

ORDOS DESERT

Yellow River

QIN

Xianyang (Xi'an) •
Mausoleum of Qin Emperor

• Luoyang

Yangtze

South China Sea

Extent of Qin Empire 206 BCE
--- Frontier Walls

The Terracotta Army:

Pit 2
Pit 3
Pit 1

The Terracotta Army

Mausoleum Precinct plan:

Bronze birds and terracotta musicians pit (K0007)

Mausoleum precinct

Outer wall

Prayer halls and Afterlife Palace

Inner wall

Possible remains of government office buildings

Remains of government offices

Bronze chariots and horses pit

Sacrificial animal pit

Stable pit

West gate

Officials pit (K0006)

Funeral mound

Acrobat and weightlifter pit (K9901)

Stable pit

Stone armour pit (K9801)

East gate

Sacrificial pit

Concubine cemetery

5

What You Find When Digging a Well[1]

The birth of the Qin dynasty in China was traumatic and violent. From 771 BCE (around the time the ancient Greeks in the Mediterranean began the Olympic games), through until 221 BCE – a period of 550 years – the inhabitants of a vast expanse of Asia (which we know today as modern-day China) were at war with one another.[2] At the start of this period there were 170 independent states fighting each other for survival. And by the end there would be just one: the state of Qin. Having gobbled up all its defeated opponents, the now-vast empire of Qin was ruled over by King Zheng, who declared himself Qin Shihuangdi: the First (Shi) Emperor (Huangdi) of Qin. In proclaiming himself Emperor, he began a new age in Chinese history: that of Imperial China.

It was a bloody conquest: estimates are that over a million men, not including Qin casualties, had died fighting in the final power struggle.[3] King Zheng had come to the throne as king of the state of Qin in 246 BCE, at the age of just thirteen.[4] He became the First Emperor of Qin in 221 BCE aged thirty-eight, but he would be dead just over a decade later. The entire Qin dynasty collapsed in 206 BCE, four years after Zheng's death, with the Han dynasty finally rising from the ashes of renewed rebellion and civil conflict in 202 BCE. The Han dynasty would last for over four hundred years, successfully governing over a once-more-united empire until 220 CE.

We are thus much more likely to be familiar with the Han dynasty – given its longevity – than with that of the Qin, which lasted for just fifteen years. And yet the impact of the Qin dynasty, and that of Qin Shihuangdi in particular, on the development and identity of China – in both ancient and modern times – has been no less important than that of the Han. In fact the Qin dynasty, and its ruler, set the tone against which everything and everyone measured themselves going forward.[5] In particular, as we shall see in this chapter, Qin Shihuangdi created one of the most well-known and evocative monuments in all of Chinese history. It is not without irony that King Zheng was named after the month in which he was born: the first month of the Chinese year – the start of everything.

*

Before King Zheng became the First Emperor of this huge, unified empire, his home state of Qin existed on the western edge of a group of warring states that fought for survival and supremacy in China.[6] This peripheral position may actually have been of great benefit to the Qin, allowing them to remain on the sidelines of the over-five-hundred-year raging civil war that consumed the more central states, waiting for their moment to weigh in.[7]

While others had to focus all their energies on fighting for survival, the Qin state was laying important groundwork for its later role as the ruling power. In the first half of the fourth century BCE, the then-Qin ruler, Duke Xiao (great-great-great-grandfather of King Zheng), engaged the services of a new strategic advisor called Lord Shang. Shang was an expert administrator of the law and had a very particular view of where the balance of power should lie in a state between its people and its rulers: 'if the people are stronger than the government, the state is weak; if the government is stronger than the people, the army is strong'.[8] Shang saw to it that the Qin adopted administrative and legal reforms that enabled the government not only to keep strict legal control, but also to develop a formidable centralised state power structure, which was in turn used to develop a powerful military.[9] Shang's approach would later became emblematic of the Chinese philosophical school of 'Legalism', one of the so-called '100 Schools of Thought' about how best to govern that were circulating at this time. As the warring states struggled for survival, each was attempting to discover the magic formula not just for success on the battlefield, but also for strong and stable governance of their territory.[10]

It was no accident, following the enormous leaps forward in centralised administration and military power that had occurred in the state of Qin, that the successor of Duke Xiao, Huiwen, ruling in the second half of the fourth century BCE, was the first Qin ruler to feel powerful enough to do away with the title of Duke and instead take the title of King.[11] Nor that one of his first acts was to condemn Lord Shang to death to ensure that no one advisor was more powerful than his king. Shang suffered one of the cruel punishments he had been in favour of: his limbs were tied to four chariots, which pulled away in different directions until his body was brutally torn apart – quite literally limb from limb.

King Huiwen then made use of his powerful military to begin the task of Qin expansion at the expense of its neighbouring states to the east. According to the famous ancient Chinese historian writing in the later Han period, Sima Qian, Huiwen captured dozens of cities and beheaded hundreds of thousands of defeated troops.[12] He was even said to have been offered a prophecy by his strategic counsellor: 'With Your Majesty's ability, the multitude of your offices and people, the readiness for use of your chariots and cavalry, and their instruction in military tactics, you may annex the feudal states, absorb all under Heaven, and rule with the title of Emperor.'[13] Despite significant expansion, Huiwen did not however quite succeed in conquering 'all under Heaven'. The next three generations of rulers – King Zheng's great-grandfather, grandfather and father – continued the assault successfully, enfolding further territories under Qin rule until, in 246 BCE, King Zheng came to the throne at the age of just thirteen years old.[14] And the youngster, despite the gains of his ancestors, still had a significant fight on his hands to incorporate 'all under Heaven' under Qin rule.

The Han historian, Sima Qian, painted a description of King Zheng in his first decade on the throne:

> The King of Qin, with his arched nose and long eyes, puffed-out chest like a hawk and the voice of a jackal, is a man of scant mercy who has the heart of a tiger or a wolf. When he is in difficulty he readily humbles himself before others, but when he has gotten his way, then he thinks nothing of eating others alive.[15]

Growing into adulthood as the king of a state fighting for supremacy in the end-game of over five hundred years of continuous war, Zheng needed every ounce of his tiger-like heart to sustain him. But he seems to have learnt his role well. From 230 to 221 BCE, King Zheng, in the words of Sima Qian, conquered his remaining enemies 'as a silkworm devours a mulberry leaf'.[16]

Now as Qin Shihuangdi, Zheng ruled over a population somewhere in the region of 30 million people. The title 'Huangdi', however, carries the connotation of more than just a mortal ruler. In particular, the 'di' part has a divine resonance. More than 1,000 years earlier, the inhabitants of what is now China had worshipped 'di' as their supreme god. Legendary sages and rulers during that thousand-year period had also been credited, posthumously, with the title of 'di' in recognition of their elevated divine status.[17] But here, for the first time, was a living ruler who claimed for himself a divine status, as the holder and executor of *tian ming*, the 'Mandate of Heaven', to 'stand in the centre of the kingdom, and tranquillize the people within the four seas'.[18] It was a claim that would be made by every Chinese ruler from 221 BCE all the way until 1911.

Though he had already achieved so much in establishing a unified empire, Zheng had the unenviable task of trying to rule a vast land composed of recently conquered enemies. He was guided, as his forebears had been, by the administrative approach of Lord Shang and Legalism: tough laws, centralised control and robust government leading to a strong military.[19] But the task awaiting him was on a scale no one had attempted before.

Zheng made some smart strategic moves: he divided his new realm into thirty-six new provinces, cutting across the previous state lines, and appointed for each province a governor, army commander and inspector who owed their advancement to their king.[20] He had in effect done away with the feudal system of state rulers and created instead a civil administration. Having eradicated the traditional power bases of his potential rivals, he then insisted that all the former ruling elite families move to the Qin capital at Xianyang (the modern-day city of Xi'an, nestled between mountain passes in Guanzhong province). Around 120,000 elite families were brought from all over the empire to Xianyang, where the city was transformed with the construction of hundreds of palaces to accommodate them, alongside a palace bigger and better than all the rest, which was fit for Qin Shihuangdi (known as Epang Palace).[21] At the same time as keeping his enemies close (and making them dependent on him), he also sought to remove any group's ability to fight back. He ordered that all weapons be brought to the capital, where they were melted down to make bronze bells and twelve bronze statues of giants, which were then placed in the palaces across the city.[22] Only the Emperor's army would henceforth have access to weaponry.

Alongside these moves to castrate any potential rivals and rebellion, Qin Shihuangdi also moved swiftly to create greater unity and communality within his empire, which had been at war with itself for over half a millennium. The Chinese writing script was standardised, as were all weights and measures. Even carriages had to be of the same gauge width.[23] Nor did his efforts to ensure uniformity stop there. The First Emperor was also interested in uniformity of thought. One of the by-products of the lengthy conflict had been the development of a plethora of philosophical schools of governance mentioned earlier, the '100 Schools of Thought', of which Qin's Legalism was one and Confucianism another. But such variety did not sit with the now dominant philosophy of Legalism (which in particular saw the ideas of Confucianism as antithetical to the military success of the state), nor with the First Emperor's desire for uniformity within his new empire. According to the Han historian Sima Qian, in 213 BCE one of the First Emperor's councillors suggested that:

> apart from those copies which the scholars of broad learn-ing are responsible for in their official capacity, anyone in all under Heaven who dares to possess and hide away the *Songs*, the *Documents*, and the sayings of the hundred schools, should hand them all over to a governor or commandant and they should be indiscriminately burnt. If there is anyone who dares to mention the *Songs* or *Documents* in private conversation, he should be executed. Those who, using the old, reject the new will be wiped out together with their clans.[24]

This has been seen as evidence of the First Emperor's decision 'to burn the books' and wipe out alternative thought and memory of the past, a policy pursued equally by the modern Chinese Communist Party under Chairman Mao in the 1950s during the 'Cultural Revolution'. However, this view overlooks the fact that, crucially, court scholars were allowed to keep studying all the material. The First Emperor was not attempting to delete knowl-edge and thought entirely, as Mao has been argued to have sought to do many centuries later, but rather to centralise control over it.[25]

With such a vast population, stretching across more than 2 million square kilometres, to control, the First Emperor then began a massive road-building programme, with approximately 6,700 kilometres of new roads radiating out from his capital across the empire, like spokes from the centre of a wheel. These roads made administration and control of provinces much easier for the centre. They were closely guarded and taxed: only those who had permission from the First Emperor were allowed to use them and move around the empire.[26] The most famous of them is known simply as 'Straight Road', and runs for over 1,000 kilometres from near Xianyang north towards Inner Mongolia. It was laid out in a straight line in 212 BCE, cutting through mountains and reaching across valleys thanks to a series of manmade embankments – a potent symbol of the First Emperor's power to remake the world.

At the same time as seeking to eradicate conflict within his new empire, the First Emperor also sought to minimalise conflict with the enemies outside his domain, particularly the nomadic tribes to the north. These tribes, renowned for their horsemanship, specialised in lightning raids into Qin territory to plunder what they wanted – normally smaller portable high-value items such as precious metals – disappearing again before the Qin forces could muster to defend against them. To deal with the problem of these frequent and disruptive attacks, the First Emperor turned to his trusted advisor, the general Ming Tian.[27] The idea to build a wall was born.

Individual states had in fact been building walls across their northern borders for several centuries, but now Ming Tian's job was to connect them up in one Great Wall that would defend the entire northern boundary of the new Qin Empire. He employed over 300,000 men, creating a defensive wall roughly 5,000 kilometres in length from Lintao (Gansu Province) in the west to Liaodong (Liaoning Province) in the east, utilising former walls built by individual states and natural barriers such as mountains, and linking them where necessary with walls composed of earth and rock, interspersed with ramparts, watchtowers and garrison stations.[28] This grand engineering project you may be surprised to hear is not the Great Wall of China we know today, which was actually constructed by the Ming dynasty during the fourteenth to seventeenth centuries CE (although the Ming wall follows the route in many places of the much earlier Qin wall).

As well as defending the newly formed Qin realm from attack, the wall had another goal: it gave the Qin Empire a defined border, strengthening further the notion of Qin identity. In the little over a decade that Zheng was the First Emperor of the Qin dynasty, he had thus not only established an unprecedented empire in China, but also sought to create a unified culture, writing system, school of thought and legal system, as well as connecting isolated provinces and defining the empire's physical borders.

However, the First Emperor's ambitions were not limited to the here and now. Inspired perhaps in part by the semi-divine status implicit in his Imperial title, he also invested a great deal of time and energy in searching for the key to immortality. He sent several expeditions to search for the fabled 'Islands of the Immortals', supposedly located in the Bohai Sea off the east coast of China, where it was thought the herbs and drugs conferring immortality could be found.[29] While waiting for these expeditions to return, he had experimented, at the suggestion of his court alchemists, with swallowing the traditional Chinese materials of immortality: jade and mercury.[30] In fact it is likely that it was mercury poisoning that killed him in 210 BCE.

Yet while the First Emperor did not succeed in living for ever, he certainly succeeded in ensuring he had a magnificent home to move to after his death. The moment he ascended the throne in 246 BCE as a thirteen-year-old boy, work had begun on his tomb. This was traditional practice, born out of the long-held concept that the deceased needed to be able to carry on in death as in life, and so needed a home and surroundings commensurate with those they had enjoyed in life. For a king, that meant a palace tomb. For the First Emperor of Qin, the first ruler of his kind, that meant a tomb unlike any other that had been created before:

a place from which he could continue to rule all under Heaven. Ancient sources tell us that work to build his tomb increased exponentially over the eleven years of his Imperial rule, with up to 700,000 convicts and forced labourers working simultaneously on both his new palace in Xianyang and the tomb (his homes in life and the afterlife).[31]

The tomb itself was built 35 kilometres outside of Xianyang, between the Wei River and a sacred mountain, Mount Li. This magnificent tomb is another example of how the First Emperor remade the world. A four-sided stepped pyramid that reached 120 metres high, it stood within a double-walled compound, with the outer wall running for a total of 6 kilometres.[32] It was nothing less than another palace, from which Zheng could rule for eternity in the afterlife.

Historians have long known about the First Emperor's tomb because the historian Sima Qian wrote about it, as well as about the funeral itself. It seems that on Zheng's death, the First Emperor's son declared that all his father's concubines who themselves had no sons should be buried with the First Emperor. Equally, it is recorded that in order for the workmen, who completed the tomb and oversaw the burial, to never be able to reveal its contents, they too were buried alive when the tomb was closed. Trees and bushes were then planted over the tomb so that it would blend into the landscape and appear like a natural hill. This obsession with ensuring the secrecy and undisturbed sanctity of the interior of the tomb, as well as its unbelievable grandeur, is captured in Sima Qian's description of what was inside the Emperor's tomb itself:

Craftsmen were ordered to make crossbows and arrows which would operate automatically, so that anyone who approached what had been excavated was immediately shot. Mercury was used to represent the various waterways . . . and the great sea . . . And above were ranged the heavenly constellations and below was the layout of the land. Candles were made of whale fat, for it was reckoned that it would be a long time before they were extinguished.[33]

After the First Emperor's death, his prime minister, Li Si, along-side another trusted official, Zhao Gao, conspired to fake a letter supposedly written by the First Emperor to his intended heir urging him to commit suicide. This would leave the First Emperor's younger and more impressionable son, whom Li Si and Zhao Gao hoped to lead by the nose, to become ruler. The plan was success-ful, and the younger more impressionable brother became the new Emperor, Qin Er Shi ('Qin Two Emperor'). He diverted extra resources to finishing his father's tomb and oversaw his burial there seven to eight months after his death. But soon afterwards, the new Emperor was murdered and his nephew, another impres-sionable young ruler, placed on the throne. He survived only forty-six days before the Qin Empire completely fell apart. While all court eyes had been focused on the internal machinations for the throne, rebellions had started outside of the capital without the watchful eye of Zheng to keep tight control over the empire. One major rebellion was led by a warrior called Xiang Yu, who eventually forced his way into the Qin capital, killing the last Qin Emperor and setting fire to the entire city.[34] The Qin dynasty was over just fifteen years after it had begun – a flash in the pan in the grand scheme of history, but burning with such a fierce flame that its impact would last much longer.

The First Emperor's tomb survived not only the civil war that engulfed the empire after his death, but also every era of Chinese history through to the present day. Ming dynasty writers (four-teenth to seventeenth century) visited the site, and photographs exist of the tomb from as early as the beginning of the twentieth century. In 1962, the tomb and its surrounding 6 kilometres of precinct walls were surveyed. Today the tomb stands as a not-quite-so-tall artificial hill (just 64 metres instead of the original 120 metres), and the precinct walls are likewise in a significantly more meagre state.[35]

An artist's impression of Napoleon coming face to face with ancient Egypt in Cairo.

The Rosetta Stone, with the ancient Greek text at the bottom, the 'cursive' / 'enchoric' / 'demotic' text in the middle and the hieroglyphic text at the top.

Portrait of Jean-François Champollion, who cracked the code of the Rosetta Stone in 1822.

Marc Aurel Stein with his dog Dash II/Dash the Great and the expedition team on his second expedition to the Taklamakan Desert.

Paul Pelliot, the French scholar, in the manuscripts cave at Mogao.

The monk Wang Yuanlu, photographed by Stein.

The soldier, Sergeant Carrasco, and local Quechua inhabitant, Pablito Richarte, at Machu Picchu, photographed by Hiram Bingham.

Hiram Bingham III in 1911.

Machu Picchu, following the clearing conducted by the Yale team during their second expedition in 1912.

The 3.5 million year old footprints left in the ash by a group walking on two legs (as well as by many other creatures) at Laetoli, Tanzania.

Mary Leaky excavating with her beloved dalmatians watching her.

A Terracotta Warrior
with colour restored.

Terracotta Army, view
of Pit 1, where 6000
warriors, spread across
11 'corridors', have been
found standing guard
and all facing East.

Clearing of sand from around the surviving
cargo of the Uluburun shipwreck,
45 metres underwater.

The 'On-Shore' camp and laboratory during
the ten-year excavation in Turkey.

The replica of the Uluburun ship, sunk in the Kaş underwater archaeological park.

The area of the kurgan that once covered the underground burial chamber of the Altai Princess on the Ukok Plateau.

Dr Natalia Polosmak inside the burial chamber of the Princess, surrounded by the original logs of the chamber's walls and floor.

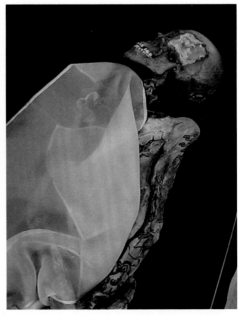

The preserved body of the Princess, with her vibrant tattoos still showing on the flesh of her arm.

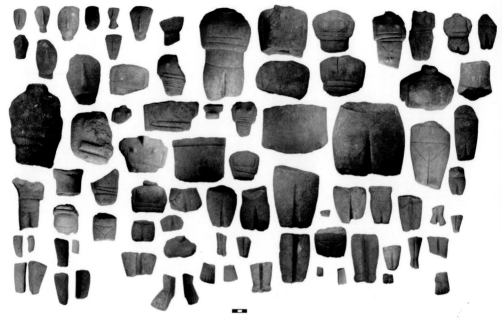

A collection of the many purposefully broken Cycladic
figurines found in excavations on Keros.

A photograph taken at Trench F on the islet of Dhaskalio, looking east towards
the excavation area of Kavos on the island of Keros.

But throughout the centuries up until the very recent past, no one had any clue that the hill and compound walls were only the tip of the iceberg of Qin Shihuangdi's underground realm.

*

On a crisp March day in 1974, a group of agricultural workers set out into the fields to start the important annual task of digging a new well to ensure they had enough water to nourish their crops through the coming spring and summer. Armed with the basic tools of their agricultural trade – hoes and shovels – the workers concentrated their search in fields in the shadows of Mount Li, an area sown with fragrant pomegranate and persimmon and known locally to be riddled with underground springs and watercourses. The group of workers comprised six brothers from the Yang family and a neighbouring friend, Wang Puzhi, who all knew the area well as they lived in a village nearby. The close-knit group chose a promising site just under 2 kilometres away from the artificial hill of Qin Shihuangdi's mausoleum (although it is unclear whether the group knew what the hill really was), and began to hack into the dry topsoil. By day two of digging, at about 2 metres down from ground level, the group hit a layer of unusual thick harder red soil. On day three, one of the brothers, Yang Zhifa, then forty-one years old, digging with the metal hoe that he used to tend crops, heard it hit something solid. What he uncovered surprised the entire group – it was a piece of terracotta in the shape of a human neck. No head or body was attached.[36]

The group decided to proceed carefully as this might be the site of an old kiln, and any terracotta jars they unearthed could be re-used in the village and on the local co-operative farm. But instead of jars, over the next two days they uncovered more terracotta body fragments, as well as a number of bronze objects including arrowheads.[37]

The finds soon drew a crowd. Perhaps this was some kind of ancient temple site, with statues of ancient gods? Worried that they might incur the ill will of the spirits, the locals urged the group to put the finds back in the ground. As Yang Zhifa later recalled, some villagers feared these statues of gods did not want to be disturbed, and that their removal would ruin the area's Feng Shui and bring trouble for the village. But the diggers thought there might be some reward for reporting these finds to the authorities – even if, as one joked, it was only extra tobacco for Yang Zhifa's beloved pipe.[38]

What happened next depends on who you believe. Yang Zhifa tells the story in a later interview of how his group prepared three two-wheeled carts, onto which they hauled their terracotta and bronze finds, and set off for the Lintong Cultural Centre (the local district museum) several kilometres away. Yang recalls being phlegmatic about the potential of their discoveries as the carts bounced across the rough field tracks and along the long roads to the museum. If the items did not turn out to be anything special, he thought, he would chuck them in the local river, go home, wash, and come back the next day to get on with the well.[39]

Other accounts differ. When the Yang brothers began digging their well, the sole curator of cultural relics and archaeology at the Lintong Cultural Centre was a certain Zhao Kangmin. Appointed in 1961, he was originally a farmer but had taught himself to read ancient Chinese scripts and then how to conduct archaeological investigations as part of his role at the museum. But he also knew only too well the precarious position of the past and of those who studied it within Communist China. He had experienced first-hand the Great Proletarian Cultural Revolution of 1966, during which Chairman Mao had encouraged his Red Guards to destroy the 'four olds' (old ideas, old culture, old customs and old habits of the exploiting classes): a Qin-era statue at the Lintong Cultural Centre had been destroyed by Mao's Red Guards, and Zhao Kangmin had been forced publicly to criticise himself for 'encouraging feudalism' because he had studied and cared for it.[40]

According to Kangmin, on 25 April 1974, about a month after the Yang brothers had first dug up the terracotta body parts, he received a call to inform him that the finds were still in the fields where the well had been dug. It was, according to Kangmin, he who put two and two together: that this field was just under 2 kilometres east of where the tomb of Qin Shihuangdi still stood in the landscape, and that, potentially, these finds could be related to the First Emperor. Kangmin rushed to the site. There, he collected as many terracotta pieces as he could find, retrieving some that were being played with as toys by village children, and took them to the Lintong Cultural Centre.[41]

Whatever the truth, Yang Zhifa and his team were compensated with thirty Chinese yuan – then the equivalent of three annual salaries for agricultural workers – which they paid over to their local production unit, as required by the Chinese Communist state at the time. In return, each man received points equivalent to half a day's pay, which they could use to buy food and other goods.[42]

Meanwhile, Zhao Kangmin started to put the body parts discovered by the farmers together in his workshop at the museum. There, before his disbelieving eyes, a fully life-sized human came to life. Kangmin managed to reconstruct the entire body of what he nicknamed a 'Terracotta Warrior', given that the terracotta figure was wearing armour. He was convinced that the figure was linked to the tomb of the First Emperor of Qin – despite the fact that not a single ancient source mentioned anything about a terracotta warrior being associated with the tomb. But Kangmin made no official report. Still shaken by his personal experience of the Cultural Revolution, and hearing stories of how the Red Guard had in 1969 ripped open the burial place of the sixteenth-century Ming Emperor Wangli – even dragging the skeletons of the Emperor and his wives out of their graves to publicly denounce and burn them – he wasn't prepared to risk a similar reaction. What if declaring the find led to the destruction of the figure, the potential desecration of the Qin Emperor's tomb, or even further public humiliation of himself?[43]

So the lone Terracotta Warrior stood silent in the Lintong Cultural Centre. There he might have remained, had not a journalist, Lin Anwen from the Xinhua News Agency, China's official state-run media outlet, come to see local relatives. Lin heard about Kangmin's treasures in the local museum and decided to visit. And although Kangmin implored him not to write about the warrior for fear of the Red Guard, Lin went ahead and published a thousand-word report in an official state journal in June 1974. But instead of a visit from the Red Guard, within days the report had been read by the Vice-Premier of the State Council and on 6 July, China's Director of Cultural Heritage flew to Xi'an to see the warrior for himself. By 15 July, an archaeological team from the Shaanxi Institute of Archaeology in Xi'an had been dispatched to investigate the field where the figure had been unearthed, and to work out just how large an archaeological site they were dealing with. They had expected to be there for a week or so. Instead, they were still there eight months later. Drilling borehole after borehole radiating outwards from the original well, they continued to find more and more of the same warrior figures, as well as original bronze swords and even a terracotta horse. In March 1975, a year after Yang Zhifa had stumbled on the first shards of terracotta, they finally reported back to their Institute and on upwards to the Department of Cultural Heritage that they thought there could be an entire underground chamber of warriors as big as 230 metres by 62 metres: an underground army.[44]

What the journalist Lin Anwen had realised, which Zhao Kangmin had not, was that the Communist Party's attitude to cultural heritage, and particularly to antiquities relating to the Qin Empire, had changed dramatically in just the few short years since Kangmin had himself felt the wrath of the Red Guards. The Han Empire, having taken power back in 202 BCE after the Qin leadership had disintegrated, had set itself up as the antithesis of the Qin, particularly in terms of its chosen philosophy of government (it followed Confucianism in place of Legalism). The subsequent Han Emperors had equally set themselves up as the opposite of the First Qin Emperor. The Han had thus ensured that the reputation of the Qin era that would go down in history was a unanimously negative one. As a result, for just over two millennia up until the final collapse of Imperial rule in the Chinese Revolution of 1911, the First Emperor of Qin had been considered the model of a bad ruler and Qin culture as the antithesis of civilised Chinese society.

The denigration of the Imperial past – not only of Qin but also of Han and indeed of every Imperial dynasty – of course became standard practice following the Revolution and intensified especially with the creation of the Communist People's Republic of China by Chairman Mao in 1949. And it got even worse when Mao launched the Great Proletarian Cultural Revolution in 1966, seeking to purge the Chinese Communist Party of corruption and encouraging the Red Guards to destroy the 'four olds'. But in reality the effects of the 1966 Revolution were devastating for China; it kicked off a bitter civil war across the country, which brought the national economy to its knees and promoted increased factional struggle at the heart of the Communist Party, particularly between Chairman Mao and the head of the People's Liberation Army, Lin Biao (effectively Mao's heir apparent). Having previously been Mao's right-hand man, Lin, together with his wife and son, died in a mysterious plane crash in 1971. Soon afterwards, rather conveniently, details of a plot to assassinate Chairman Mao, allegedly drawn up by Lin Biao's son, were released, which included several comparisons of Chairman Mao with the (supposed) worst of the Imperial rulers: the First Emperor of Qin.[45]

The response of Mao's supporters (and indeed the wider Communist Party machine), instead of simply denying these associations, was extraordinary: nothing less than a prompt and total rehabilitation of the First Emperor's historical reputation. In 1972, the President of the Chinese Academy of

Sciences, Guo Moruo, who had two decades earlier written articles about how awful the First Emperor of Qin was, now wrote a new article praising the First Emperor as a positive historical figure who had pushed history forwards by sweeping out the old to usher in the new (as Chairman Mao was now doing). This was accompanied in 1973 by the 'revelation' that Lin Biao had apparently been a closet follower of Confucius – not only something looked down on within Communist culture, but of course also deeply associated with the Han dynasty. A campaign followed that summer entitled 'Criticise Lin, Criticise Confucius', which argued that Lin had picked up all his faults from studying Confucius. Over the winter of 1973 and into 1974, this campaign was bolstered by further publications, which sought to simultaneously criticise Confucianism and Lin Biao, while also extolling the First Emperor of Qin and, as a result, Chairman Mao. By 1974, the campaign's title had morphed simply to 'Criticise Confucianism, Appraise Legalism', the guiding philosophy of the Qin Empire.

It is in many ways bizarre that the Chinese Communist Party, seeking to create a new society antithetical to that of the former Imperial order, and having recently encouraged the destruction of cultural heritage during the 1966 Revolution, should end up in the early 1970s framing the debate about the Communist future of China through the lens of two former Imperial dynasties and their guiding philosophies. Yet it also underlines just how deep an impact the Qin and Han empires had had on China that they ended up being the chosen reference points in this debate even centuries later.

The result of this complete 180-degree turn on the Qin era was nothing short of miraculous for the Terracotta Warriors. When Lin Anwen published his article about Zhao Kangmin's find in June 1974, not only was the ruling Communist Party over the worst of its excesses of cultural heritage destruction (and keen to develop new tourist revenue streams for its failing economy), but it was also in the grip of First Emperor mania following his

radical reappraisal and the simultaneous denigration of
Confucianism, associated with the Han Empire. In many ways,
though Yang Zhifa and his farmer friends who had dug the well,
as well as Zhao Kangmin who had pieced together the first
Terracotta Warrior, could not have known it, they had together
discovered the best-kept secret of the First Emperor of Qin at a
crucial moment. This was the only window in time over the previous more than two millennia when the public mood towards the
First Emperor was positive, glorifying even. If the discovery had
happened even just a few years earlier, it is entirely possible that
the first Terracotta Warrior would have been forgotten, or worse,
destroyed. As it was, every resource was now made available to
uncover what would soon be called the Eighth Wonder of the
World.[46]

Since the first fragments were found in the soil by the well
diggers in 1974, work has not stopped on uncovering even more
astounding secrets of the tomb of the First Emperor of Qin.
Following the discovery of what is now called 'Pit 1' in 1974–5,
the decision was made to build a new museum at the site. Even as
they broke ground for the museum, the Shaanxi Institute of
Archaeology team discovered two further pits of buried warriors
– now called Pit 2 and Pit 3 – alongside another pit (Pit 4) that it
appeared had been excavated in antiquity but then seemingly
backfilled without any objects being placed in it. In roughly twelve
years, the vast scale of the First Emperor's underground army
came to light. In Pit 1 (its final extent measuring 362m by 62m),
spread across eleven underground corridors, they found 6,000
terracotta warriors standing guard, all facing east, (with nearly
2,000 warriors still to be properly excavated today). In Pit 2 (measuring 124m by 98m) they found 89 horse-drawn chariots standing
ready alongside over a hundred cavalry riders, as well as numerous standing and kneeling archers (with perhaps as many as 1,400
warriors still to be excavated). In Pit 3 (a smaller chamber, measuring almost 29m by 25m) a single chariot was found pulled by
four horses, alongside 68 warriors and a larger number of senior

officer figures, leading to its identification as the army's 'command centre'. In total, experts now estimate that the First Emperor's Terracotta Army numbered more than 8,000 warriors, with 140 battle chariots and 520 horses.[47]

These warriors have captivated every audience that has laid eyes on them ever since. For those lucky enough to see them *in situ*, it is the sheer number of them that dazzles – enough to fill roughly half of the entire seating at the O2 Arena of the Millennium Dome – as they stand there on eternal silent guard. But they equally dazzle when you get up close. The first thing you notice is their height: at an average of around 1.8 metres, they tower over many today, as they probably did when first constructed. They ooze confidence, not just thanks to their athletic build and armoured costumes, but also through the calm straight stare of their eyes. They are on the one hand perfectly balanced and still in their stances, yet, on the other, somehow full of potent energy: poised for action. That sense of them coming alive at any moment is enhanced by the lifelike details of their dress, hair and facial features. The closer you are drawn in, the more of those details you notice: on one kneeling archer in Pit 2, even the tread pattern on the sole of his rear shoe has been rendered visible.[48] The overall impression when faced with these warriors is thus, I think, deliberately unnerving: made of terracotta and yet so real; immobile and yet so full of life.

Over the course of further multiple excavations in the past thirty years, we have also now realised that the warriors, horses and chariots are by no means the only secret underground elements of the First Emperor's gigantic sprawling funerary complex. The warriors stand just under 2 kilometres to the east of the First Emperor's tomb. In between the warriors and the Emperor's tomb, archaeologists found 101 underground stable pits complete with both terracotta horses and the remains of real horses that had been chained up and buried alive at the time of the Emperor's burial over 2,200 years ago. Bowls of water, grain and straw had been provided for both the real and terracotta horses, which were buried alongside terracotta figures of grooms, court officials and stable workers. It is estimated that perhaps another three to four hundred real horses still remain to be excavated. And it seems it wasn't just real-life *animals* that were buried – just over a kilometre to the west of the tomb precinct archaeologists discovered tombs full of real bodies: most likely craftsmen and convict-workers who had died during the construction process (rather than those craftsmen who were buried alive at the time of the Emperor's funeral, as recorded by the historian Sima Qian).[49]

Even more extraordinarily, about a kilometre to the northeast of the Emperor's tomb and its walled precinct, excavation work in 2001–2003 uncovered what is known as Pit K0007. At over 900 square metres, this pit contains an underground artificial lake and manmade tributary streams. Along a 60-metre stretch of riverbank were forty-six life-size bronze swans, cranes and geese, each engaged in a different activity, exquisitely cast and detailed (even down to the worm in one crane's beak).[50] Opposite them, on the other side of the riverbank, were fifteen terracotta figures, who could represent musicians, engaged in a variety of poses.

More spectacular secret underground finds have come to light within the 6-kilometre-long outer walls of the Emperor's tomb precinct. Excavations between 1998 and 2003 revealed Pit K9801, situated between the inner and outer walls of the tomb precinct, which was filled with eighty-seven complete suits of armour and forty-three helmets – all made of stone – alongside a complete suit of stone horse armour. Much of this pit is still to be excavated, and it's thought there may be a further 6,000 suits of stone armour inside it. Just to the south of the armour store, eleven more terracotta figures were found in Pit K9901. Though nowhere near as numerous as the thousands of warriors, these figures portray intricate characters dressed in short, toga-like garments over bare legs and torsos – they have been labelled 'acrobats' and 'entertainers' – as well as a number of huge muscular figures with big bellies who seem to be practising weightlifting.

Nor have finds within the inner tomb precinct wall been any less intriguing. In 1980 a small pit was discovered just 20 metres west of the Emperor's tomb containing two painted bronze chariots each drawn by four horses, thought to have been for the use of the Emperor in the afterlife. The detail of the chariots is staggering – they are made up of over 3,000 individual bronze parts and the terracotta horses had been provided with large quantities of real hay. To the north of the Emperor's tomb mound, a vast array of prayer halls was discovered in 2012, and in 2013, just next door, a cemetery area filled with 105 tombs was revealed, all with female corpses buried in them – thought potentially to be the burial place of the Emperor's concubines.[51]

The tomb complex of the First Emperor of Qin is now thought to cover something like 50 square kilometres stretching out on all sides from the Emperor's tomb itself at the centre.[52] The sheer extent of the tomb complex – the vision required to imagine it, let alone the manpower to construct it – reveals to us the true power, might and magnificence of the First Emperor of Qin. We can now start to bear witness for ourselves to what the 700,000-strong workforce, as mentioned by Sima Qian, achieved in the little over a decade that Zheng was the First Emperor of Qin (building on the two decades of work on his original tomb, which was begun when Zheng came to the Qin throne at the age of thirteen back in 246 BCE). While the First Emperor was busy undercutting old territorial allegiances, unifying his empire's language and systems, and knitting it together with new roads and border walls, those workers were struggling feverishly to construct an entire world for their Emperor in his afterlife – a tomb on a scale and complexity previously unimagined (while simultaneously of course building the First Emperor a new palace in his capital unlike any seen before). All for a man who hoped he might never need it as he sought the keys to immortality, but who was clearly planning to be well prepared if only his spirit could live on.

*

What I find most extraordinary about the discovery of the Terracotta Warriors and all the accompanying treasures is the fact that we had no clue about any of it until Yang Zhifa went looking for a well in that dry spring of 1974. While the ancient sources talk in detail about all the different unifying and building activities the First Emperor undertook, as well as the huge effort put into building the First Emperor's tomb – and even about the internal decoration and protection mechanisms of the tomb of the Emperor himself – there is not a single mention of the thousands of figures who were buried around him. This must be a candidate for one of human history's best-kept secrets.

Why, though, did the First Emperor feel the need to go to such lengths to preserve the secrecy of his tomb? To understand this deep mystery, we need to reflect once again on the newness of the Qin Empire. The preceding five hundred years of conflict and destruction would not have been easily forgotten in the short few years that the Qin Empire blazed in triumph. As Lü Buwei, an advisor in the early days of King Zheng's rule (before he became First Emperor), put it: 'From antiquity until now there has never been an imperishable state. Since there are no imperishable states, there are no unrobbable tombs.'[53] The First Emperor was caught between wanting to create something larger, grander and more noticeable than had ever been envisioned before and wanting to ensure its survival for eternity. He did that in part by booby-trapping his tomb, and in part by keeping its full extent and extraordinary nature a secret from everyone (reportedly by burying alive those workmen who sealed up the tomb to make sure they would not tell anyone either).[54]

Archaeological investigation of the different pits shows us that Zheng only in part got his wish. To construct the space for the underground army, corridors within each of the Terracotta

155

Warrior pits were first dug, then a wooden roofing system was constructed over them. Earth was then piled on top of the roof, raising it back to ground level, leaving just an entrance ramp down into the vast corridored chamber created below the ground. The warriors, horses and other figures were then brought in and positioned underground before the ramp itself was sealed. But it is clear from the archaeology that these pits – and the warriors – have suffered badly since they were set up and sealed underground, and not due simply to the ravages of time. Burnt red earth, and the charcoaled remains of wooden ceiling beams, have been found in the pits – it seems sections of the underground pits were set on fire.[55] Around the tomb of the Emperor himself excavators have found scattered ashes, fired earth, broken bricks and tile fragments, indicating that anything visible above the ground was smashed and burnt.[56] It seems likely that this destruction occurred soon after the tomb was sealed, when the Qin Empire disintegrated and the rebel Xiang Yu laid waste to the Qin capital. Following this early damage and the weakening of the underground supporting structures, millennia of rain, snow, mud and other natural onslaughts caused the ceilings to collapse and crush the many wonderful figures and objects buried inside. Not a single warrior or terracotta horse was found intact during the twentieth-century excavations of Pits 1 and 2: they all had to be painstakingly pieced back together.

The teams in charge of this huge puzzle have had to develop a whole series of new techniques for carefully excavating, fitting back together, and studying the broken elements of the First Emperor's tomb complex. But the upshot of this hard work is that, in the process, we have discovered to an even greater extent how extraordinary a display it is.

One of the things that people often comment on in relation to the Terracotta Warriors is their individuality. Every warrior of the 8,000 or so made is different – almost as if they were supposed to resemble individual people. Yet studies of the figures have now unlocked the mass-production processes by which such individuality could be achieved on such a monumental scale.[57] Using local clay, the central torsos were built up in sections before other components – the arms, hands, heads, legs – were added (all of which were made using wooden moulds). These standardised figures were then subjected to specific kinds of individualisation. There are in fact only eight face shapes among the thousands of warriors, but they have been adapted into thousands by the addition of particular hairstyles and the varied incising and adding of other facial features like ears, eyes, eyebrows and facial hair.[58] The 16,000 surviving hands, too, were all formed in just two standard moulds, but were attached to the figures at different angles and then the fingers were bent into different positions before the figure as a whole was fired to enhance the sense of individuality.[59] Yet where exactly (and how) such a large number of life-size figures were fired in kilns big enough to handle them remains a mystery.

Every Terracotta Warrior, post firing, was originally covered in lacquer and then painted. While the colours remained safe hidden underground, in the modern arid Xi'an air, the ancient lacquer on a statue curls in under fifteen seconds after exposure to the outside world, destroying the paint in the process. But now a multi-step process (using both complex science and low-tech solutions such as cling film) has been evolved that can protect each figure from the moment of discovery through to conservation and display, so we can today admire recently excavated figures in their original bright polychromy. As a result, we have come to realise both how expertly the figures were painted and how the colour choices intensified still further the experience of looking at a forest of individuals. Previously unexcavated parts of Pit 1 were tackled in a fresh campaign in 2009–11 using these new colour-preservation techniques. One warrior's face was decorated with black eyelashes only 0.02 centimetres wide (applied probably with a single brush hair).[60] More widely, the study of the paint has revealed that the warriors – while in standardised armour – were painted to be shown each wearing different-coloured clothes beneath their armour.

A slightly different kind of mass-production process seems to have been used for the bronze weapons (swords, lances and arrows) with which the Terracotta Warriors were armed. On the one hand, weaponry was produced solely for the purpose of arming the Terracotta Army. Scholars now think that a vast assembly-line process was set up, with multiple teams working in parallel to produce the weapons. But what astounded those examining the materials employed in the weaponry was two things. First, that despite multiple teams working in parallel, the metallic consistency of all the arrows was near identical. This could only have been achieved through the multiple teams working under a strict centralised command alongside an even stricter quality-control process – unlike anything seen before. The second was that the weapons – made to be placed in the tomb – were also created to be especially deadly and long-lasting. The arrows were found to contain a high percentage of tin, making the bronze harder (and thus the arrow more devastating). The swords were coated in chromium salt oxide, which had ensured they had not rusted and were still gleaming when discovered.[61]

Yet in among the weaponry produced especially for the tomb, archaeologists also found weapons – particularly the heavy duty items like lances and axes – that had been created much earlier. Analysis of makers' marks on the weaponry showed that some groups of weapons were made in the period 244–237 BCE (particularly the dagger-axes) while another (the lances) was produced in the period 232–228 BCE.[62] Scholars now think that the unexpected early death of the First Emperor – and the rush to finish his tomb – led the organisers to raid the real-life palace armouries of the Emperor for weaponry (made during different periods of his reign) to supply to the Terracotta Warriors alongside the weapons that had so far been created especially for the tomb.[63]

This extraordinary underground population of the First Emperor's tomb complex, with lifelike individualisation of the figures, has no precedent in Chinese history and had never been seen before on such a scale in Chinese art and statuary. Many scholars have tried to explain the sudden innovation in style by pointing to the arrival of new knowledge (and perhaps even new groups of craftsmen) into the Qin Empire from the West. In particular, scholars have sought to make the case for a link with the lifelike styles of painting and statuary that existed in the expanded Hellenistic world of the Eastern Mediterranean and Central Asia. In this period – the third century BCE – the realms of Greece and Persia had been united by the conquest of Alexander the Great almost a century before and vast imperial Hellenistic monarchies now governed from Greece to Afghanistan. Less than a century after the creation of the Terracotta Warriors – by the 140s BCE – we have direct literary evidence from the ancient Chinese historian Sima Qian of a Han Chinese ambassador, Zhang Qian, making his way to the trading emporiums of ancient Afghanistan and seeing with his own eyes Chinese goods for sale.[64] It is thus very possible that at the time the Terracotta Warriors were being created, there was at the very least some awareness of cultural and artistic styles between China and Central Asia.

Scholars have pointed in particular to possible links between the art of the Hellenistic world and the twelve giant bronze statues the First Emperor of Qin had sculptured from the molten weapons of his defeated enemies in his capital, as well as with his Terracotta Warriors, and in particular the heavily individualised and lifelike bronze sculptures that were found in Pit K9901 (the 'acrobat' and 'weightlifter' figures).[65] The evidence is currently inconclusive for a direct link between these particular sculptures and those of Hellenistic Asia. It is clear, however, that whether we ascribe the strides forward in individualisation and lifelike sculpture represented by the Qin creations to outside influence or internal artistic development, they represent the very pinnacle of artistic creation in China at the time. Nothing but the best for the First Emperor of China.

Thanks to Yang Zhifa and his team and their well digging, and the thousands of excavators, scholars, conservators and other specialists who have worked on the tomb complex since 1974, we now have a permanent new picture of the First Emperor of Qin. Beginning with the Chinese Communist Party's rebranding of the First Emperor as a role model after 1971, the wonder of the Terracotta Warriors revealed to us over the last five decades has ensured that the First Emperor has enshrined his place as a new favourite of – indeed, perhaps the most well-known figure in – Chinese history. His tomb complex was supposed to stand as a mirror image of his living world in the afterlife. His armies stood guard, facing east towards the barbarians on the borders of his realm. His chariots stood ready to take him wherever he needed to be. His armouries were full of beautifully made stone armour, specially made to fend off evil spirits.[66] His stables were full of horses ready to pull his chariots and carry his cavalry. His civil servants and officials were awaiting his commands, as were his concubines. He had diverting meadows full of animals, musicians and acrobats to entertain him. He had recreated the rivers of the world flowing around his eternal tomb home and etched the stars into his own Underworld sky. Though his empire fell in real life, in many ways he has succeeded in achieving immortality: not least as we – over two millennia later – continue to gasp in admiration at the extraordinary wonder of his eternal resting place.

Ironically enough – given that Zheng ruled as Emperor for such a short time over a dynasty that collapsed just fifteen years after its creation, and that spent the best part of the next two millennia being held up as the antithesis of respectable Chinese culture – the Terracotta Warriors and the man for whom they were created are now arguably China's globally best-known piece of (at least ancient) history. The first overseas exhibition of the Terracotta Warriors was staged less than a decade after their initial discovery: in 1983 in Sydney, Australia. Since then, multiple exhibitions around the world dedicated to the Terracotta Warriors have been packed out.[67] Journalists now refer to China's 'terracotta diplomacy' alongside their 'panda diplomacy': Terracotta Warriors are sent out around the world for exhibition, just like pandas are leased to zoos, as part of China's global networking.[68] The site of the mausoleum was made a UNESCO World Heritage Site back in 1987, and continues to be a massive draw for high-profile visitors to China as well as foreign tourists and the Chinese. Over just the three-day holiday period for Chinese New Year in 2021, despite Covid restrictions hampering travel and permitted visitor numbers, 35,000 people came to see the site.[69]

The same success and fame cannot be said to have befallen the tomb's discoverers. The village of the well digger – Yang Zhifa – was uprooted and forcibly moved thanks to the authorities' decision to build a museum at the site. Yang Zhifa himself, like his fellow villagers, is said to have received 5,000 yuan compensation for his 167-metre plot of land and was moved to a new village, 'the Qin warrior village', where he was given a three-bedroom flat. But many villagers resented the forced upheaval and blamed Yang Zhifa as the root cause of so much unwelcome change. In the end, the criticisms from his community got so bad that Yang Zhifa had to move further away to escape their rain of insults.[70]

Likewise, Zhao Kangmin, head of the Lintong Cultural Centre, who was the first to put a Terracotta Warrior together, did not directly benefit from his work, at least publicly. He was not posted to the new museum but spent the rest of his career at the Lintong Cultural Centre, which, despite his efforts, did not attract the flood of tourists who came to see the warriors down the road. Although he continued to excavate across China and to publish, he remained a quiet and reserved man up to his death in 2018.

Between Zhao Kangmin and Yang Zhifa and the rest of his well-digging party, there was also a good deal of rivalry over who really deserved the title of discoverer of the Terracotta Warriors. Zhao Kangmin liked to sign his title as 'The very first man who discovered, determined, restored and unearthed the world-famous Terracotta Warriors and horses'. In 2003, a group of the well diggers officially asked the museum authorities for a certificate that would declare them as the discoverers of the Terracotta Army. This was finally refused in 2009, on the basis that while the well diggers had been the first to find the pieces, it was Zhao Kangmin who realised their significance.[71] Today, on many Chinese websites, that distinction is maintained: between the well diggers who 'found' the statues and Zhao Kangmin who 'discovered' them (together with the wider archaeological team who then – over decades – both uncovered them and made the discoveries of all the further incredible figures in the different pits across the tomb complex).[72]

Yang Zhifa, and a number of the well-digging party, did, however, get a job at the Terracotta Warrior site – signing autographs for tourists. He even famously signed his autograph for Bill Clinton when he visited in 1998.[73] Some of his neighbours, too, managed to change with the times and benefit from the world-celebrity status of the warriors: early labourers on the main excavation later built kilns to create replicas of the warriors to sell across the world at handsome prices, while others sold handmade Chinese cultural items to the tourists.[74] But not all adapted. Yang Zhifa's neighbour and joint well digger, Wang Puzhi, was driven by poverty and illness to suicide in 1997. Two of Yang Zhifa's brothers, also there on those fateful days in 1974, have died early after being unable to fund the medical care they needed.[75]

Now himself retired and without income, Yang Zhifa is diplomatic about the ways in which the warriors changed his community's way of life: 'That's life', he says.[76] But one of Yang Zhifa's sisters-in-law is quoted, back in 2007, as wondering whether it would have been better for Yang Zhifa and his colleagues to have left the fragments they found that day buried in the ground.[77] The gift of immortality for the First Emperor of Qin, which Yang Zhifa and his well-digging colleagues gave through their discovery and the subsequent uncovering of the Emperor's extraordinary preparations for the afterlife, has come at a cost, in many ways highest for those closest to the discovery.

The tomb of the Emperor himself still remains to be excavated. In part it has been left undisturbed out of respect for the final resting place of such a (now) hero of Chinese history. In part, it is out of need for the scientific techniques of excavation to advance still further to ensure we are properly prepared and will not squander this once-in-eternity excavation opportunity. But it is also in part out of fear of the booby traps, which Sima Qian told us await those who enter the tomb, and of the potentially lethal presence of mercury from those underground rivers the First Emperor had created. Initial tests show high levels of mercury in the tomb itself. Perhaps the First Emperor – in his quest for immortality – has not yet claimed his last victim.

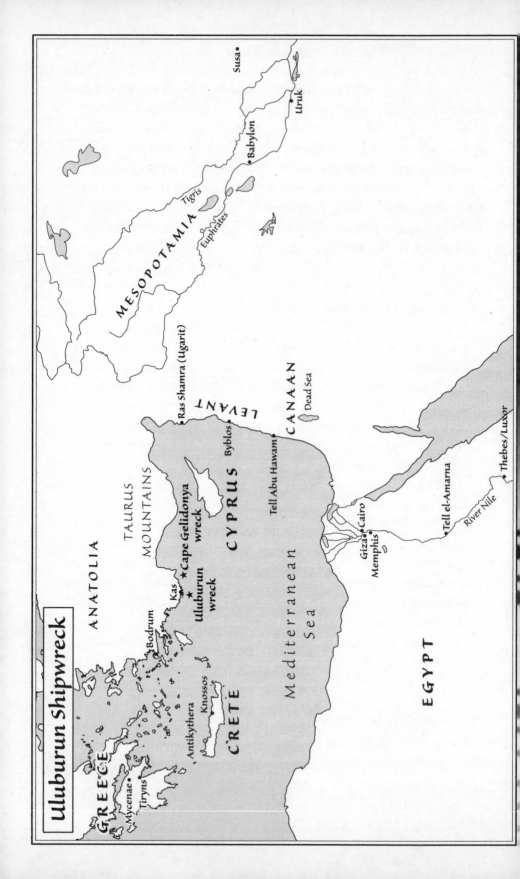

6

Metal Biscuits With Ears[1]

'A metal biscuit with ears.' That is how Mehmed Çakir described what he had seen to his captain in 1982. Little did he know then that what he had found would lead to the recovery of what was at the time the oldest seagoing vessel ever found. In so doing, the archaeologists leading the investigation would be pushed to the very limits of human endurance. But their efforts would not only change for ever our understanding of the Mediterranean world at the time King Tutankhamun was ruling in Egypt but would also confirm the creation – and potential – of a whole new field of archaeological investigation: underwater.

Mehmed was a young barrel-chested sponge diver from a town called Yaliçiftlik. Yaliçiftlik lies on Turkey's Aegean-facing western coast, not far from Bodrum, and is famed still today as a starting point for luxury '*gulet*' Turkish sailboat cruises. Mehmed told me that, growing up, he had always felt related to the sea. By the time he was eighteen, he was free-diving to depths of between 6 and 15 metres, searching for sponges on the sea floor. Since ancient times people have sought out natural sea sponges for their subtle mix of softness and abrasiveness, and their extraordinary longevity, as the ultimate body-cleaning tool. Demand for sea sponges exploded in the early twentieth century as a must-have product of the burgeoning middle classes, leading to massive over-harvesting, and in the aftermath of the Second World War the remnants of the Turkish sponge-diving fleet, based out of ports around

Bodrum, were forced to sail ever further afield to secure their goods. In the summer of 1982, Mehmed's captain had therefore taken his crew to the shores of Turkey's southern coast, facing towards Cyprus, in the hope of a good haul.

Mehmed, then in his twenties, told me that he had only been hired as a professional sponge diver the year before, having impressed a local sponge-boat captain with his diving ability. At that time, there were different ways in which the sponge-fishing fleet collected sponges. The first method was known simply as 'dragging', meaning the ship had a net with a metal chain attached along its lower edge in order to scoop up sponges nestled on the muddy sea floor. It was common for these draggers to net ancient amphoras (ceramic jugs) and, more rarely, statues. In 1953 a bronze statue of the Greek goddess Demeter had been pulled from the seabed by one of these draggers off the coast of Bodrum, where it was subsequently dumped on the beach by the ship's captain. Fortunately it was eventually taken to the Izmir Archaeological Museum where it can be seen today, but this statue was lucky.[2] Most dragging captains saw no value in these ancient objects. In fact they were seen as a hazard, potentially causing damage to the dragging nets. The crews were often instructed to break up the ancient amphoras before throwing them overboard so that they would not get caught in the nets again in the future.

Dragging for sponges is done in waters that are too deep for diving. But on shallower seabeds (and the rockier and more uneven seabeds where nets would be useless), divers are the only ones who can successfully collect the sponges. There were three forms of sponge diving in operation by the time Mehmet was learning his trade. The most ancient was that of the 'naked' sponge diver. Using a rudimentary kind of telescope to examine the sea floor from the boat, the sponge diver's job, once a sponge had been located, was to dive without any form of underwater breathing apparatus (this is the 'naked' part) to the bottom, cut the sponge loose, bag it, and ascend again. A barbed weight was first sent down attached to a rope to mark the spot where the sponge had been seen. The diver, holding a heavy stone to speed up his descent, then dived down – normally without even wearing a mask – using the rope as a guide.[3] Arriving quickly at the sea floor, the diver worked on the sponge until he could feel the precious oxygen in his lungs beginning to run out. The most dangerous part of the job was the ascent. Ascending too quickly risked 'the bends' – the build-up of gas bubbles in the blood – causing strokes, paralysis and death. But ascending too slowly meant being starved of oxygen, leading to brain damage – and again death.

Alternatively, there was the helmet diving method. The helmet diving suit, originally invented back in 1837, was a rubberised canvas suit topped by a large metal helmet and breastplate. The helmet was connected via a long hose to the boat on the surface, where a machine delivered compressed air down to the diver, filling his helmet and the suit down to his waistline. This was crucial because it meant the diver's lungs were filled by air at the same pressure as that in the environment immediately surrounding them (the air around his upper body inside the suit). Without that equality of pressure inside and outside the area of the lungs, a diver's lungs, throat and nasal cavities would be crushed by the pressure differential.

The great advantage of this system of course was that the diver could spend much longer on the sea floor working on the sponges, as he had a ready supply of oxygen delivered to him via the hose. The disadvantages, however, were multiple. The helmet diving suit meant that the diver was at risk of floating to the surface, in part thanks to the fact that his upper body was being inflated. To counter this the diver wore heavy lead shoes, along with weights strapped around his waist and his lower back to weigh him down. But he also had to keep his upper body upright at all times, otherwise air would rush from around his upper body to his feet and he would be swung upside down. Maintaining this delicate balance was almost impossible if there was a strong current, as the danger of being pushed forward (and thus flipped upside down by the air imbalance) was too great. And the suit had yet another unfortunate side effect – thanks to those heavy lead shoes, the diver destroyed almost anything he stepped on.

In 1943 a gamechanger arrived on the scene: the aqualung was invented by the explorer and filmmaker Jacques-Yves Cousteau and engineer Emille Gagnan. Carried on the diver's back, the aqualung delivered compressed air to the diver, meaning they were free of a hose tethering them to the surface. But the really key invention was not the aqualung itself, but the regulator, which sat between the aqualung and the mouthpiece in the diver's mouth. The regulator was able to alter the pressure of the air being delivered to the diver's lungs to ensure it equalled at all times the pressure of the water around them. This meant the diver had much greater mobility, and, without weighted shoes, did not crush everything under his feet. The downside was that the aqualung could only carry so much compressed air. To get around this time limit, sponge-diving fleets increasingly connected the regulator directly to a hose leading back to the boat on the surface, rather than rely only on the aqualung container. The sponge diver could therefore move around easily and delicately, while still remaining under water for extended periods of time.

Mehmed worked with the last of these systems: diving with a regulator connected via a hose back to his ship. He took to sponge diving like a duck to water. Being on the sea floor was, he described to me, like being in a cheerful, coloured aquarium – more impressive and wonderful than any landscape above the waves.

Sponge divers, much like the captains of sponge-net dragging ships, had traditionally seen little value in any ancient artefacts they came across on their journeys into the ocean deep. Sponges were much more valuable than any ancient object they could retrieve (and hope to sell), so while they did not deliberately break up the ancient artefacts they found, they did not normally investigate or attempt to excavate them either. That did not mean, however, that they never reported back their findings. In 1900, a sponge-diving team reported a 'heap of statues in the sea' off the coast of Antikythera, a tiny Greek island between Crete and the Peloponnese. At the time there were no amateur or professional diving clubs – and certainly no diving archaeologists – available to investigate further (the aqualung would not be invented for another forty-three years) and so the Ministry of Education in Athens hired the sponge divers themselves to salvage the statues. This is how the very first underwater 'dig' took place. The sponge divers must have had tremendous courage – they were working in depths of up to 180 feet (over 50 metres) using the techniques of helmet diving and naked diving – but there were terrible consequences. One man died of the bends and two others were paralysed from the waist down in the pursuit of the ancient relics.[4]

Between 1901 and 1959, inspired by the advances in diving technology during this period and by the realisation, following the successful recovery of the Antikythera statues, of how much could still survive from antiquity on the sea floor, there was increasing global interest in what could be learnt about the ancient world from its remnants hitherto thought unrecoverable beneath the waves. This academic interest in turn led to calls for the development of safer techniques not just for salvaging ancient artefacts from the sea floor, but for conducting proper excavations under water. In 1959, a young American archaeology student called George Bass was asked by his supervisor to learn to scuba-dive – the aim was to assist photojournalist Peter Throckmorton in investigating the remains of a shipwreck that had been found by sponge divers at Cape Gelidonya off the southern Turkish coast. With just six weeks of scuba training under his belt, George led the first ever complete excavation of an ancient shipwreck on the seabed. It was also the first time that a trained archaeologist (even though he was still a PhD student) had actually worked on ancient finds *in situ* under the water.

Flushed with this success, in the early 1970s Dr George Bass left his (by now) tenured position at Penn University and sold everything he owned in order to found the American Institute of Nautical Archaeology, based in Cyprus. The goal of the Institute was to locate ancient shipwrecks, and then conduct full excavations, as they had done at Cape Gelidonya. However, the Institute and its staff were evicted from Cyprus following the outbreak of war there in 1974 and instead established a new home back in the US at A&M University in Texas, where it was renamed simply the Institute of Nautical Archaeology (INA).[5] What the INA realised was the huge potential of sponge divers to help archaeologists identify ancient wrecks. They calculated that if they spoke to the crew of twenty sponge-diving boats in any single year, they were gaining access to 10,000 hours of time spent under water, and all the knowledge that came with it. What they needed to do then was ensure that the sponge divers could recognise all the telltale signs of an ancient wreck and its cargo, and that they knew where to report what they had seen. Throughout the 1970s, the INA spoke to nearly every active Turkish sponge diver in the ports and on their boats, as well as visiting their homes during the down season. Alongside pictures of amphoras, the INA team showed the sponge divers images of the main cargo item that had been aboard the Cape Gelidonya shipwreck they had excavated during the 1960s: the 'oxhide' ingot.

You may be as mystified by this term as the sponge divers themselves were at the time. An ingot is the technical name for a thin square slab of metal weighing about 25 kilograms. This metal slab nearly always has projections or 'handles' at each corner to make it easier to carry, and scholars called this shape 'oxhide' because it was thought to resemble the shape of the dried skin of an ox. Such a shape made the metal both easy to stack (horizontally and vertically) and, thanks to its handles, easy to pick up/put down. This was the traditional form in which raw copper and other metals were transported during the Bronze Age (in the Aegean, roughly the period 3000–1200 BCE) and the INA team asked the Turkish sponge divers to keep an eye out for such ingots as they could provide a clue in discovering ancient shipwrecks.

*

In 1982, Mehmed, just a year after starting as a professional sponge diver, had travelled with his crew and captain round from Bodrum to the southern coast of Turkey, to a place where a sea plant, called '*puçera*' in Turkish, grew in abundance, and around which sponges often grew. Mehmed had a successful dive. As he told me, he already had a net full of sponges, when, forty-plus metres under water, he noticed some metal on the sea floor. He says he tried to pick it up but couldn't move it. Swimming to the surface as quickly as he could without risking the bends, he described to his captain that he had seen: a 'metal biscuit with ears' – his name for the oxhide ingot. The location was just 100 kilometres away from where the Cape Gelidonya wreck had been found. His captain immediately jumped into the water to see for himself. Could it be from another wreck that had been dashed against the rocks millennia ago?

Mehmed and his captain put in at Kaş harbour, a sleepy fishing village on the southern coast of Turkey, after a hard day's work at sea. They were discussing who to tell of their find, the oxhide ingot, when they saw someone they recognised in the café by the harbour.

Dr Bahadir Berkaya was an archaeologist working for the Museum of Underwater Archaeology in Bodrum and he had met many of the local sponge divers over the years.[6] The Museum of Underwater Archaeology had been formed as part of the birth of underwater archaeology in the 1960s – after the Cape Gelidonya project, the INA team had worked with Turkish officials to secure the first ever grant from the Turkish government for a museum. The building in which the museum was housed is testament to the region's extraordinarily rich history. What is now a museum was once a castle, built by the Knights of St John in the early fifteenth century on a promontory that is thought to have also been the location of the palace of King Mausolus, who ruled in the fourth century BCE – one of the most famous ancient kings of Bodrum (then known as Halicarnassus). While no part of Mausolus's palace has survived, the Knights of St John did use material for their castle from another building constructed by Mausolus nearby: his tomb. This burial place was so big and luxurious, standing 45 metres tall, that not only was it recognised as the Seventh Wonder of the Ancient World, but Mausolus's name was adopted for this type of building: a mausoleum.

On this summer's day in 1982, Bahadir Berkaya told me that he had been sent by the museum director to investigate a potential archaeological site further along the coast of southern Turkey, and he was now making his way back to Bodrum, stopping overnight in Kaş. So it was completely by chance that he was sitting in Kaş harbour that evening when Mehmed stepped ashore. Hearing about what Mehmed had seen, Bahadir suggested that they take the discovery to the museum's director, Dr Oguz Alpozen. Within a week, a team was dispatched to the location to confirm what Mehmed had seen. Bahadir was part of the team, as was Mehmed, who was there to guide them to the exact location. Bahadir remembers how the first diver came up after just a short time under water. When he saw the diver coming up so soon, Bahadir's initial thought was that the diver had been unable to reach the bottom because of a technical problem, or else that he had seen nothing. His heart sank. But then he heard the diver's screams of excitement: 'We've found it!'

Over the course of two more dives, the team realised that they were looking at not just one or two artefacts, but an entire ship's assemblage. On the third dive, they brought to the surface one of the many oxhide copper ingots they had identified. The presence of the oxhide copper ingot proved that this was a ship from the Bronze Age, and that it would perhaps rival the ship found at Cape Gelidonya for the oldest ship ever found. The group were so elated that evening as they celebrated together in the harbour town of Kaş that, according to Bahadir, one of them completely forgot that his wife was due to be going into labour at the hospital in Ankara. A quick telephone call to the hospital confirmed that not only had his wife gone into labour, but that he was now the proud father of a baby boy. On the spot, he declared the boy's name: 'Tunç', which is Turkish for 'Bronze', named in honour of the find they had just confirmed. Today, Tunç is almost my age, and still lives in Bodrum, where he runs a diving school.[7]

A few days after the first dive and Tunç's birth, George Bass heard news of the discovery from his colleague Dr Cemal Pulak, who had been called by the Director of the Bodrum Underwater Museum.[8] 'I think we have another Bronze Age wreck,' Pulak told Bass. The timing was not ideal though; the diving season was drawing to a close as the autumn weather swept in and the pair were forced to wait until the following year to conduct their own survey.[9] In 1983 Pulak led a ten-day inspection of the site. He recalls the water becoming colder and darker as he descended the 45 or so metres down to the seabed – a depth equivalent to roughly ten double-decker buses stacked on top of one another.[10]

One of the strangest effects of diving – which I experienced when I learnt to scuba-dive myself – is how the water affects the perception of colour. Water progressively absorbs the different colours of the spectrum as the depth increases. Red is the first to go, followed by orange and then yellow. Everything that is left is greenish-blue – even your own blood if you are unfortunate enough to cut yourself. At a depth of 45 metres, Cemal Pulak was in this greeny-blue world when he saw the wreck for the first time. Out of the darkness rows and rows of copper oxhide ingots swam into view. He counted 84 of them. Alongside the ingots, Cemal saw large *pithoi* (storage jars) and, after fanning off the sand with his hand, he discovered the ship's stone anchor at a depth of 51 metres. The ship had come to rest on a steep part of the seabed with its bow facing downwards. Cemal managed to raise to the surface a collection of small finds from the wreck: an amphora, a small flask, a wall bracket, samples of what later was shown to be tin and even an ancient twig, once carried in the ship's hold, which turned out to be from a pistachio tree. The finds that Pulak raised were used to give a rough initial date for the ship: from 1400–1300 BCE. That made it between 3,300 and 3,400 years old, beating the Cape Gelidonya wreck by at least a full century and perhaps two. This was, at the time, the oldest seagoing vessel ever found.[11]

It was soon named after the nearby Cape that the ship had failed to round and probably been dashed against: Cape Uluburun.[12] Full-scale underwater excavation began on the Uluburun shipwreck in 1984 and continued every season for the next ten years. The magnitude of the task ahead was enormous. The Cape Gelidonya shipwreck, which George Bass had excavated during the 1960s, had been considered up to this point an incredible achievement against all the odds. The small team had pitched their camp on a narrow strip of beach, surrounded on all sides by unscalable cliffs, twenty miles from the nearest town. They had slept on mattresses spread out on the sand, fearful that rockfalls from the cliffs might hit them while they slept. Flies hounded them at every moment and the heat had been intense. Food was brought by boat once a week and there was no way to keep it refrigerated. And this was all before anyone had stepped into the water. Portable generators on their boat compressed and pumped air through hoses down to the divers, where the precious regulators ensured it matched the pressure around them. Someone kept a wary eye open to make sure that the air intakes were never downwind of the generators or the boat's engines for fear that the carbon monoxide exhausts could enter the air stream sent down to the divers and poison them. The team's emergency portable decompression chamber – intended to be used in the event that a diver came up too quickly and began to suffer the bends – was still being held in customs in Istanbul. As a result the team had to shorten the length of the dives to ensure their safety, with divers working in pairs to look out for one another and with a timekeeper keeping a watch on things from the surface.[13]

At 28 metres down, the Cape Gelidonya diving team also had to deal with some of the inherent difficulties of being under water.

When I learnt to scuba-dive, I imagined that you might feel the weight of all that water pressing down on you from above, causing a kind of claustrophobia. I was relieved to find out on my first proper dive that this was not the case at all. You feel instead an immense sense of freedom in the water. But I was confronted by a whole series of effects I had not been expecting: the greeny-blueness of the underwater world, for instance, and how the refractive properties of water disorientate you. Or how the glass of your face mask and the air that sits between the mask and your eyes all combine to distort your sense of distance and size, not to mention the face mask giving you tunnel vision. The lack of horizon – you are surrounded on all sides by the greeny-blue of the sea – robs you of your directional sense. Underwater currents can buffet you around. All of this adds up to the uneasy feeling of being in an alien environment. On a recreational scuba dive, marvelling at a wreck or brightly coloured fish for only a short period of time, these feelings are minimal and easily brushed aside thanks to the excitement of the experience. But when divers go under water for lengthy periods, repeatedly, in order to perform serious tasks, especially at depth, psychological studies have shown that this sense of being in an alien environment can inhibit confidence in one's ability and cause performance to slump.[14] With time and practice, of course, divers go a long way in conquering these difficulties, but the most experienced speak of their constant respect for the dangers of the world in which they swim. A careless diver is a dead diver.

But at least in the Aegean, two things were on the team's side. First, water clarity in the Aegean Sea is high thanks to the absence of plankton. Second, they didn't have to be too worried about sharks.

As George Bass began the official excavation of the Uluburun shipwreck in 1984, he knew that what had faced the Cape Gelidonya team in the 1960s paled into insignificance compared with what faced them now. The crucial difference was depth. The Cape Gelidonya wreck had been located in water 28 metres deep.

The Uluburun shipwreck was between 44 and 55 metres down – almost twice the depth. At these depths, a whole new series of problems come into play. It's not just the need for longer periods of ascent with more frequent decompression stops and more time between dives to ward off the bends; crucially, it's also the powerful impact of the air the divers breathe. Air is composed of 80 per cent nitrogen and 20 per cent oxygen. At such depths oxygen can become toxic, and nitrogen becomes narcotic. That is to say, at depth, the very air we breathe intoxicates us. George Bass's diving rule was that for every 50 foot of depth, the effect of the nitrogen was equivalent to drinking a gin martini. Divers at Uluburun would be starting their work in an alien cold greeny-blue world on the sea floor, effectively three and a half gin martinis down.[15]

The work that lay before them on the seabed was immense. The team had already realised that the Uluburun ship lay bow down spread out along a steep uneven section of sea floor. At Cape Gelidonya, for unknown reasons, the remains of the wreck were almost all incarcerated in what the excavators labelled 'a hard marine concretion'. Old-fashioned helmet-suit divers had been employed to swing heavy axes under water to break up the concretion into segments. These segments were then brought to the surface, reassembled into place according to the maps the teams had created of the site under water, and then individually, carefully taken apart on the beach. At Uluburun, however, apart from in a few places, such a concretion had not formed, so the team had the opportunity to map, draw, photograph and then excavate the wreck item by item *in situ*. It would be methodical, careful, intense work that the divers had to conduct while semi-intoxicated. But George Bass knew at the outset that the Uluburun shipwreck was an opportunity to do more than simply uncover a new piece of the past. It was the chance to prove once and for all that archaeologists could themselves undertake serious deep-water excavation without the need to hand the task over to professional divers who lacked the archaeological background. To this day, the Uluburun excavation remains the deepest large-scale diving project ever conducted with normal scuba-diving equipment.[16]

Over the course of the ten-year-long excavation of the Uluburun shipwreck, a total of 22,413 dives were made to depths between 42 and 61 metres, with divers spending in excess of 6,600 hours on the seabed working on an area just 250 square metres in size.[17] Their first priority in the initial season of excavation was to sink an underwater telephone booth close to the wreck so that divers could communicate with the command ship during dives. They also set up an 'air lift', a kind of elevator powered by compressed air, to bring up heavy finds. The next crucial step was to establish a system for recording the location of items on the sea floor. In a normal land-based excavation, a grid would be laid out using pegs and string, which nowadays is achieved by capturing the GPS co-ordinates of every find on computers. But how to do that in over 40 metres of water?

The team's choices were further complicated by the fact that the ship had sunk onto a steep and very uneven underwater slope, with the result that the wreck now sat at a 30-degree angle and was listing by 15 degrees to starboard.[18] As the ship had disintegrated over the millennia, its contents had then slid further and further down the slope. The latest techniques at the time – using a measuring bar and photogrammetry technology – proved insufficient and the team had to resort to old-fashioned triangulation of the main areas of the site by metre tape.[19] A series of 1.5-metre by 1.5-metre metal squares were bolted together to form a web that covered the whole of the wreck, fixed at its edges to the sea floor. This metal grid helped orientate the divers – important not just because of the lower light conditions at 44 to 51 metres below the surface, but also because of that semi-intoxication experienced by the divers. The metal bar system was crucial to ensuring that the divers did not get lost and could steady themselves when needed.

In the first season in 1984, the team dived twice a day.[20] Every dive was timed – in terms of both duration and the rest required between dives – and depths were monitored to ensure that the team were not exposing themselves to long-term damage. The work was exhaustingly difficult. Divers had to carefully uncover finds, record their position, sketch them using special waterproof versions of pen and paper, assess their condition, remove them delicately and secure them for transport to the surface. They had to use long suction tubes to suck huge quantities of sand away from parts of the wreck to uncover the remains. And in certain areas, the solid marine concretion that had covered the whole site at Cape Gelidonya had also developed. Described in the initial excavation reports as 'rock-hard', it had formed around various objects, which the divers sought to release with careful chisel blows.

In excavation everything happens in reverse from the way we do things in life: excavators find the last things put in a location first, and the first last as they dig down through the layers. And in this case the original levels of ship storage had been complicated by the ways that the sand, water and the occasional nosy sea creature had pushed and pulled the objects over three millennia on the steep underwater slope. Nonetheless, the divers slowly uncovered level after level of objects, finally reaching the Lebanese cedarwood timbers of the ship's hull, still preserved under the weight of their cargo.

When not diving, the team was split. Half lived on the research vessel provided by the Institute, which was also the command centre for the dives. But the boat was not big enough for the other half of the team, who camped out that first summer and in subsequent years on the nearby inhospitable south-east-facing rocky promontory, against which the ship had almost certainly crashed almost 3,400 years before. On the cliff edge, too, was a space for the initial study and preservation of finds brought up from the seabed.[21] Photos of the cliff camp reveal the team to be living in a sort of shanty town. Rough wooden beams were crammed into gaps between rocks in order to hold up ragged sheets that were providing protection for the artefacts from the glare of the sun and the spray of the waves as they crashed against the rocks below.

At the end of each season, the team then had to carry out what must have been a heartbreaking task. When the weather conditions became too rough to maintain the diving and living arrangements, the team, no doubt with sighs of agony after all their painstaking work, had to cover the wreck over again with tons of sand, to ensure that no looting could take place in the months between excavation seasons. Tons of sand that would have to be carefully removed at the start of the following season. So at the end of every season, Uluburun disappeared back into the seabed, as if she'd never been found at all.

*

Over ten years of persistent excavation, an astounding picture emerged of this extraordinary vessel, and of the pulsating corridors of ancient Mediterranean trade and cultural connectivity of which it was a part.

The Cape Gelidonya wreck – dating to 1200 BCE – had been just 9 to 10 metres long, carrying a mix of thirty-four copper oxhide ingots, tin ingots and broken bronze tools. At one end a cabin area had contained the personal possessions of the crew, including a pair of ancient goat knucklebones, which could have been used for foretelling the will of the gods (like runes) or simply for playing dice, alongside the official seal of a Near-Eastern (roughly the area of today's Middle East) merchant, who most likely commanded the ship. It seems that this merchant's business was the buying of scrap copper, tin and bronze in order to sell it on to be melted down and made into new bronze implements.[22]

The Uluburun shipwreck has been shown to be of a different class altogether – in terms both of size and of content and prestige. It measured 15–16 metres long and would have carried an estimated twenty tons of cargo. Estimates have recently been made on the total worth of that cargo, coming out at roughly 12,000 Ugarit shekels of silver, one of the central trading currencies of the Eastern Mediterranean at this time. Compared to the average salary of a working man at the time, the Uluburun ship held a cargo equivalent in worth to a thousand years' salary. Or put another way, given that the ancient town of Ugarit, which now lies as rubble in northern Syria, had a population during the ship's lifetime of around 8,000 people, the value of the ship's cargo would have been enough to feed the entire town for a year.[23]

The heaviest element of that cargo were those 'metal biscuits with ears' first seen by the sponge diver Mehmed. There were 354 copper oxhide ingots on board the Uluburun ship (as well as 121 'bun shaped' copper ingots), weighing in total about 10 tons. To give a sense of how large and extraordinary this haul is, the total number of copper oxhide ingots in museums across Cyprus, Greece, Sardinia, Italy, Britain and the US (and in private collections) is still less than those recovered from the Uluburun shipwreck.[24] The ingots were arranged on board in four layers, spread out across the length of the ship in a herringbone arrangement to provide maximum stability and minimise their movement while at sea. Underneath the ingots was a thick layer of brushwood and sticks, which cushioned the dead weight of the metal against the ship's timber hull. When analysed, the copper in the ingots was found to have come most probably from Cyprus.[25] The ingots all bore a variety of incised markings, including some artistic images of fish, a trident and even a boat.[26] We think these are the favoured identifiers of different traders, scratched into the copper when they received it into their possession, much like a graffiti tag today.

Along with the copper, there were also 120 pure tin ingots weighing in at just over a ton – the other crucial ingredient required to make bronze. The copper and tin on board would have been enough to make eleven tons of bronze. This was the crucial and prestige product of this period: not for nothing has the ship, which sank around 1400–1300 BCE, been dated to what historians have labelled 'the Bronze Age'. The Bronze Age began in the Eastern Mediterranean around 3300 BCE, when inhabitants of the preceding 'Stone Age' learnt how to construct kilns capable of reaching temperatures over 1,000 degrees centigrade, the crucial melting point of copper. From that point onwards, communities in the areas of the Near East and Levant (the modern-day Middle East) were able to mix copper and tin to make bronze – a material harder and more durable than any other readily available at the time. With this advantage, those communities were able to make better weaponry and other technological inventions, leading to the creation of more successful and substantial communities. Such leaps forward were paralleled also at this time in agriculture, writing, art and trade, creating the earliest known civilisations and empires, which spread around the wider Eastern Mediterranean in tandem with the knowledge of these technological and cultural advancements. By the time of the Uluburun ship, the Eastern Mediterranean Bronze Age was already almost 2,000 years old. Great civilisations and empires, many with their own already long and illustrious histories, jostled with one another around the Eastern Mediterranean and into the area of the modern-day Middle East: from the dynasties of Egypt on the Mediterranean's African coast, to the great Sumerian, Babylonian and Assyrian empires covering parts of today's Iraq and Turkey, to the Hittite Empire spanning portions of today's Turkey and Syria, to the Mycenaean kingdoms of Greece. While often at war with one another, they were also trading ferociously – and that is where the Uluburun ship fits into the picture.

It is incredible to think that the Uluburun ship, and the civilisations and empires it was serving, existed so long ago. As a measure, I always find it useful to remember that the Uluburun ship was sailing well over a thousand years before the time of the Roman Empire. And the ship's contents stand as testament to the incredibly diverse and rich networks and trade that connected these flourishing civilisations in this period. Analysis of the tin on board the Uluburun ship, for example, shows that it originally came from mines in the Taurus mountains of Turkey and also from Afghanistan.[27] It had travelled a great distance across land before it even started its journey by sea. In fact the Uluburun tin ingots were mostly cut into halves and quarters, possibly to make them easier to carry on pack animals down from the mountains and across land.[28]

On board the ship, the copper and tin ingots were balanced and wedged in by another ton of ballast made up of stones. But whereas the copper had maintained its shape and consistency under the pressure of all that salty sea water over the last 3,300 years, the tin had not fared so well. Cemal Pulak speaks of the tin having the consistency of toothpaste and the underwater excavators having to scoop it up using teaspoons.[29] Just imagine having to scoop up a ton of toothpaste with a teaspoon while 45 metres under water . . .

Resting on top of the heavy (and now toothpasty) ingots were 149 Canaanite jars, recognisable by their little circular handles that jut out like small ears either side of a large oval face. The jars are called Canaanite as this shape was popular in the northern part of modern-day Israel/further north into Syria. The boat's cargo included three sizes, with the largest able to hold 26.7 litres. The majority of the jars were found to still contain a yellowish substance, which was chemically identified as terebinth resin, a gum made from the terebinth tree. This resin was used as a wine preservative, as it helped kill the bacteria that turn wine into vinegar, and as a way of colouring perfumed oils. The ship was carrying about a metric ton of resin in total – the largest ancient deposit of the material ever found.[30] Analysis of the pollen extracted from the resin suggested it was gathered from trees in northern regions of the Dead Sea in Israel.[31]

Alongside the Canaanite jars were nine large Cypriot ceramic storage jars known as *pythoi*. These are much more bulbous than Canaanite jars, resembling a person with a very flabby belly, and their handles are placed much higher up near the mouth of the jar, which is itself much wider than that of a Canaanite jar. This wide mouth makes them ideal for the transport not of liquids and resins (as with the Canaanite jars), but instead of smaller solid items. Inside each were carefully packed smaller Cypriot pots, jugs, wall brackets and oil lamps, as well as preserved foods in small jars, such as olive oil. There were also over a 175 glass disks (also known as glass 'ingots'), weighing a total of 350 kilograms, in four different colours – dark blue, turquoise, purple and yellow – which would be sold and eventually cut into beads or used as inlays for jewellery, as well as 70,000 pre-cut beads made of glass or faience. This remains the oldest and largest-known collection of glass ingots to have ever been excavated.[32]

And this is only the beginning of the list. Also on board the ships were twenty-four ebony logs, a collection of ostrich eggshell vases, seashell rings, carved wooden and ivory boxes, as well as cylinder seals from Mesopotamia, which were covered in designs and could be rolled in wet clay to produce a kind of administrative signature of ownership on an object. Divers also found an ivory elephant tusk and fourteen hippopotamus teeth (eight incisors and six canines). While elephant tusk was the preferred form of ivory for trade in this period as it yielded larger quantities of solid ivory to sculpt, hippopotamus teeth were more commonly used because they could be more easily obtained and – to the nonspecialist – looked identical to elephant tusk ivory (although I do not envy whoever's job it was to obtain a hippo's tooth).[33] One hippopotamus incisor tooth on board had already been carved into a trumpet!

The jewellery found was made up of gold, silver, bronze, tin, glass and faience, and the recovered cargo also included figurines, vessels and weapons fashioned from the same materials. Mixed in with the jewellery was one piece of gold that caused quite a stir when it was first found: a gold scarab from Egypt with the cartouche of Queen Nefertiti inscribed on it. Nefertiti was the wife of the Pharaoh Akhenaten, who ruled in the second half of the fourteenth century BCE. Akhenaten had attempted to abandon Egypt's traditional pattern of worshipping a wider plethora of gods, and instead insisted on the worship of just one: Aten, the disc of the sun, by which Akhenaten claimed, in his own Great Hymn to

Aten, all life was created. This new religious direction was not widely embraced and was dismantled after Akhenaten's death. In fact some have argued that Nefertiti ruled alone as Pharaoh after Akhenaten's death for a short while before power passed to the most famous Pharaoh of them all: Tutankhamun, who proceeded to do his best to wipe the memory of Akhenaten from the official records. The fact that the scarab with the cartouche of Nefertiti was found on board the Uluburun ship means that the vessel must have sailed after (but not long after) Nefertiti's death, which has helped, alongside the analysis of the timbers and pottery, to place the ship's date more precisely at the end of the fourteenth century BCE.[34]

The ship also reveals what other goods were being traded between the flourishing Bronze Age civilisations gathered around the Eastern Mediterranean 3,300 years ago. On board was a cargo of perishable goods, including acorns, pine nuts, pine cones, wild pistachios, olives, almonds, grapes and figs, not to mention a selection of herbs and spices including coriander, black cumin, sumac seeds and charred barley, as well as a selection of pulses and seeds. One Canaanite amphora contained more than 2,500 large olive stones.[35] But perhaps the most common perishable item to have been identified on board was the pomegranate. Remains of pomegranates were found in a quarter of all the areas the excavators sampled across the shipwreck for food remains. The pomegranate was an exotic product originating east of Mesopotamia, which, by the time of the Uluburun shipwreck, was still relatively rare on the coast of the Mediterranean, making the ship's haul of pomegranates an expensive and sought-after luxury cargo. But the pomegranate was not simply desired as a rare food choice. Its juice was used to enable oil to bond better with a scent to create a strong-smelling perfume, which would have been very popular with the elites of the time to anoint themselves with or have burning like a modern-day scent diffuser. Far more importantly, however, by the Bronze Age the pomegranate also had clear associations with both fertility and death. It is often depicted in funerary iconography or recreated in glass or precious metal to be put into graves, as an item needed by the deceased on their journey to the Underworld (a pomegranate-shaped silver vase, for example, was found in the burial chamber of King Tutankhamun in Egypt's Valley of the Kings, buried at around the same time the Uluburun ship was sailing). The Uluburun pomegranates may therefore have been intended to satisfy the needs of both the (elite) living and the recently dead.[36]

Clues were also unearthed in the equipment of the crew itself: their cooking and drinking utensils, lamps, fishing tackle, tools to fix the ship, as well as musical instruments to entertain themselves with during the long hours at sea. Divers found seven sets of balances and weights (some in the shape of animals like lionesses, bulls, ducks, frogs, the Sphinx and even a fly) with which to conduct business at the different ports the ship docked in. The design of the weights and instruments suggests that the people using them were of Phoenician/Canaanite origin – areas today covered by Lebanon, Israel and Syria. We have even been able to identify one particularly ornate set of weights and measures as probably belonging to the captain (as well as an expensive Canaanite sword made of bronze with an ivory handle).[37]

Some of the most recent analysis has suggested the ship's final port of call before it sank was one of the ports of the Ugarit kingdom, either Minet el-Beida or Ras Sharma, today to be found just north of the Syrian port of Latakia. This last stopping point was suggested not simply by the goods the ship had on board, but amazingly by one of its unintended stowaways. Snuggled in among the copper ingots lying 45 metres under the water was part of a jaw of a mouse – with its molar tooth still in place in the jaw. The shape of the molar has been linked directly to that of today's Syrian house mouse population.[38] Little did their ancestor mouse know it had made a poor choice in boarding this particular ship . . .

The unfortunate mouse was not the only animal stowaway on board the Uluburun ship. The underwater excavators also found, recorded and brought to the surface thirty-six shells of terrestrial gastropods: or in other words, snails. World snail experts have examined the finds and in the *Journal of Molluscan Studies* (this is the best journal title I have ever encountered) they reported that four of the shells belonged to local sea snails that had ended up exploring the wreck, but that thirty-two were land snails that had at different times made their way onto the ship during its fateful journey around the Eastern Mediterranean coast. Some it seems had got trapped in the terebinth resin as it had oozed out of the trees and then ended up being incarcerated in the Canaanite jars. Indeed it was because scientists were able to identify the origins of some of the snails found in the resin (alongside the pollen residues) that they have been able to pinpoint where the resin came from (about 50 kilometres from the Mediterranean coast, near the Dead Sea in modern-day Israel). The other molluscs were all found among the spiny bushes, twigs and branches that were packed under the copper and tin ingots to protect the ship's hull from the weight. Cruelly ripped from their hiding places, these poor snails – which, unlike their resin brothers, were probably still very much alive at the moment of impact on the rocks – had been transported against their will on a fateful voyage, only to end up at the bottom of the ocean. But they have as a result gained celebrity: they are the earliest direct evidence for the overseas transport (albeit inadvertently) of land snails in antiquity.[39]

It is thought that the boat itself was made in, and probably first set sail from, the port city of Tell Abu Hawam (modern-day Haifa in Israel), but the goods on board the Uluburun ship come from nine to ten different ancient civilisations across a massive geographical area.[40] What this diverse and valuable cargo, from glittering glass beads to precious comestibles and tons of bronze and iron, makes clear is that the ship represents a snapshot of the pulsating international trade links that joined the wealthy, diverse and sophisticated Bronze Age civilisations living around the Eastern Mediterranean. Indeed, the ship is testament to one of the most active trading periods of the Bronze Age Mediterranean.

This period, at the end of the fourteenth century BCE – at roughly the same time as the great Cyclopean city walls were being built at the palace of Mycenae in Greece, and King Tutankhamun ruled in Egypt, his infamous golden and bejewelled death mask subsequently being fashioned for his mummified corpse – is known as the 'Late Bronze Age'. It was the time when the ruling powers of Egypt, Mesopotamia, the Levant, Anatolia, Cyprus and the Aegean were intensively interacting with one another on diplomatic, military and political levels as well as through trade.[41] We can even link the Uluburun ship to depictions and records of international trade from the period. Under the rule of the Egyptian Pharaoh Amenhotep III in roughly the mid-fourteenth century BCE, a man called Ken-Amun was the 'superintendent of the granaries', essentially meaning he was the man in charge of the royal pantry and responsible for maintaining stock levels. On Ken-Amun's tomb in Thebes, there is an inscribed portrait of a Syrian merchant fleet arriving into an Egyptian port, shown unloading Canaanite jars, with *pithoi* vessels on its deck, just like those found on the Uluburun ship.

But the cargo of the Uluburun ship wasn't simply for trade – there was something grander going on here. In the second half of the fourteenth century BCE, Amenhotep III's successor Akhenaten came to power (the husband of Nefertiti whose cartouche inscribed onto a gold scarab was found on board). Dating to his reign, 350 clay tablets from the Egyptian city of el-Amarna – today known as the Amarna letters – detail Egypt's diplomatic relations with Assyrian, Hittite and Cypriot rulers as well as with others in Syria and Palestine. This cache of clay tablets underlines how trade was often conducted at the level of the ruler as part of an intricate diplomatic game of royal gift exchange. The Amarna letters reveal how kings sent to one another large quantities of copper ingots (the King of Cyprus, for instance, is recorded as sending 200 talents worth – roughly 8,000 kilograms – to the Egyptian Pharaoh), as well as ebony, elephant tusks, gold and silver: all items matching the cargo aboard the Uluburun ship.

So the traders on board our ship were not working simply within a commercial market, but one that was also under the influence and direction of the royal households of the ancient Mediterranean, who used and supported a network of long-distance trade to facilitate their inter-royal gift exchange and diplomatic relations. The Uluburun ship was therefore most likely carrying raw and finished goods for such long-distance royal gift exchange as well as others that were being commercially traded by the crew between the ports it stopped off at en route.[42]

We can guess the ultimate destination of the ship by the non-Aegean nature of the majority of the cargo; this gives us the ship's direction of travel (towards the Aegean). If it were coming from the Aegean we would expect a much larger proportion of Aegean goods on board to exchange around the Eastern Mediterranean. The ship's destination can also be inferred by a small number of the personal and professional possessions and items of interest found on board. While the overwhelming majority of these were of Phoenician/Canaanite origin, belonging to the ship's main crew, a smaller number came from the Aegean (Aegean-style drinking vessels, swords, knives and glass plaques), and from areas further to the north and west (Baltic amber, for instance, and an Italian-style sword). Given that a number of these objects appeared in pairs, the excavators have suggested that there must also have been on board the ship two people from the Aegean. These people, however, were most likely not traders themselves, because no sets of Aegean balances and weights – essential for trading – have been found. Instead, they may have been official ambassadors sent by an Aegean ruler, there to oversee the safe transport of luxury goods heading towards the Aegean as part of a gift exchange between ruling households.[43] Piecing together all these parts of the puzzle leads us to think that the ship was probably heading from the ancient communities based in the area of today's Lebanon towards the Mycenaean kingdoms of Greece.

The Uluburun ship presents a vital picture of the pulsating flow of goods and raw materials circulating around the Eastern and

Central Mediterranean in the Late Bronze Age, and is testament to the high degree of connectivity between the different communities that lived like frogs around this giant pond. But for me what is most special is that it also gives us a rare glimpse into the lives of the men who crewed this ship. Not simply the personal choices they made in the shape and design of their weights and balances (the lioness, the duck, the fly!); there were also musical instruments on board, including a lute with a tortoiseshell soundbox. I wonder if one of the crew was playing, and the others listening, rapt, while they rounded Cape Uluburun and subsequently got caught by the strong north-westerlies that blow in that region, with the result that the crew didn't realise until it was too late how close to the rocks they had come.

While the crew – as far as we can tell – never made it to their ultimate destination in the Aegean, in one way the ship has: its remains are being conserved, studied and displayed in the Bodrum Museum of Underwater Archaeology, not far from where Mehmed Çakir, the sponge diver who originally discovered the wreck, still lives. Mehmed continued as a sponge diver until 2000 when he retired; he told me that finding the Uluburun wreck made him as happy as when he found the most desirable massive '*melat*' sponges. He has been to see the ship in its new museum home. The ancient blocks of Mausolus's mausoleum, now part of the Crusader Castle in which the Museum of Underwater Archaeology is housed, have a new – and equally precious – body to guard into eternity. Back off the coast of Kas, an underwater archaeological park was also established in 2006. A replica of the cargo of the Uluburun ship was created and sunk, and then the grids used by the excavation team were positioned over the top of the sunken items to replicate the 'archaeological site' as it was originally explored by George Bass and his team. At the same time, a full scale hypothetical model of the Uluburun ship was built using similar wood to that available in the late fourteenth century BCE, sailed to the coast off Kas and then sunk within the archaeological park (both the replica find site and the replica ship were sunk this time only at a depth of about 20 metres). This has not only allowed tourists to dive and visit both the replica 'archaeological site' and view the ship as it may have looked just after sinking, but it has also allowed archaeologists to monitor the pace of decay of the replica ship to give new insights into the process of disintegration of ancient vessels underwater.[44]

But for me, the most important elements of this story are the collaborations and extreme endeavour that made this discovery possible. Archaeologists exchanged knowledge and began collaborations with Turkish sponge-diving crews in order to pool their collective insight, resources and coverage to increase their chances of finding underwater treasures. This collaboration enabled the discovery of Uluburun. At the same time, an international team of archaeologists, by constantly innovating and pushing themselves to the limits of human endurance and beyond what had ever been attempted before, ensured the discovery's study and conservation. In the most inhospitable of places 45 metres under the water, over ten years of constant effort, such collaborative and innovative efforts unveiled a detailed and insightful picture of human life and interaction from over 3,300 years ago. Archaeology – and the archaeologists – proved that their capability to uncover the past had made a quantum leap forward with the excavation of the Uluburun ship. Underwater archaeology has continued ever since to go from strength to strength – penetrating deeper and deeper under the waves to depths where humans could never hope to dive, with the help of scanning technologies and remote-controlled craft, to uncover ever more wonderful – and indeed in some cases older – examples of the human desire to cross the sea and interact with one another.

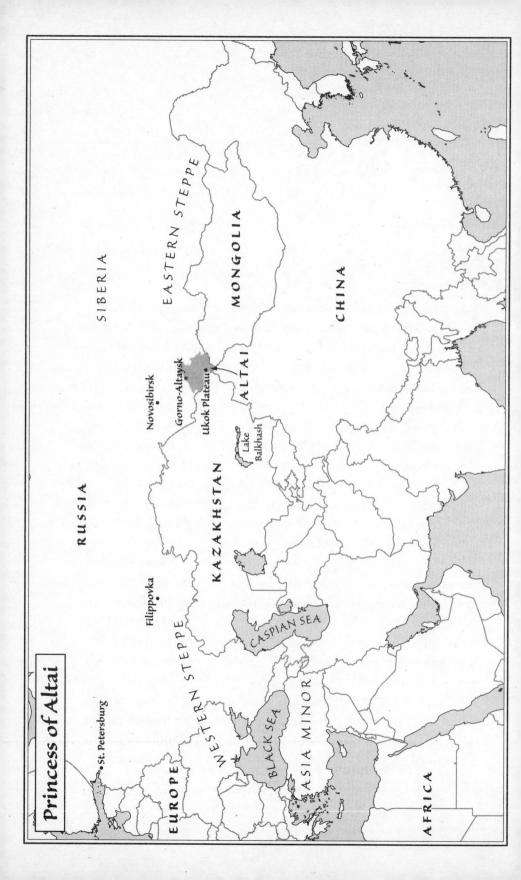

7

Back from the Ice[1]

In southern Siberia, in an area where the borders of Russia, China, Mongolia and Kazakhstan converge, lies the Republic of Altai. It is part of Russia, and the least populated republic of the country, as a large majority of its territory is composed of inhospitable mountains, vast tundras, inaccessible alpine meadows and lakes.

In April 2020, when much of the world was entering into full lockdown, this was the only area of Russia not to register a single Covid-19 case. The Regional Deputy, Yerzhanat Begenov, told the press then that there were no cases among the 200,000-plus inhabitants thanks to the republic's early implementation of self-isolation and restriction on travel. Also, as he went on to explain, 'we have protection. The Altai people worship the mummy.'[2]

The 'mummy' supposedly offering this protection is in fact the ancient remains of a woman who lived several thousand years ago in the Altai region. She is known by many names. In the republic, she is often referred to as the 'Princess of Altai'. And for many, she is also more than just a princess. The powerful community of Altai shamans and tribal elders from the region have claimed that the mummy is none other than Ochi-Bala – a warrior woman of Altai epic and legend, who defended her land and people from invading evil. According to the story passed down through tens of generations, on her death she was buried in Altai land in order to provide a continual barrier against the evil spirits of the Underworld.[3]

The mummy/Princess of Altai/Ochi-Bala was first discovered in 1993 on the Ukok Plateau, one of those inaccessible alpine meadows that make up the Altai region. Her remains were excavated by a Russian-led team of archaeologists, who took her by helicopter back to their research base at Novosibirsk, outside of the Altai Republic. Her body remained there over the next nineteen years, undergoing a series of investigative examinations and procedures for preservation. Throughout that time, many people from the Altai protested that the princess should never have been dug up in the first place. They pointed to a series of local and national misfortunes over that time period that had, according to them, been brought about because of the disturbance of the princess's final resting place and her removal from the Altai region. First there was the helicopter crash when the archaeologists tried to move her to Novosibirsk in 1993; then the major earthquake in the Altai region that occurred soon after her body was removed; followed shortly afterwards by Russia's constitutional crisis in late 1993 when Boris Yeltsin ordered Russian tanks to shell the Russian parliament. Her removal also supposedly led to Russia's subsequent economic difficulties and even the outbreak of war in Chechnya in 1995.[4]

Nor, they claim, has the rest of the world been spared. Hillary Clinton, while visiting Russia in November 1997, was given an exclusive chance to see the princess's body, followed by a vodka toast with the local governor and then a meeting with a traditional Siberian family. Two years after this visit, the governor lost his post, and the local family split and moved to Canada. Before that, in January 1998, the Monica Lewinsky scandal had broken, bringing personal and political misfortune to Hillary Clinton. Local Altai newspaper headlines even claimed that Hillary Clinton's run for the presidency in 2016 was thwarted by the 'curse of the mummy' she had met back in 1997.[5]

The Republic of Altai was so angry at the excavation and removal of the princess's body from the Ukok Plateau that its state assembly banned all further excavation there – a ban that has remained in force to this day.[6] Following almost decades of ardent protests from the republic, on 20 September 2012 the princess's body was finally returned to the Altai to be housed in the national museum in Gorno-Altaysk, Altai's capital.[7] And while some – including the region's Deputy – seemingly now believe in the mummy's power and willingness to protect the Altai Republic from evils as modern as Covid-19, there are many who also believe that the mummy is *still* unhappy with her current resting place in the museum. They fear her displeasure has led to a series of forest fires, high winds, and the Altai's worst flooding in over fifty years, all occurring since the princess's return to Altai. 'Naked and defenceless', they say, 'Ochi-Bala is freezing from inexplicable shame.'[8]

The ultimate solution, for those who believe the princess remains unhappy, is to re-bury her. On 18 August 2014, the Council of Tribal Elders of Altai officially voted to re-bury her on the Ukok Plateau in order to 'stop her anger which causes floods and earthquakes', and also to enable her to continue to perform her long-held role of keeping the evil spirits of the Underworld at bay.[9]

Even among those who don't subscribe to the view that the mummy is Ochi-Bala, itching to return to her role as guardian of the gate between realms, there are many who sympathise with the need to re-bury her body out of common decency and respect for the (long) dead. As one of the campaigners for her re-burial has put it: 'Who puts up the naked corpse of their mother for public display? She knocks into our hearts, seeking compassion.'[10] The response from the regional government (which oversees the museum) offers a different perspective: 'Can you, for example, bury some vase from the Hermitage museum? Of course not. The mummy, though it can sound quite rude, is still a museum exhibit; that is why we cannot just bury it.'[11]

An uneasy compromise has been reached: although the princess remains in the museum and has not been re-buried, her mummified remains in the museum in Gorno-Altaysk, out of respect for the beliefs of the Altai shamans, can only be viewed at the time of the full moon.[12]

*

The princess's original resting place, the Ukok Plateau, is a strange otherworldly place. From the plateau you can see parts of the territories of modern-day Russia, Mongolia, China and Kazakhstan. But for somewhere seemingly at the meeting point of many worlds, it is simultaneously cut off from everywhere. The name 'Ukok' means 'the end of everything' – everything human. Locals believe that the Ukok Plateau represents the 'second layer of heaven' – a place above ordinary humans and events, a gateway between worlds. Indeed, since time immemorial, it has been considered sacrilege to shout on the Ukok Plateau in case you offend the spirits that reside at this spiritual crossing point.[13]

Today, the Ukok Plateau can only be reached by helicopter or, in warmer seasons, by heavy-going dirt roads that wind through precarious mountain passes. While the winter is long and cold, with the passes covered in snow and prone to avalanches, the summer is short and mild with temperatures not quite reaching 20°C. But summer thaws bring different problems for those attempting to access the plateau by road: swamp mud from the fast-thawing snow and mass mud slides down the mountain.

If you do manage to reach the plateau, you find yourself in a place of 'overwhelming sky'.[14] Sitting at around 2,250 metres above sea level and surrounded by peaks that ascend to between 3,000 and 4,500 metres, the plateau offers a wealth of grassland even in the depths of winter thanks to harsh winds that prevent the snow from settling, as if a giant were moving around with a leaf-blowing machine strapped to his back. Even in severe winters the Altai herdsmen fight their way through to the plateau grassland with their sheep and horses to ensure year-round feed.

The same was true well over two thousand years ago, during the first millennium BCE – when the Princess of Altai was not a mummified corpse but a living, breathing individual. The Ukok Plateau is part of the great Eurasian Steppe. This is the arterial corridor of low and mountain grasslands stretching from the Black Sea in the west to Mongolia and China in the east, along which huge communities of nomads (nowadays referred to more correctly as nomadic pastoralists) roamed with their horses and other livestock. These communities that lived across the vast expanse of the Steppe in the first millennium BCE are sometimes, as a single group, called the Scythians, or the Scythian-Siberians, or else simply Early or Iron Age Nomads/Nomadic Pastoralists. But they were in reality a diverse range of peoples with different languages and cultural behaviours, who were regularly interacting with one another and with the great empires that surrounded them to the west, south and east.

What bound them together, as the terms 'nomadic' and 'pastoralist' suggest, was that none of these groups living along the Steppe built permanent settlements and cities like the sedentary ancient civilisations of Greece, Persia, Central Asia and India or China that surrounded them. Instead, these groups moved on a seasonal basis with their livestock, setting up temporary settlements wherever they went.

Unlike their sedentary neighbours, they never wrote down any of their communities' histories or stories. Nor did they ever produce their own coinage. Therefore what we know about them comes principally from two major sources. The first is what those sedentary civilisations that interacted with them, and who did write down their histories, thought about them. The Greek historian Herodotus, for example, writing in the fifth century BCE, was fascinated by the nomadic pastoralists living on the north-eastern edge of the Greek world, between the Black and Caspian Seas. He calls these peoples 'Scythians', and reports on their culture, traditions and behaviours. Indeed, he is so well informed about their practices that he is able to describe in detail their burial practices, revealing how, during the funerary procession of a Scythian king conducted by the tribal groups under his sway, the men in each group cut off a bit of their ear, lacerated their arms, noses and foreheads, and thrust an arrow through their left hands in his honour. When the corpse eventually was placed into its grave, alongside it was placed the body of the king's concubine (freshly strangled), as well as that of his cup-bearer, cook, groom, attendant, messenger and some of his horses. A year after the initial burial, Herodotus recounts, fifty of the king's Scythian servants, as well as fifty horses, were killed, and then set up, using a complex series of wooden stakes to keep them erect, in a circle around the king's burial mound.[15]

From the great Persian Achaemenid Empire of western and Central Asia, at its peak from the sixth century BCE through to the late fourth century BCE when it was conquered by Alexander the Great, we hear about nomadic pastoralist tribes, known collectively as the 'Sakas', who ranged across the Steppe from just north of the Caspian Sea in the west to the Altai Mountains of modern Russia. Persian sources distinguish two groups based on what they drank and what kind of headgear they wore and considered them formidable enemies with whom they were frequently at war (in fact the legendary Persian king Cyrus the Great was killed campaigning against them in 529 BCE).[16] Equally, we hear about the nomadic pastoralists from the eastern end of the Steppe from the great Chinese historian of the Han dynasty, Sima Qian. Writing in the second century BCE, Sima Qian focuses on the military might and daring of the fast horse-riding tribes like the Xiongnu on Han China's north-western frontier, who frequently raided into Han territory. In an attempt to prevent these raids, the Han (and previous Chinese dynasties like the Qin) had begun building walls, the very first versions of the Great Wall of China. Over time, an uneasy truce was developed in which the Han bought relative peace with the Xiongnu through the offering of goods and even a Han princess for the Xiongnu ruler.[17]

In addition to contemporary accounts from neighbouring empires, another major source of information about these different groups of nomadic pastoralists comes from their burials. While these communities did not invest in permanent settlements and cities, many of them did invest in lavish burials and funerary monuments for their elites, as indicated by Herodotus's descriptions of funerary practices. Explorers and archaeologists over the last two centuries have found and excavated some of these burial sites, allowing us not only to compare and contrast the literary accounts of writers like Herodotus and others with the physical remnants of these cultures, but also to examine these communities at first hand for the first time. What has emerged is not only corroboration for many of the literary details (a pointed hat, for example, has been found in a Saka grave at Issyk, south of Lake Balkhash, dating to the fifth century BCE, echoing the Persian description of the 'pointed-hatted Sakas'), but also a much deeper understanding of the extraordinary level of interaction, particularly through trade, that these nomadic pastoralist communities had with one another and with the sedentary communities around them. Scythian tombs on the western end of the Steppe are filled with huge quantities of gold finery made by Greek craftsmen, incorporating scenes from nomadic life and mythology. From a nomadic burial in Filippovka in the southern Urals, golden amphorae and a silver rhyton (drinking cup) of Persian manufacture have been unearthed. Numerous other burials have revealed items of Persian and Saka origin, incorporating ideas and emblems of each culture, lying side by side.[18]

So often in the past, because they chose not to build cities and write lengthy histories, these nomadic pastoralist tribes of the Steppe have been considered a kind of poor barbarian relation to the sedentary empires in the south, west and east from the same period. We now realise nothing could be further from the truth. Not only was there a great deal of mutual respect between the nomadic pastoralist and sedentary communities for each other's skills and abilities, but there was also a steady and ever-increasing stream of interaction between the different tribes of nomadic pastoralists, as well as between them and their sedentary neighbours, particularly through trade. By the end of the first millennium BCE, the continuous arteries of trade stretching across the Steppe from the Mediterranean to China became established as what we now know as the Silks Roads.

The discovery of the remains of the nomadic pastoralists began in the time of the Russian Tsar Peter the Great in the early eighteenth century. The Tsar was impressed by a golden plate fashioned in the shape of a panther, which had been discovered in a tomb in the region. Russian high society mimicked the Tsar's reaction, becoming enchanted with this kind of ancient material. There was a thirst for more, fed by robbers who quickly became adept at identifying the markers of nomadic pastoralist tombs in the landscape and raiding them for the gold they might contain. Peter the Great himself tried to stem the tide of such thievery, by demanding all finds be given (for free) to his newly built museum, the Kunstkamera. He also founded the Russian Academy of Sciences in 1724, which would spearhead a more professional examination of these burial sites.[19]

Exactly two centuries later, in 1924, researchers working at 1,600 metres above sea level in the eastern Altai Mountains discovered a new phenomenon: a nomadic pastoralist grave that was frozen in solid ice. How had these buried tombs been turned into eternal ice cubes? It seems that rainwater and snowmelt, seeping into the underground burial chamber soon after it had been created, had been turned to ice by the bitter temperatures of the following winter. The large collection of stones above ground covering the burial had then deflected the mild heat of the many subsequent summers, preserving the ice hidden inside. The burials had therefore become – and remained – thick blocks of ice for over two thousand years. Up until 1924, the survival of ancient material in these nomadic graves excavated from the Black Sea through to China had been at the mercy of the natural conditions of the ground and the climate: hard-wearing metals had mostly survived but only occasionally had more organic materials like clothing been found, and no one had ever unearthed the remains of an actual human body. Here, frozen in time in the ice in the Altai, there was now the possibility of discovering a tomb with everything still preserved inside. The Altai region contained potentially not just one but a whole series of deep freezers waiting to be unlocked.

The first of these frozen tombs was excavated (or rather melted) in 1929. Then, between 1947 and 1949, two Russian archaeologists, Drs Mikhail Gryaznov and Sergei Rudenko, uncovered many more while working in the heart of the Altai Mountains. They explored five burial chambers, and although some of them had been partly robbed at some point over the previous two thousand years, the frozen nature of the burials ensured that many parts of the burial assemblage had remained untouched. What emerged were the first examples of what the archaeologists termed the 'Pazyryk culture', their label for the particular group of nomadic pastoralists who had inhabited the Altai region in the second half of the first millennium BCE. The frozen conditions of the burial allowed Gryaznov and Rudenko to bring to world attention an astonishingly rich picture of nomadic burial. The skeletons of horses, wearing elaborate harnesses decorated with gold and bronze plaques, were laid next to the burial chambers. The chambers themselves were square rooms with walls made out of double layers of logs and a floor covered in felt or gravel. The coffins inside the burial chambers were made out of the trunks of larch trees, and were surrounded by the organic materials put into the burials with the deceased over two thousand years earlier, including wooden tables, stringed instruments, leopard-skin fur boots, embroidered Chinese silk cloth, the world's oldest surviving wool carpet, richly and intricately decorated with central Asian/Persian themes, and even the dismantled parts of a Chinese four-wheeled carriage.[20]

More than this, Gryaznov and Rudenko's discoveries enabled

us to come face to face, for the first time, with the embalmed bodies of the nomadic pastoralists themselves. Four bodies were discovered within the burials: two men and two women. In one tomb, the female corpse had been dismembered by robbers, most probably in ancient times before the tomb had frozen solid. The male corpse, however, was preserved enough for experts to understand that, just like the Egyptians had started to do to mummify their dead more than two millennia earlier, all his internal organs and muscles had been removed. The Pazyryk body had then been stuffed with herbs and other vegetation in order to dry out the remaining flesh before being sewn up and placed in the coffin. The man's flesh had then received a second (unintended) kind of mummification process that no corpse in Egypt had ever been subjected to. It had been frozen in the ice of the tomb for two thousand years. Now once again thawed out, the surviving flesh revealed that in life he had been heavily tattooed across his arms, chest, back and legs, featuring real animals like deer, fish and leaping stags, alongside fantastic beasts such as griffins. The man and woman in the other tomb were buried together, similarly embalmed and tattooed, with coats placed over their shoulders, and stockings and shoes on their legs and feet.[21]

Thanks to Rudenko's further excavations in the 1950s more 'Pazyryk culture' tombs were discovered at several different sites across the Altai region, enriching still further our understanding of this particular group of nomadic pastoralists who were, in the middle and second half of the first millennium BCE (approximately sixth to third centuries BCE), a thriving part of the much wider continuum of tribes and communities that ranged across the vast landscape of the Steppe. However, the Pazyryk are special, because it is only in this region of the entire Steppe that environmental conditions and ancient practices conspired to create the wonder of these tombs frozen in the ice. The summers were warm *enough* that the ground thawed *enough* to allow the ancients to dig and install the burial chambers in the first place. The winters were also cold *enough* to ensure that water, once it had seeped into the underground burials, turned to ice. And it was the nomadic practice specific to this region of covering the surface area of the underground tomb with a large collection of rock boulders (known as a 'kurgan') that deflected the heat in the subsequent summers and prevented the frozen tomb from ever thawing again, unlike the uncovered earth all around it.[22]

As a result, only here in the mountainous region of the Altai could this – and did this – miracle of ancient freezer technology happen. This isolated and otherworldly region offers us a unique chance to peer into the lives of the people who were part of a much larger interconnected ancient world.

*

Dr Natalia Polosmak knew this better than most. In 1990 she was a researcher at the Institute of Archaeology and Ethnography, an extension of the Russian Academy of Science originally founded by Peter the Great, in Novosibirsk, Siberia, just over 1,000 kilometres north of the Altai and its frozen tombs. Since Rudenko's excavations in the mid-twentieth century, the Institute had dedicated itself to improving the archaeological techniques of excavation (or 'controlled thawing' as Natalia likes to call it) for these icy tombs. But they hadn't actually excavated any more tombs – over the previous few decades the focus had been on building up expertise and refining techniques.

So in 1990, Natalia was ready to lead the Institute's charge back into the field. She had identified an untouched area to begin her search for new frozen tombs to excavate: the Altai's Ukok Plateau.[23] She was of course aware of the local legends and powerful meaning of the Ukok. She was also aware that no one had dug there before despite the cultural importance of the location, mainly because of the difficulties of access; the challenges of working at such high altitudes (no one from the Institute had ever worked an excavation at Ukok's altitude); and the potential perils of working in a region where the borders of four nations, who were not always on good terms with one another, came together.

Natalia left Novosibirsk by helicopter in the summer of 1990 accompanied by her intrepid cocker spaniel Peter (named after Peter the Great) and a team of willing excavators. Five hours later, hovering over the vast expanse of the Ukok Plateau, the helicopter pilot asked Natalia where she wanted to land. She simply pointed at a random spot. That night, with the helicopter (their only way out) gone, the team camped by a river, feeling more alone than they had ever felt in their lives.[24]

They woke the next morning to the arrival of the Russian army border patrol, which had come to check out their documents. Natalia asked the patrol guards if they knew of any nearby kurgans – the manmade rock-boulder mounds that were the tell-tale signs of a Pazyryk tomb. Lt Mikhail Cheponov, head of the border patrol, replied at once: 'Get in the truck, we'll show you kurgans.' With Cheponov's help, that summer Natalia struck (golden) ice, in the Ak-Alakh river valley of the Ukok Plateau, just 14 kilometres from China's border with Russia.[25] Over that summer excavation season, the team thawed out and excavated a frozen tomb containing not just the skeletons of horses in beautifully wrought bridles and a range of impressive organic finds, but two preserved corpses – the first to be found since Rudenko's excavations in the 1940s to 60s. The first body was that of a man in his late forties, wearing a jolly pair of bright red trousers, with a wood, leather, bronze and gold necklace (known as a torque) around his neck, and a pickaxe, dagger and arrows by his side.[26] The second body was initially thought to be that of a young woman aged just seventeen, but later analysis of DNA showed it to be a young man, related to the older one (perhaps as uncle and nephew). He too was kitted out for war.[27]

Back in Novosibirsk at the end of the season, the Institute team were delighted. Not only was this the first successful excavation from the ice of Pazyryk corpses since the time of Rudenko, but the Institute team had successfully operated in such an inhospitable and remote environment. The tombs themselves revealed what Natalia calls a 'middle-level nobility'.[28] The individuals buried were important enough to have the tomb created and the horses slaughtered for them, but at the same time no gold or silver was found, nor any imported item. These were what we might think of as 'middle-class' Pazyryks.[29]

After such a successful season, Natalia returned to the Ukok Plateau in the following summers. The excitement caused by her initial discoveries had upped expectations, and in the first subsequent summer a Japanese TV crew came with her to document any new discoveries. But in 1991 they found nothing; and in 1992 they found only a disturbed burial that had not had a sufficiently large kurgan boulder covering to keep it frozen. Spring came late in 1993: the mountain passes through to the Ukok Plateau were clogged with snow until the end of May, and even then the supply trucks could not break through. Natalia had to move her focus of study to be nearer the trucks, in another part of the Ak-Alakh river valley. The first night after setting up camp it snowed so hard that no one in the morning could open the doors of their thin plywood huts they had built for shelter.[30]

Once again, Natalia turned to her Russian military patrol contacts for information on known nearby kurgans. This time the one they pointed her to lay on the other side of a barbed-wire fence. This fence represented the internal border of Russia. The kurgan on the other side was in a no-man's-land buffer zone between the Russian and Chinese borders. Encouraged by the Russian border patrol's assurance that the group would be within firing range so that the soldiers could protect them if anything should happen, the team crossed the wire fence into no-man's-land.[31]

The kurgan, some 18 metres in diameter, was itself in a bad state – already partly demolished after having been used as the base for a previous border defence system.[32] It took the team two weeks to remove the remaining boulders to open up the centre of the kurgan. Natalia's trained eye could see immediately that a 5-metre by 4-metre burial area of disturbed earth lay at its heart, but equally quickly she could see that this area had been intruded into at some point by grave robbers, probably in antiquity. Over twenty-five years later, in 2017, Natalia reflected on this moment in an article she wrote called 'The Ukok Diary'.[33] In it, she explains that she is still not sure why she pressed on with the excavation at that point back in 1993. In part, it was practical. It was early days for the digging season, and if the kurgan turned out to be empty, they still had time to excavate another. But partly there was something else: Natalia felt intuitively that they should dig there.

The team that summer was an eclectic one. Alongside Natalia and her cocker spaniel was a team of labourers, excavation specialists and students. One student, Elena Kunznetsova, was an undergraduate in Novosibirsk completing her field experience for her degree, and the helicopter ride to Ukok had been the first in her life. Others appeared seemingly out of nowhere. Natalia cannot remember how the strong and able Genny from Harvard University came to be part of their team, or how the German tourist Frau Gerda, by chance exploring the Ukok that summer, ended up staying as the camp cook and washer of excavated finds. Nor can she remember where Tei, a Japanese postgraduate student, or Karla, a German undergraduate, appeared from.[34] But together they bonded as they removed the boulders atop the earth, and now began to excavate the earth itself.

Many of the team found being on the Ukok Plateau a surreal experience. The team's dig illustrator, Elena Shumakova, recalls feeling lost on the 'immense serving-plate of the Plateau, with nothing but stars above it'.[35] Border guards would occasionally appear and equally serenely vanish. The silence was pristine. When not working, many of the team went on outings to pick rhubarb and the camp made its own rhubarb jam – a well-known

Ukok delicacy. Other provisions would arrive when a lorry or helicopter could get through. Sometimes it was food, sometimes it
was equipment for the dig or for the camp. One time, Natalia
remembers in her Ukok Diary, the helicopter brought gas masks,
although she is not sure why: 'it seemed as if we were on an island
lost in the ocean, and sometimes waves would wash ashore bread,
tins and letters, and one day even a fridge'.[36] At night, despite the
summer months, the temperatures were cold enough for a thin
skin of ice to form on the nearby lake and for frost to gather on
the flowers and grass of the alpine meadow. These disappeared as
the rising of the sun brought everything back to life for another
day, but as soon as darkness fell, the ice and frost regained the
upper hand once more.[37]

Natalia's memories of the daily life and practicalities of
surviving on the Ukok are so hazy because of her increasing
focus on the burial they were excavating. As she later explained
in her diary, 'every minute of our existence belonged to it, and
it was the pulse of my life'.[38] She was in a sort of trance, 'the
world shrunk to the . . . grave'. At the depth of about a metre
into the ground, the team discovered the skeletons of three
horses, fragments of gold leaf clinging to their still-surviving
harnesses, lying on top of a series of stone slabs. The team
could tell they were not the first to disturb the slabs – ancient
tomb robbers had also got this far. Beneath the slabs, there was
a burial chamber – they found that the body within had been
ruthlessly disturbed, stripped and mangled by tomb robbers on
the hunt for items of value. Next to what remained of the
tangled skeleton lay some sheep bones and a clay drinking cup,
along with some knives – evidence of the meal left for the
deceased in the afterlife.[39]

This disturbed burial sat on top of a series of neatly aligned
logs. Natalia's team could see that the ancient tomb robbers
had not broken through this log floor. Perhaps this was because
they had assumed this was the only burial in the kurgan and
that the logs were its floor. Perhaps, also, it was because the

logs were frozen, placed at just the right distance underground for the magical 'freezer' effect of the Altai kurgans to kick in. But Natalia realised that the logs did not represent the floor, but were the roof of something buried – and frozen – further down. From here on downwards, Natalia's team would be thawing, not excavating, their way into an untouched tomb frozen in time.[40]

As the logs were thawed and removed, revealing a large block of solid ice in the ground underneath, it seemed as though the universe itself was lending a hand in the excavation: the sun, now bearing down directly on the hard, frozen ice, gently turned it soft and granular. The team initially hacked and lifted blocks of loosening ice out of the ground and dumped them at the side of the grave, Natalia's dog, Peter, continuing to demolish them by licking them. Dark shadows began to loom below – the first signs of objects trapped under the ice. The team, conscious that they were nearing the heart of this new burial, turned to subtler thawing techniques. Taking water from the nearby lake, they heated it in buckets with blowtorches, and then scooped up the warm water in metal drinking cups to pour it slowly onto the dissolving ice. The team recall the overwhelming memory of thawing the tomb as having constantly wet feet, sinking into the melting ice, surrounded by rivulets of blowtorched-warmed water mixing with ice-water frozen for millennia.[41]

The dark shadows began to form discernible shapes, before at last becoming free from the ice. A wooden sarcophagus, measuring 2.73 metres long, made out of the trunk of a single larch tree, came into view. Alongside it were two small tables, which had been suspended in the ice off the floor of the tomb. When the rainwater had initially poured into the tomb, the tables must have floated upwards, before being frozen into the ice, as if suspended in the air. On the tables were surviving cuts of rotting meat over 2,000 years old, kept from completely decaying by the ice. On one was a slab of mutton, on the other horsemeat, with a knife stuck into it as if the deceased had been about to cut themselves a piece. The knife's handle was decorated with wolves' faces and ibex horns. The overwhelming sensation for the team now moved from wet feet to the pungent odour of warmed water mixing with two-thousand-year-old defrosting rotted meat, creating a broth of decaying meat juices that ran around the ice floor of the tomb.[42]

They pressed on, melting the ice in the rest of the chamber, but still leaving the larch coffin untouched. More exquisite utensils came into view, all suspended in the ice after having been raised from the floor by the rising tide of rainwater that had cascaded into the tomb over two millennia before. A drinking goblet made of horn cut so thinly it was translucent; jugs decorated with incised designs and leather appliqué in the shape of cockerels; a wooden beaker with a handle carved in the shape of two snow-leopards; the first surviving example of a Pazyryk stirring rod, used to beat milk into kumiss, the preferred yoghurt-like drink of the region in antiquity, as now (the remains of the drink were later discovered inside the wooden beaker). Some of the objects showed signs of repair in antiquity and thus of long use before they had been placed into the tomb.[43]

The tomb itself, located almost 3 metres below the surface of the ground, was made of wooden logs on all four sides, measuring 3.6 metres by 2.3 metres, with a height of just over a metre: like a miniature Swiss chalet buried in the earth. Up against the outside of the northern wall of the tomb, the team discovered more horse burials: six horses laid out in two neat layers of three. The hair of their manes was still intact, as were their plaited tails, the decoration of their harnesses and even parts of their saddles. Their warming remains added to the pungent mix of smells in the damp tomb, not helped when their stomachs were sliced open to remove their contents for analysis. The team, Natalia remembers in her Ukok Diary, came to refer to this heady mix as 'the grave smell: the aroma of a bygone world'.[44]

News about the find spread fast from the Ukok Plateau back to civilisation. By the time the team were ready to open the larch coffin, on 19 July 1993, over a month since they had started excavating the site, they had been joined not only by more colleagues, but also by television crews from National Geographic, Brussels Royal Museum of Art History, as well as Russian state television.[45]

With the cameras rolling, six-inch-long bronze nails, which had held the coffin lid in position, were pulled out and the lid was removed to reveal a coffin full of opaque white ice. Good, Natalia thought, no one had ever found an un-looted coffin full of ice – it boded well for the condition of the body frozen within.[46] Confusion gripped her though when, while patiently melting the ice with cups of warmed water, the top third of the coffin revealed a black shape. What could it be?

At 10.35 a.m., a jawbone emerged through the ice with preserved cheek flesh on it, almost in the middle of the coffin. The body of the deceased, Natalia realised, occupied only two-thirds of the nearly 2.7-metre-long coffin; the remaining third was occupied by the black shape Natalia had seen through the ice. As the ice thinned, this shape turned out to be a tall black felt headdress. More joyously, Natalia could see that flesh had survived on the body, and by that afternoon, a shoulder had appeared covered by a fur blanket. Flesh! Clothes! Natalia caught her breath as she pulled back the fur blanket to reveal the flesh of the shoulder and saw for the first time a bright blue tattoo of a griffin, clear against the still-pale skin.[47]

Over the next days, the full extent of the spectacular nature of the burial find became clear. The three-foot-long headdress was speckled with scraps of gold foil that, Natalia later described, 'lit the dark coffin like candles', and was decorated with fifteen little wooden birds as if they were nesting in a tall tree.[48] A dish of coriander seeds had also been placed in the coffin. The body was not only covered in a fur blanket, but dressed in a surviving maroon and white wool skirt tied with a red wool belt, a yellow silk blouse with a red braid around the neck, as well as white felt stockings on the legs and still-supple leather riding boots on the feet. The body – as the headdress, skirt and blouse made clear – was that of a woman. A mirror lay by her left thigh, as well as some strings of beads. She had gold hoop earrings and a gold-leaf-encrusted wooden necklace in the shape of winged snow-leopards. Her tattoos covered not just her shoulder but both arms from shoulder to hand, as well as her finger joints, representing a series of mythical and real animals inked in dark blue against her creamy white flesh.[49]

Natalia oversaw the investigation of the tomb and of the body of what she and the team now referred to as simply 'the Lady'. Over that summer the Ukok Plateau had, in Natalia's view, never supported so many wildflowers. Nature, she felt, was exalting in her find. At the beginning of August 1993, she oversaw the transfer of the Lady's body from her coffin to a stretcher and covered it in muslin. The body was then lifted on the stretcher out of the grave and carried by six student pall-bearers to a plywood hut on the plateau. The helicopter due to transport the Lady and the team back to Novosibirsk was due on 2 August, but because of a freak heavy snowfall that turned the Ukok into a place of 'blinding whiteness' it could not land for another five days. Everyone felt close to the Lady, checking on her in her plywood home while they waited for Nature to allow them to leave.

After finally boarding the helicopter with the precious cargo and successfully taking off, ninety miles from Novosibirsk, Natalia heard an explosion. The engine had failed and the helicopter had to glide to the ground in an emergency landing. Thankfully, everyone survived. The Lady made the rest of the way by bus to her new home at Natalia's Institute, where she was put in a freezer.[50]

*

Over the next two decades, the myths surrounding the Lady began to swirl around back in the Altai (that she was Ochi-Bala of Altai heroic epic, meant to defend the world against the evil spirits of the Underworld). Then the debate caught fire about whether the 'Princess of Altai' should be returned to her homeland, and the ban on any further excavation on the Ukok Plateau was imposed. Stories of 'the mummy's' mystical power to cause harm to those who crossed her path (starting with the story of the helicopter crash) began to gather momentum.

In the midst of all this, Natalia and her team continued to use every scientific avenue of investigation possible to better understand the Lady and her life story as well as the nature of her ancient Pazyryk community.[51] By conducting analysis on the logs of the tomb's walls, as well as the larch coffin itself, the team realised that the wood for the tomb and coffin had been brought from a forest over fifteen miles away. From the tree rings, they could tell that the wood had been felled (and thus the burial taken place) around the end of the fourth century BCE – a few decades after Alexander the Great had conquered the Persian Achaemenid Empire to the west.[52] The logs from the burial walls had been felled some years before those of the larch trunk coffin: likely they had been used to construct huts for the Pazyryk to live in before they were used to construct this tomb. Even more specifically, Natalia's team could tell that the larch wood trunk for the coffin had been felled in the early summertime. This was confirmed by the contents of the horses' stomachs; inside they found a partially digested mix of grass, twigs and pine needles, and close analysis of their stages of cellular growth, along with the pollen residues, as well as the presence of larvae of horse flies, indicated that the horses' last meal had been in mid-June. They had been deliberately killed with blows to the head, and then lifted neatly into the space by the side of the tomb.[53]

A June burial makes sense: this was the time when the ground on the Ukok Plateau was unfrozen and soft enough to be diggable. Yet when the post-mortem was conducted on the body of the Lady soon after her bumpy journey to Novosibirsk, the specialists concluded from the state of her skin that the Lady's death had actually taken place some three to six months before she was buried, in the middle of winter. The body had also been entirely mummified. The pathologists found that all her internal organs, including her brain and her eyes, even the mucous membranes of her nose, had been removed and her body stuffed with a mix of earth, dry grass and horsehair to preserve it. In among the dried grass and horsehair a peat-like substance was found, which was later discovered to be the mashed-up remains of her organs. Her skin had even been treated with a resin-like substance (later discovered to be mercury) to aid its preservation. This Lady had died and her body been mummified and treated, then kept in the community, until the ground was soft enough to dig up. Only then was it possible to construct her tomb and conduct the funerary ritual.[54]

Natalia was sure the Lady was someone important to her community. This entire tomb, including the enormous larch trunk coffin, had been constructed just for her – with significant effort from the community to bring the wood required from over fifteen miles away. It was set in a prominent part of the Ak-Alakh river valley on the Ukok Plateau. Moreover, it was not, as with other Pazyryk tombs that had been discovered, amid a cluster of other tombs as part of a cemetery, but instead stood all on its own (bar the burial of the man directly above her). It had been filled with a range of well-made beautiful objects and a magnificent meal. Six healthy and ornately harnessed horses had been sacrificed on her behalf. The Lady herself had been buried in a magnificent gold-leaf-flecked headdress, and her clothes – especially the silk blouse – spoke to her being the recipient of expensive goods traded across the Steppe (the silk, originally thought to have come from China, was later identified to have come from northern-eastern India).[55] The coriander seeds found by her head (which had previously only been found in very elite Pazyryk burials) were analysed and shown to have come from western Asia Minor, perhaps even bordering on the Mediterranean.[56] The dyes used to colour her skirt, like those used for a number of Pazyryk textiles discovered in other elite tombs, came from various far-flung places, including the Eastern Mediterranean, modern-day Iran, India and China.[57]

More mysterious was the male burial found directly above hers. Initially it was thought that the presence of this body indicated there was later reuse of the burial kurgan by another nomadic group. But on further examination it appeared the man had in fact probably been buried simultaneously with the Lady below. The man, a post-mortem revealed, had been intentionally killed by a blow to the back of the head with an obtuse object. The pathology of the blow showed that it had been delivered as the man bent his head and provided no resistance. Like the horses, he had, most likely, been sacrificed to accompany the dead woman. Detailed analysis of the surviving bones (which had been disturbed by tomb raiders) revealed evidence that there had in fact originally been two people buried in this upper tomb: the man and an adolescent girl aged just nine to ten years old (although it was impossible to ascertain the cause of her death). Perhaps not just one, but two lives had been sacrificed for the Lady?[58]

The Lady was no 'Amazonian' warrior – no weapons were found buried with her. She was not engaged in heavy manual labour, as the post-mortem had also made clear from the study of the condition of her skin and bones. Her heavily tattooed body – something only seen in the more elite Pazyryk burials discovered – put her on the same level of importance as the male 'chieftain' body covered in tattoos discovered by Rudenko in the 1940s. Was she a princess, the daughter of a ruler? Or was she, as Natalia began to believe, a member of the Pazyryk community who had been revered for her special knowledge: perhaps as a storyteller or healer?[59]

The study of the Lady's body, particularly the fissure lines of her skull, revealed she had been just twenty-five to thirty years old when she died.[60] Yet the post-mortem conducted soon after her body was taken to Novosibirsk could not establish her cause of death. It was only later that MRI scanning of her surviving body parts revealed what had probably killed her: the Lady had developed breast cancer. She had suffered for many years before her death with a tumour in her right breast, spreading to her lymph nodes, which seems to have finally caused her demise, no doubt bringing with it severe pain and trauma.[61] Yet this was not all – it seems the Lady also suffered damage to her right hip, knee joint and shoulder during her lifetime, perhaps from falling off a horse.[62] A special technique called synchrotron X-ray fluorescence – which allows for the identification of minute quantities (down to a single atom!) of individual elements – was applied to the Lady's hair and nails. It revealed that she had not only often breathed in hemp vapour, which has a narcotic effect (perhaps helping to ease her pain), but that, in doing so, because the hemp had been burnt in a bronze incense burner, she had also been gradually poisoning herself with copper vapour.[63]

Nor was she the only person to have suffered pain during her lifetime. The male buried above her (and seemingly sacrificed as part of her burial) suffered from spina bifida throughout his life, preventing him from walking in an upright posture without incredible difficulty and distress. The stresses on his bones and pelvis suggest that he had compensated for this by spending most of his days on horseback.[64]

For Natalia, the job of piecing this picture together has defined her career. She believes that the Lady – perhaps because of her constant pain and suffering thanks to her cancer – was considered by her community as a kind of shaman: 'The illness, with unexplainable supernatural origin, made her stand out from the crowd.'[65] The scholar Mircea Eliade, an expert on Shamanism across different ancient societies, has said that the figure of the shaman was one who 'experienced the sacred with a greater intensity than the rest of the society'.[66] The Lady was, in Natalia's words, perhaps regarded as 'the Spirits' Chosen One' because of her illness and affliction, becoming a respected and important figure in the community, who required a magnificent and in many ways unique burial. Perhaps this explains the sacrifice of the man, similarly suffering and thus perhaps thought in some way to be another chosen by the Spirits, buried with honour above her. His (and the young girl's who was buried with him) was a respectable, if less elite, burial than that of the Lady's. Perhaps he was her assistant, accompanying her in life and in death. If so, he can be said to have made not only the final sacrifice in the form of his life, but to have successfully protected her after death. After all, it was his tomb that grave robbers found and desecrated, before giving up and not bothering to probe further to discover the Lady beneath.[67]

Natalia believes that the Lady was near death from her breast cancer when her Pazyryk community, in the late fourth century BCE, made the annual winter move in October time up to the Ukok Plateau to make use of its exposed grassland through the winter. She would have been moved on horseback, and, because of her extremely ill state, perhaps this was when she sustained her fall, damaging her hip, shoulder and arm. From the October through to her death, probably in the following January, she may have been largely bedridden and in agony. Following her death, the community mummified her body and kept it, waiting for the ground to thaw in June and for her burial to be undertaken.[68] It is not without irony that both her burial and discovery 2,000 years later were accompanied by an enforced period of waiting: in the fourth century BCE, for the summer to come and the ground to thaw in order to bury her, and in 1993, following a freak summer snowstorm, for conditions to improve before the corpse could be taken from the Ukok to Novosibirsk. We are, it seems, always at the mercy of the elements.

*

Since that unforgettable summer of 1993, Natalia and her team have not just been at the epicentre of an extraordinary story of discovery (the first mummified and tattooed body, in an undisturbed frozen burial, to be found in the Altai in nearly forty years), but have, thanks to their own pioneering scientific work, only added to the value of their discovery with their piercing, and emotive, insights into the life and death of this important woman and her attendant. Their work has been celebrated accordingly: in 2004, Natalia was announced the winner of the State Prize of the Russian Federation, and in 2006 she was awarded the National Heritage Award – two of the most prestigious academic awards in Russia. Natalia has also dedicated considerable time to ensuring that the wonder of her discoveries is communicated far outside the academic community: through articles at the time of the discovery for *National Geographic*, to TV documentaries with PBS and an ongoing series of articles in the public-facing journal *Science First Hand* explaining each stage of the scientific investigations into the Lady. What impresses me most about these articles is Natalia's openness about her thoughts, feelings and emotions during the journey – from her first helicopter ride to the Ukok, to the intense experience of discovery, to the patient slow ongoing work of scientific analysis.

Given the spectacular nature of the discovery and the thorough ways in which it has been communicated to the world by Natalia, it is perhaps no surprise that it has been the excavation, removal and study particularly of the Lady, as opposed to any of the other Pazyryk bodies found in this tomb and in others across the Altai both before and after 1993, that has become the focus of so much public consternation, debate and legend. The Lady – and Natalia – have been victims of their own success. To a certain extent, Natalia accepts this. She understands, as she has put it in her own writings, that 'history needs personalities' in order for our past to remain relevant to today'.[69]

I spoke with Natalia by email in May 2021 to follow up with her on the latest developments surrounding the Lady and her reactions to them. Natalia reiterated to me that she did not begrudge the decision, in 2012, to return the mummified body of the Lady/Princess of Altai/Ochi-Bala to the Altai, even though she did not attend the return ceremony.[70] What she minds is that, since 2012, the Lady has, as a result, not been made available for further scientific investigation, but has been kept rather, as she put it to me, as an 'object of worship and as a sensational exhibit'. She feels frustration that as new questions and scientific techniques of discovery arise, she and her team won't be able to apply them to the Lady: 'We can do nothing,' she says. Moreover, she believes the ongoing decision to ban further excavation of burials on the Ukok Plateau is 'unreasonable' and has 'brought nothing but harm'.[71]

The ban on excavation on the Ukok Plateau is further muddied by a geopolitical controversy that has lasted almost as long as that of the Princess of Altai. In 2006, the Russian company Gazprom – the world's largest producer of natural gas – signed an agreement with the China National Petroleum Corporation to build a 2,600-kilometre gas pipeline from north-west Siberia, through the Altai, and specifically the Ukok Plateau, into China. The proposal was heavily criticised, not least for the plan to run the pipeline through the Ukok Plateau given the spiritual importance of this place for the Altai elders, the ban on excavation there and its designation as a 'Quiet Zone' by the Altai regional government, as well as its designation as a UNESCO World Heritage Site. But after Gazprom put up 697 million roubles (out of a total cost of 746 million) to fund the brand-new Anokhin National Museum, located in the Altai's capital of Gorno-Altaysk – the museum that clinched the deal for the return of the princess's body to the Altai in 2012 – the regional government subsequently dropped its opposition to Gazprom's plans and gave them permission to begin construction.[72] It is only legal and regulatory challenges by Greenpeace-Russia and others that has prevented construction starting. Since then, the possibility of a gas pipeline across the Ukok Plateau has hovered worryingly in the background.[73] While Gazprom currently say they have no active plans for this, in 2019 they opened the 'Power of Siberia' pipeline, which crosses into China further to the east as part of a 400-billion-dollar deal with

China to supply them with gas for the next ten years. In order to supply the amount of gas agreed, Russia will need to build more pipelines.[74] The 'Power of Siberia 2' pipeline is earmarked to run through the Altai and potentially once again through the Ukok Plateau.

This is not the only threat hanging over the Ukok Plateau. Climate change is causing a destabilisation of the permafrost cycle in the Altai. While this has a range of problematic impacts for the region's ecology and biodiversity, it also presents a special threat to the as-yet-unexcavated frozen tombs that are unique to this region. The gradual warming of the planet means that the delicate balance in the Altai region that has, for over 2,000 years, kept frozen the tombs hidden beneath rock-boulder kurgans is starting to tip. The tombs, frozen in ice for so long, are starting to thaw in the summer months. That means their contents – kept up to now in pristine condition, like that of the Lady's burial, for so long – will start to decay. The potential for discovery about the communities that roamed this important part of the world in antiquity is, quite literally, slipping through our fingers.

Urgent research projects have sought to identify still-frozen tombs across the Altai (over 9,000 were identified) as a first step towards potentially artificially maintaining their frozen state using cooling technology until they (or at least some of them) can be excavated. All of this puts a question mark on the usefulness of the ongoing ban on excavation of the Ukok Plateau, which, while seeking to protect this hallowed ground, may well, if no compromise can be found, end up forcing us to stand on the sidelines as the remains of the past that have been preserved there for so long now thaw out and decay.[75] Indeed, Natalia commented to me when we spoke that she is not sure we can still assume there are any frozen tombs left untouched by the changing climate.[76] The clock is clearly ticking.

Natalia, when she first came face to face with the body of the Lady as it emerged from the ice back in 1993, remembers saying,

'Forgive me', as she disturbed the princess's millennia-long slumber.[77] She still worries about her role in bringing the Lady to such world attention. An ethnographer friend once told her: 'If She [the Lady] had not wanted it, you would never have found her.'[78] Natalia agrees, but still wonders why the Lady wanted to be found. Was it to rise again as a figure of mystical power, cursing those who came into contact with her and protecting her realm from modern-day evils, such as Covid-19? Was it to stand once again as a symbol of the Altai in a period when it is under threat from national and world politics, not to mention climate change?[79] Or was it, as Natalia believes, to tell us something about her world of the past?

Our job, not only as archaeologists but as humanity in general, Natalia says, is to listen.[80] Natalia has listened to what the science could tell her about the body of the Lady and her effects. Since 2012 and the return of the Lady to Altai, she has combined what the Lady revealed with knowledge gained from other Pazyryk excavations to understand better their culture. And while the Ukok Plateau remains out of bounds, Natalia's latest investigations have taken her up to Kashmir, India, following up on archaeological and anthropological evidence pointing to this part of the world being one of the origin points of the Pazyryk people.[81] Who knows what she might uncover next?

The case of the Lady is clearly an important one in the evolving debate about how, where and by whom the past should be managed and cared for. Crucially, it has thrown into sharp relief the very difficult and delicate ongoing balancing act that is required after an object is returned to its place of discovery: between exciting wider public interest in the past, acting on the beliefs and desires of local communities, and the preservation of space for ongoing research. And for me, the Lady in the twenty-first millennium, well over 2,000 years since she died, has highlighted another increasingly crucial element to factor into that ongoing balancing act. The story of her survival and discovery demonstrates how past – and potential future – discoveries are at the mercy of wider geopolitical, and now climatic, shifts, affecting not just when and how they will be uncovered and studied, but whether they will survive at all. It remains to be seen whether we will choose to listen to the Lady in time.

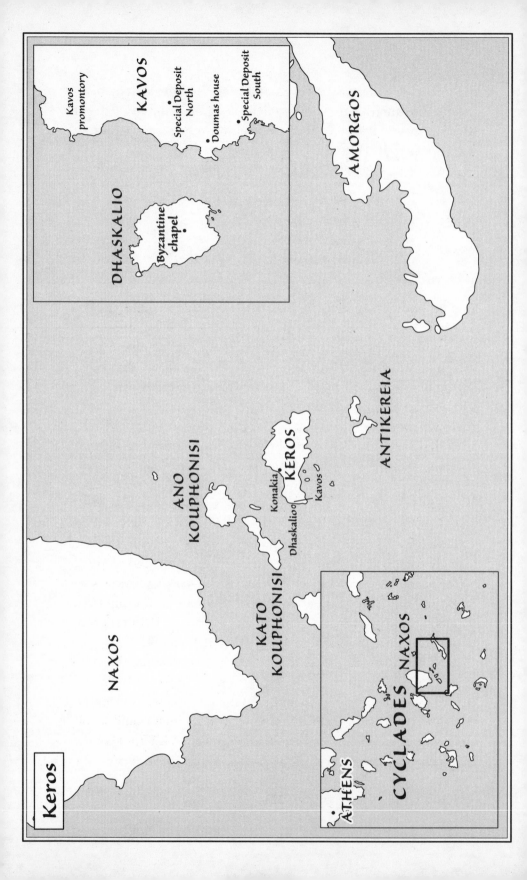

8

A Find Over Time[1]

In the Louvre Museum in Paris sits a mysterious and ancient object. It is a bewitchingly beautiful thing to look at: an oval head almost 30 centimetres tall carved in smooth shining marble with just the nose protruding from the front and two small ears jutting out from the back of an otherwise flat faceless head. The face's smooth surface is marred only by a chip in the marble over the lower right jawline, as if it has recently been in a fist fight. The head has been carved with light-touch attention to human features, and this somewhat simplified and ennobled representation of the 'essence' of humanity has led to comparisons being drawn to the work of modern sculptors and painters like Matisse and Henry Moore.

However, this marble fragment is far from modern – it was lovingly carved in the third millennium BCE and lay undiscovered on the island of Keros, a speck of rock in the Greek Cyclades, until 1873, just over fifty years after hieroglyphs had been deciphered thanks to the Rosetta Stone. We call this period in the Mediterranean during the third millennium BCE, when this marble head was created, the 'Early Bronze Age'. It was the period when the great Minoan and Mycenaean palace civilisations of Crete and mainland Greece were still only in their embryonic stage; and was well over a thousand years before either the Uluburun cargo ship would set off on its voyage around the Eastern Mediterranean (c.1300 BCE) or the Mycenaean Greeks gathered to besiege Troy (c.1250 BCE).

A decade after this first fragment was discovered, in 1884 Ulrich Köhler, who ran the German Archaeological Institute in Athens, found two more figurines on Keros. This time they weren't monumental in size like the Louvre head, they were tiny. But it was their small size and exquisite detail that took the breath away. One depicted a seated lyre player and the other a standing double-flute player, both, like the Louvre head, dating from the third millennium BCE.[2]

No one had ever imagined that cultures this old were capable of such creations. In the decade after these discoveries, the label 'Cycladic civilisation' was coined – given Keros is part of the Cycladic islands of the Aegean – to describe the people who had created these wonders. But no surviving literary sources spoke of the meaning and purpose of such figurines. Were they linked to religious worship? Or were they 'artistic' work, part of everyday living?

Despite these mysterious discoveries, no further investigation was conducted on Keros, partly because no one could believe it had itself ever been an important cultural centre. Keros today is one of the largest uninhabited islands in the Mediterranean, home to wild rabbits, hares, rock pigeons, dense scrub and dwarf juniper. There is only one mention of Keros in all the surviving written sources from antiquity: as an island that paid tax as part of the Athenian Empire in the fifth century BCE: the paltry sum of 10 drachma and 3 obols.[3] Seemingly insignificant to the historical narrative, even its name, Keros, was only officially noted, for the first time since antiquity, thirty years before the discovery of the Louvre head. And for much of the nineteenth century the island belonged to the monastery on Amorgos, a larger nearby island, which used it for pasture for sheep and goats. Not exactly a beacon of civilisation.

But one man in particular, with the help of an ever-expanding team of specialists, would change our knowledge – and the reputation – of Keros for ever, and with it open our eyes to the extraordinary achievements of early Mediterranean civilisation.

*

In 1949, Colin Renfrew, aged twelve, travelled with his parents in his dad's red MG sports car from their home in Stockton-on-Tees near Newcastle to France and Italy for their summer holidays. It was Colin's first visit to the Continent. They went to the Louvre in Paris and Colin stood in front of the marble head from Keros. When I spoke to now-Professor Lord Colin Renfrew by Zoom in February 2021, he recalled how this moment was the first time in his life he came face to face with the Early Bronze Age.[4]

Their journey then took them on to Italy, towards Pompeii and Herculaneum, and when their MG's engine broke down, they passed the time waiting for it to be fixed by visiting the Etruscan site of Cerveteri. Colin was hooked on the past. Returning home, as a schoolboy he took part in excavations at Canterbury each holiday, and he and his father visited medieval parish churches together by bicycle whenever they could.[5]

As so often happens, however, Colin felt the pressure to study something more immediately 'relevant' to the world. He focused on the sciences in his last years of school and in 1958, after completing his military service in the RAF, he began a degree in Natural Sciences at Cambridge. But it only takes one moment to tip the balance of a life's direction. Colin spent the summer of 1960 on an exchange with Perugia University. Inspired by his impromptu visit to Cerveteri back when he was twelve, he decided to attend a course of lectures on the Etruscans. He recounted to me with a chuckle how, on returning to Cambridge that autumn, he surprised everyone with the bold and unusual decision to drop Natural Sciences and study Archaeology and Anthropology instead.[6] And it is lucky for Keros that he did.

In the 1928 Greek census, Keros was listed as having just twelve inhabitants. It was used by Greek and Italian soldiers as a refuge during the Second World War and suffered a series of earthquakes in the late 1950s that cut off access to most of the natural water sources on the island, making habitation there all the more difficult. By 1961 the Greek census recorded just eight people living on Keros.[7] But that was not the worst fate to befall the island.

The 1950s were a crucial period for the worldwide recognition of the beauty – and modern-day value – of ancient Cycladic figurines. In part this was the inevitable outcome of the greater academic study, discovery and excavation of Early Bronze Age ('Cycladic') civilisation, which had kicked off since the discovery of that first Keros head back in 1873. But it was also thanks to the way in which the focus and passion of the modern art world in the 1950s, bewitched as it was by the abstract sculptural work of artists like Henry Moore, Jean Arp and Constantin Brâncuşi, chimed with the style of these enigmatic and yet enchanting Cycladic figurines. Private buyers now wanted these ancient pieces, inspired by the ways in which these millennia-old sculptures echoed modern ideals of the essence of beauty and humanity. Shady dealers were willing to sell them. And looters now had a market to fence them to. The robbing of unprotected archaeological sites where these figurines had been found took off.

Keros, already known as the font of some beautiful examples of Cycladic figurines and practically uninhabited and definitely unprotected, was a prime target for looting. Aerial reconnaissance photos taken during and after the Second World War show that between 1945 and 1960 areas of dense scrub on the western edge of the island were brazenly cleared by looters to make their illegal excavations easier.[8] In a recent Greek TV documentary, elderly inhabitants of the nearby island of Ano Kouphonisi, who were kids back in the 1950s, recall the shadowy comings and goings by boat at night.[9] It was an all too familiar occurrence, which they were advised to simply ignore. Sometimes they were even given ancient marble Cycladic figurines to play with and make clothes for, 'like dolls'.[10] Keros, with a declining population and no one to defend it or the antiquities buried within it, was, it seems, systematically ravaged.

Colin, now in his final year of his undergraduate studies in Archaeology and Anthropology, still did not know how much his life would become entwined with Keros. In 1962 he was casting around for a subject area for his PhD. His first thought was the Etruscans – the reason he had got into archaeology. But again, one's life course can sometimes depend on single moments. In the summer of his final year, Colin visited the National Archaeological Museum in Athens and saw for the first time the sheer numbers of Cycladic figurines in their collection. His response was both emotional and intellectual: as he explained to me in our Zoom interview, he was captivated by their beauty but also inspired by the lack of concrete knowledge about them and the culture that produced them.[11] Here was a topic an ambitious young scholar could make waves with.

The first job was to survey all the known sites in the Cycladic islands where these figurines had been excavated to understand more about the figurines and their contexts. Colin's PhD supervisor introduced him to Christos Doumas, who since 1960 had been part of the Ephorate (the Greek Archaeological Department) responsible for Athens and the Cycladic islands. At a dinner in Athens, Doumas mentioned to Colin the island of Keros as a site he should visit, even though Doumas himself had not yet been there.[12] But friends of his – the very wealthy Greek philanthropists Nikolaos and Dolly Goulandris, who had seen how disturbed the ground on Keros was from aboard their luxurious private yacht while cruising around the islands – had told him about it.[13] Dolly and Niko, as they were known, had an eye – and a concern – for Cycladic sites, having recently started, with the permission of the Greek state, their own private collection of Cycladic art. If Keros was a site attracting looters, as Dolly and Niko's observations seemed to suggest, then it was one the Greek archaeological authorities wanted to know more about. Their resources, however, were stretched thin across multiple islands – roughly two hundred and twenty at the last count. Asking Colin to include the site in his PhD survey was a good way of covering more ground.

So, on 24 July 1963, Colin Renfrew hired a small boat to take him from the island of Ano Kouphonisi, an island then without electricity, to the even smaller island of Keros. He landed at Konakia, an area on the island's north side, where a small group of people still lived during the summer season. He asked them for directions to the area where digging had taken place. They were 'affable', he later recorded in his journal, but unhelpful.[14] Reduced to exploring the western half of the island himself, after an hour's search in the burning sun, he came across what Dolly and Niko Goulandris had seen from the sea. On a steep slope of the island's west coast, he found the epicentre of the looting activity. Renfrew was stunned by the still-plentiful ancient material strewn on the surface – unlike any other Cycladic site he had visited on his survey.[15] Visiting separately at another time, Christos Doumas described the scene as 'a true Waterloo', with fragments of ancient figurines and other pottery strewn around 'like potatoes'.[16] Renfrew recorded in his journal the scene more prosaically as 'very rich, very tragic'. Armed as he was with a permit to collect surface samples, he gathered what he could, washed it, recorded it and delivered it to the Naxos Museum (the central store for Cycladic collections). On the one hand, the sheer volume of marble material suggested to him that this site may have been an ancient workshop. On the other hand, given that this was the material the looters had left behind strewn on the surface, what kind of extraordinary finds had they made off with?[17]

Shortly after Renfrew's visit to Keros in summer 1963, Christos Doumas, as part of the Greek Archaeological Service overseeing the Cyclades, was tasked with going back to the ravaged island. In September he returned, funded by Dolly and Niko Goulandris, to conduct a short excavation in the area of the looting. He, like Colin, continued to find lots of figurine fragments scattered in the area that had been looted. Yet Doumas cast his net wider, excavating at different points across this western pinnacle of the island, but also crossing to a tiny bullet-shaped islet 90 metres off the western coast of Keros, called Dhaskalio, to search for ancient remains. On the western shore of Keros, he found the remains of a small ancient building, which has since then been known simply as 'the Doumas house'. And on Dhaskalio, at the summit, he found the remains of a (much later) Byzantine chapel.[18] Perhaps, thought Doumas, the site on the western shore of Keros was an ancient cemetery? This might account for the large number of figurines buried in the ground – maybe the figurines were grave offerings to honour and accompany the dead.

Keros was becoming a place of interest – perhaps for the first time since the Bronze Age. In November 1966, a brief survey of the entire island was conducted by the Greek Archaeological Services, and in July 1967, a full excavation team camped on the island for just over three weeks. During their time excavating, they too were overwhelmed by the quantities of ancient Cycladic material coming out of this small patch of sloped ground on the western side of the island. At the end of each day of excavation, the team filled several large wooden boxes – normally used by Aegean fisherman to pack their catch – with fragments of figurines, bowls and other vessels, and sent them for safe keeping to the Archaeological Services headquarters at the museum on the island of Naxos. Over fifteen thousand pieces of ancient pottery had now been legally excavated from this tiny site on this practically uninhabited island between 1963 and 1967 – far surpassing the quantities known from any other ancient cemetery site from the same period.

More intriguingly, no tell-tale 'schist slabs' – slabs that were normally used to cover over graves in this period – had been discovered. And even more intriguingly, there were almost no human bones. If this was a cemetery, where were the remains of those buried? And why were the figurines, bowls and other vessels all in such a fragmentary condition? Some argued that this was the result of the looting – careless breakage by thoughtless excavators. But others in the team felt this could not be the only answer – after all, looters wanted nice pieces to fence on. It was not in their interest to break everything they found.[19]

These questions demanded answers, but no one had them, nor the money or the time to conduct further investigations. Doumas was also almost totally occupied from 1968 with the site of Akrotiri on the island of Santorini, an excavation he would in turn direct from 1975, as well as becoming Professor of Archaeology at the University of Athens. The Greek Archaeological Service had quite literally a sea full of islands to look after.

And yet Keros kept turning up – sadly in darker circumstances. In 1976, an exhibition was hosted on the 'Art and Culture of the Cyclades' at the Badisches Landesmuseum in Karlsruhe, Germany, which included pieces 'from Keros', supposedly from a larger collection based in Basel, Switzerland. The Basel collectors had purchased the objects from an anonymous dealer. It was not long before this collection was being called the 'Keros Hoard' – almost certainly items looted from Keros in the 1950s.[20] Keros itself – and all the precious ancient material it still hid within its soils – remained unguarded and uninterpreted, its shores untouched by further – legal – investigation since 1967. Understanding what Keros was in the Early Bronze Age – and thus what there was to protect there – was becoming more urgent.

*

1983: Colin Renfrew was now the Disney Professor of Archaeology at the University of Cambridge – one of the most esteemed archaeological positions in the world.[21] He had led excavations at several sites elsewhere in the Cyclades, as well as in Northern Greece, and even back in the Orkney Islands. While not excavating or teaching, he had been publishing vociferously: about the sites he had been excavating; on the new techniques of radiocarbon dating and their applicability to ancient Aegean cultures; on models to explain the development of ancient societies; on the recognition of particular 'cultures' of peoples in the Aegean through the different ways in which they had carved their Cycladic figurines; as well as on the wider picture of the development of early civilisation in the Aegean. Many of his books had become seminal works in the field, and Colin's expertise and insight were in demand all over the world. And yet, in all that time, he had not gone back to Keros since his visit twenty years earlier.

Keros was, however, becoming increasingly central to academic debates on the nature of the civilisations that had existed in the Early Bronze Age. In 1983, Renfrew attended a British Museum conference, focused on the purpose and meaning of Cycladic figurines. The conference brought together all the major players associated with Keros over the last twenty years in one room: Renfrew, Doumas, Photeini Zapheiropoulou from the Greek Archaeological Service who had conducted the 1967 excavations, as well as a host of scholars with expertise from different sites around the Aegean. The attention brought to Keros by the recent flaunting of looted finds from the island only focused minds further on trying to understand what this site was. Was it a cemetery? In which case where were the bones? Where were the telltale schist slab coverings? Was it a settlement? But if so, where were the buildings and other signs of habitation? Was it a kind of religious sanctuary? Possible – but the sheer volume of material that had been found (on top of that which had been lost to looters) made this unlike anything seen elsewhere in the Aegean. And why was everything in such a broken state?

Colin remarked to me in our Zoom conversation how he still remembers the mood at the end of that conference: everyone realised more needed to be done about Keros. No longer could it sink to the bottom of everyone's to-do lists.[22] A plan was hatched to link Keros to the nearby island of Amorgos (whose monastery had controlled Keros through the nineteenth century) and include it in a new excavation project about to get underway on Amorgos. In August 1987, a team, led by Doumas, Renfrew and Lila Marangou, a Greek archaeologist who had already worked extensively on Amorgos, spent two weeks excavating on Keros.

The last semi-permanent inhabitants of Keros had left in the 1970s. The island was now used for occasional grazing for, and hunting of, animals. It was largely silent, with no easily accessible freshwater sources, shelter, drainage or food supplies. How do you excavate on an island like that? The group decided to base themselves on the nearby island of Ano Kouphonisi and replicate what Renfrew had done on his first visit to Keros: they hired Rousetos Prasinos, a local caique-boat captain, to ferry them to Keros each morning and back each evening, where they stayed in a small hotel owned by the Platis family, using one of its rooms as a makeshift laboratory for the study of finds. Colin loved the early-morning boat ride to Keros, which set off at 6 a.m. Moving through the calm waters of the crystal-clear Aegean Sea as the sun appears on the horizon and warms the air around you, he said, 'makes you feel that every day is a new beginning'.[23]

The team had two main priorities.[24] First, to investigate properly the area that had been disturbed by looters and subsequently briefly examined in the 1960s follow-up visits and excavations; and second, to conduct a full surface survey of this western end of the island to provide a context for the area of excavation. The first priority was something of a thankless task. The goal of an excavation is to map – in three dimensions – exactly where objects are found so that the 'stratigraphy' – the different levels of use of the site – can be established and the site's evolution better understood. In essence you are trying to create a picture of an area as if it were a cake and you had cut a slice through it and were looking at all the different layers of filling piled one on top of the other. Imagine doing that in an area where years of looting as well as several previous excavations have made more mess of the site than a giant in a sandpit (or indeed a toddler who had got hold of your cake!).

The second priority – the survey of the western end of the island – inspired hope that it would bring more clarity to the picture of what Keros was in antiquity. Yet both tasks actually ended up contributing further to Keros's mystery and to the debate swirling around it. Renfrew led the excavation of the looted/excavated area, which was now called the 'special deposit', because of the numbers of figurine and pottery fragments that had been found. The team were unable to tell anything about the stratigraphy of the special deposit because it had been so disturbed. But they found no traces of any kind of structure and no traces of burials. On the other hand, they continued to find new fragments of figurines and pottery – adding to the enormous amount that had already been excavated from this location over the previous decades (not to mention whatever had been looted before then). The survey team similarly found huge amounts of ancient pottery and other ancient materials across the surface of the western end of the island. In all, 18,398 pieces of pottery were collected in 1987 from the survey and excavation. What was most intriguing, though, was that the analysis showed that a large percentage of the pieces had actually been brought to Keros from elsewhere in antiquity.[25]

This new information led to even more questions and uncertainties than before. The team could not agree on what this influx of evidence told them about the nature of ancient activity on Keros – except that the island was obviously a place of huge importance in antiquity. The Keros mystery had now graduated to become the 'Keros Enigma'.

Over time, between the team members, three competing explanations for Keros continued to find favour. Doumas argued that the site may have been considered in antiquity as a mysterious entry point into the Underworld, thus attracting the dedication of so many figurines, but perhaps fewer actual burials.[26]

The survey team argued a more prosaic explanation: that the 'special deposit' was a cemetery and that the surrounding areas, given the huge amount of pottery found, could well have been the settlement. They explained the high levels of imports on the basis that this settlement on Keros was a crucial trading centre, one of the key island trading centres of the period.[27] For them, Keros was an important site, but not in any way an enigma.

Renfrew, however, was increasingly convinced that the site had little to do with the dead, or with trade. For him, the quality and sheer number of the ancient figurine, bowl and vessel finds, as well as the absence of burials and obvious structures for settlement, meant that the site felt more like a shrine, a place of religious worship. And the fact that so much of the material came from elsewhere made him think that this was a shrine that attracted people from a much wider area than just Keros and its nearby islands. But what about the fact that so much of the material was broken?

The only way to find a solution, Renfrew realised, was to examine every broken piece and look in detail at the break-lines. So began the painstakingly slow process of examining the breakage points of the thousands of figurines that had been found since the 1960s. Carefully examining each one by hand, Renfrew sought to determine whether the breakage had happened in modern times (at the hands of looters, or due to disturbance at the site) or in ancient times. For him, the evidence was clear: nearly all the figurines had been broken in antiquity. In Keros, he was looking – he believed – at a site of ritual where people had come in large numbers from many different places to deposit in the ground intentionally broken pieces of expensive figurines and pottery.[28] Such a ritual practice was otherwise unknown in the Aegean. For Renfrew, Keros was now an enigma of an even bigger magnitude: who were these people coming to Keros, where did they come from, and what were they doing by smashing pottery?

The answer to the Keros Enigma had to wait until the new millennium. In 2004, Renfrew achieved a new high in his already glittering career: the award of the Balzan Prize. This is no ordinary ceremonial commemoration – each award comes with a cheque for roughly 700,000 euros. Renfrew was sixty-seven years old and had just retired as the Disney Professor of Archaeology at Cambridge. For many, this would be the point, after such an illustrious and full career, of relaxation. But Renfrew was itching to take his new free time, and the Balzan prize money, and put them both to good use. Having spent some of the award setting up a new research post in archaeology at Cambridge, he used the rest to plan a new assault on the Keros Enigma.

So on 3 May 2006, a new team from Cambridge took the caique journey across the quiet morning Aegean Sea to Keros, captained this time by Kostas Prasinos, the son of Rousetos, who had taken the team across back in 1987. The team were staying on Ano Kouphonisi, again in the same hotel belonging to the Platis family that Renfrew had stayed in as part of the 1987 campaign.[29] I was a PhD student at the time, working at the British School in Athens, which was the base for the Cambridge Keros team before they left for the islands. I saw first-hand the careful preparations that went into the expedition. The crucial focus was on food; Keros was still uninhabited, without freshwater supplies, shelter, shade or drainage. The team would be on the island from dawn until mid-afternoon every day for six weeks. While on Keros, each member of the team had to be entirely self-reliant for food and water. That meant tinned sardines – and lots of them. Renfrew, as he told me with a smile in our Zoom interview, is a great believer in the nutritional value, taste and ease of travel of a tinned sardine.[30] As a result I saw stockpiled at the British School of Athens hundreds of sardine tins ready to transport to Ano Kouphonisi alongside the archaeological equipment necessary for the excavation. Each team member would thus take with them every morning aboard the caique their archaeological tools, some fresh tomatoes and bread, as well as bottled water, and of course, a tin of sardines.

Renfrew had a clear plan for that first season of excavation in 2006: he was determined to begin the assault on unravelling the Keros Enigma once and for all. The 1987 surface survey had indicated a potential hotspot of finds about 110 metres south of the 'special deposit' area he had investigated back in 1987.[31] Having sent in a team to clear away the harsh scrub from this area so as to expose the ground for digging (as the looters had done some time between 1945 and 1960 over the area to the north), the excavators set to work.[32] This was a difficult dig. Forget the daily transportation to and from Ano Kouphonisi or the challenges of having a large team effectively marooned on an island every day for six weeks living off sardines, bread and water. The area they were intending to excavate was on a 14- to 18-degree uneven, rocky slope descending down into the sea, without shade from the sun and perfectly positioned so as to be exposed to the whipping *meltemi* winds of the Aegean. The winds were so strong that the team's best friend – after their tinned sardines of course – was the elastic band. Bagfuls of these were needed to secure everything in order to prevent it being stolen by the nimble winds that swirled around the island – especially the precious pages of notes each team member was taking about everything they found. On certain days the winds could be so strong that they would whip up the dust, earth and sand from the exposed hillside and send it hurtling towards the team. Many chose to wear swimming goggles while they excavated to protect their eyes.[33]

What they saw through those goggles on the very first day of excavation in 2006, however, made them jump for joy. In the area they had decided to excavate, they began to find ancient figurines, marble bowls and other vessels.[34] It was another 'special deposit' – but this one had seemingly never been found by the looters and so remained undisturbed. It was everything Renfrew had hoped for and when I spoke to him over Zoom in February 2021, the excitement of the discovery still felt special: when do you ever hit the jackpot on the very first day of digging?[35]

The team now had a chance to conduct a proper excavation of an undisturbed area, and so perhaps a chance to find answers to the Keros Enigma. Over the course of the first season of excavation in 2006, followed by second and third seasons in 2007 and 2008, the team carefully recorded every find as it came into view: creating that all-important 3D stratigraphy – or cake slice – of their newly discovered 'special deposit'. But they also took regular amounts of the earth excavated and subjected it to the technique of water sieving – being completely surrounded by the Aegean Sea came in useful at last. This allowed them to effectively wash away the earth and leave behind tiny fragments of material that would never have been visible to the naked (or goggled) eye in the excavation trench. The team wanted to make sure they were missing nothing so that they could know both what precisely was in this new special deposit and – equally importantly – what was not. And it was the material that was not there that spoke at first most clearly to Renfrew. Over the course of the excavation, the team found no bones in the trenches. Bones, of course, can decay but enamelled human teeth survive for much longer. The water sieving, however, found not a single tooth. Moreover, no metal items or items of personal adornment were found – all things that should have been there if this area had been used as a cemetery.[36] The cemetery hypothesis was out.

This new special deposit area was labelled the 'Special Deposit South' and the original 1960–80s' 'special deposit' was labelled the 'Special Deposit North'. The Special Deposit South proved to be an even more impressive treasure trove than the North one had been. Between 2006 and 2008, a total of 53,639 pottery pieces, 550 figurine fragments, 2,236 stone vessels, 3,452 fragments of obsidian as well as smaller numbers of a range of different kinds of ancient material were recovered.[37] The Special Deposit South had, as a result, yielded more figurine and marble vessel fragments than had ever been recovered in an archaeological excavation in the Cyclades.[38] The material was all high-value 'choice' artefacts – either made of expensive material, or the result of significant human investment through carving and decoration. Subsequent microscopic analysis of the pottery demonstrated – as had been shown with the material recovered back in 1987 – that the over-whelming majority of it had not been made on Keros but instead originated from elsewhere across the Aegean and even from as far away as Attica and the Peloponnese in mainland Greece.[39] And crucially, all the fragments – figurines, marble bowls and vessels – were broken into pieces.

To Renfrew and the team, these breaks, just like those Renfrew had observed from the material in the Special Deposit North, seemed to have taken place in antiquity. But this time, the team could go one step further. Because the Special Deposit South had not been looted, they could be sure they had excavated everything that was there. So the team tried to fit back together the broken figurine and vessel pieces they had recovered. They couldn't – not a single complete figurine or vessel could be made from the pieces.[40] That meant that every item must already have been broken when it was first laid here. Moreover, the water sieving had failed to turn up any of the small chips of marble and other material you would expect to see if the objects had been broken at the site. That could mean only one thing: these ancient objects had not only been brought from elsewhere, but had been broken elsewhere and then brought to this area in pieces to be placed in the ground. The question that now puzzled the team was: why?

Alongside the work on the Special Deposit South, the team were also investigating the area surrounding the special deposits on this western end of the island, which is now known as 'Kavos'. Excavations showed the presence of a long natural rock terrace running roughly parallel to the sea facing the tiny islet of Dhaskalio, which seemed to mark the eastern boundaries of the Special Deposits North and South, with the natural slope of the island steepening significantly above this terrace. No built structures – bar the Doumas house, found back in 1963 – were discovered anywhere. The resulting picture was of a natural amphitheatre enclosing the slopes where the special deposits were situated, squeezed in between the Aegean Sea and the rising cliffs. 'Kavos' was a natural stage for the performance of this never-before-seen ritual deposition of already broken objects brought from afar.

Now alert to the natural stage created on the western edge of Keros, attention turned to the islet of Dhaskalio. This speck of rock faced the stage of ritual performance on Kavos. Was it the audience? Christos Doumas had excavated briefly on Dhaskalio back in the 1960s and found a Byzantine chapel. The survey team had looked there in 1987 and indicated there was more to find. But no one expected what happened next.

*

In 2007, another British academic, Dr Michael Boyd, then work-ing in Sheffield in the UK, had responded to Renfrew's advertise-ment for a research associate for the Keros excavations. His first season on the job was in 2008. When we spoke over Zoom together with Colin in February 2021, he told me how he remembers hear-ing about the 'Keros Enigma' in his studies, and then the shock and awe of coming to see the site for the first time.[41] By that stage, the team had begun to realise the magnitude of what they had uncovered, but were years away from publishing it to the world. Michael was the newest member to be admitted into their secret.

Michael's role was to manage the work on Dhaskalio – an even more challenging task than excavation on Keros as the islet itself had even steeper slopes on all sides and was separated from Keros by 90 metres of sea – it was an uninhabited island off an uninhab-ited island. Yet the difficulties were worth the reward. By the end of the 2008 season, the team had discovered that Dhaskalio – this tiny unassuming speck of rock – had been the preferred settle-ment place of those coming to Keros in antiquity. And not just settlement of any old kind – but monumental settlement. Across the summit of the islet, they discovered the remains of a grand hall, as well as a smaller summit enclosure and even an open court area, which had been fashioned out of the rocky summit. On the north and eastern sides of the island in particular they discovered plentiful manmade terraces and signs of dense occupation and settlement, with planned pathways connecting the settlement with the grand buildings of the summit. The buildings were made of marble. And 99 per cent of that marble was not from Keros; microscopic study showed it had come from Naxos, about 10 kilometres away.[42]

Perhaps most crucially, what the excavations on Dhaskalio gave the team, thanks to the mix of built structures and pottery finds, was the opportunity to create a definitive stratigraphy – that all-important cake-slice view of the site – allowing them to cement the dates during which the site was built and used. These date phases could then be applied to the material found in both of the special deposits, where the lack of built structures had hindered the ability to confidently pinpoint a date range for the material they had found. The results were dramatic. The first phase of activity on Dhaskalio and on Kavos ('Phase A') were dated to 2750–2550 BCE. The second phase ('Phase B'), 2550–2440 BCE. The final phase ('Phase C'), 2400–2300 BCE.[43] This means that people started coming to Keros before the Great Pyramids of Giza were built in Egypt or the famous circle at Stonehenge was erected in the UK, and that the entire life-cycle of phases of activity on Keros had happened before the first Minoan palaces were constructed on Crete at the end of the third millennium BCE. The Aegean – when activity on Keros was at its height – was only just waking up to the Bronze Age and beginning to develop complex communities, art and architecture. And even more strikingly, the special deposits seemed to be the earliest example in the entire Aegean of a ritual centre serving a wide regional community from across the islands and Greece. Given that people had to come to Keros by sea in order to conduct the ritual, Keros could now claim to be the oldest known maritime sanctuary in the entire world.[44]

Soon, another startling fact came to light that had never previously been realised: Dhaskalio and Keros had, in the third millennium BCE when people were coming to the island to deposit their broken figurines, been joined by a natural land causeway that today is submerged under the sea.[45] For Colin Renfrew, Michael Boyd and the rest of the Cambridge Keros team, the task was now to put together the endless streams of data they had to come up with a picture of what this place was like in the third millennium BCE and why people had gathered there to deposit these beautiful, broken figurines.

Having crossed the Aegean Sea from islands near and far, visitors would beach their boats on the causeway between Dhaskalio and Keros. Depending on the direction of the temperamental Aegean winds, either the northern or southern side of the causeway provided a sheltered spot to beach boats right at the heart of the site. They then made their way to the area of the special deposits at Kavos. They would have brought with them collections of broken marble figurines and high-value pottery, which they deposited – probably still in the bags that they brought them in – into the ground (where the special deposits are now).[46] Then they sailed away, back to their homes across the Aegean.

No evidence has been found to suggest how regularly they came. Once a year? Once every four years? Nor has any evidence come to light that this ritual was in honour of a particular divinity. The special deposits at Kavos instead seem to have been a place of pilgrimage in their own right – a place that people from across the islands, and even mainland Greece, felt drawn to. A place of 'symbolic attraction', of 'community cult'.[47] Perhaps, as Renfrew has argued, the figurine and pottery pieces that they brought with them had been, during their material lifetimes, important fixtures in rituals conducted by these visitors back in their home communities. When they had got chipped, past their prime, or simply been superseded, rather than simply discard such precious and symbolic objects, the communities instead ritually broke them and carried at least some of the pieces to be laid to rest in the special deposits at Kavos on the island of Keros.[48] In so doing, and repeatedly coming to this one island from many different places to engage in the same ritual action – the deposition of purposely broken high-value marble figurines and pottery – these visitors had developed a sense of community with one another. Though they came from different geographical areas, perhaps with diverse social and political ways of doing things, they were also increasingly united by their communal ritual practice, a bond made stronger by every visit to Keros.[49]

Renfrew has labelled this development of community feeling centred around Keros as the 'Confederacy of Keros', echoing the ways in which another Aegean island – Delos – would, over 2,000 years later, create a similar centrifugal community force in the first millennium BCE during the time of the Classical and Hellenistic Greek worlds, the time of Athenian democracy, the Parthenon, Plato and Alexander the Great.[50] He has also underlined how this phenomenon of rituals of congregation, without the need for a particular deity at the centre of it, seems to have been an important feature of early food-producing societies across the world: from Göbekli Tepe in Turkey (dating from around 9000 BCE), to Caral in Peru (c.3000 BCE), to Stonehenge in England dating from the mid-third millennium BCE, or the roughly contemporary Ring of Brodgar in Scotland.[51] Yet unlike these sites, which were defined as centres of ritual congregation by the large monuments erected at them, the marker on Keros was not a great structure, but the act of depositing symbolic materials. The most popular type of Cycladic figurine to be broken up and deposited on Keros, Renfrew notes, is of a figure with their arms folded.[52] Perhaps this was the logo, the symbol, of the community created around Keros.[53]

Having lain largely uninhabited and mostly ignored since antiquity, Keros's enigmatic past was first exploited by robbers. Thankfully, this attracted the attention of the archaeological community and eventually full investigation of the site. As a result, Keros is now the world's oldest maritime sanctuary and one of the crucial examples of humanity's earliest forms of ritual behaviour, of our desire to congregate and create community. It is a striking journey of transformation for this unprepossessing island. And that journey is not yet over – the revelations only got bigger from there.

Colin Renfrew and Michael Boyd, following the 2006–8 excavation seasons, had more questions for Keros and the surrounding area. After spending four years studying the material excavated and preparing the publications from the initial excavations, the team launched the Keros Island Survey. They wanted to know whether they could find evidence of the figurines being broken elsewhere on the island, and also to find out whether there were other sites of use around the island or whether Dhaskalio/Kavos was alone. While they found no evidence of breakage, the survey did indicate a number of hitherto completely unknown sites of occupation from this period around Keros.[54] They wait to be fully explored.

In 2015, the pair also began the Keros Naxos Seaways project. Naxos is, today, Keros's nearest large hub island, but the survey confirmed that, back in the third millennium BCE, it was Keros that was more densely inhabited than Naxos. In the third millennium BCE, it seems, Keros was at the centre of everyone's attention.

Having established this context for the unique nature of Keros and Dhaskalio, Colin Renfrew and Michael Boyd initiated new excavations on Dhaskalio in 2016. A decade on since Colin Renfrew and the Cambridge Keros team (powered by those tinned sardines) had discovered the Special Deposit South in 2006, the team returned once again to focus on understanding the chronological development of the built structures on Dhaskalio, the islet's relationship to the special deposits on Kavos and the evolution of the Dhaskalio/Kavos site as a whole. In some ways, little had changed over the decade. The caique from Ano Kouphonisi to Keros still left at 6 a.m. every morning and Renfrew, now seventy-nine years old, was always the first to appear at the dock to board.[55] The caique itself was still captained by Kostas Prasinos, who had ferried the team in 2006–8, although now his son, Rousetos (named after his grandfather who had captained the caique that took Renfrew across in 1987), also occasionally took the helm. I'm told by Colin and Michael that young Rousetos had to listen to his father reminding him constantly that he, the father, was the better boatman.[56] The team stayed in the same hotel run by the Platis family and used some of their rooms as a fieldwork laboratory. Colin and Michael are proud of the ways in which they have developed a strong bond with the local community on Ano Kouphonisi, and are even more proud of the work they have supported to change local opinions about Keros from a site that locals were willing to see (perhaps even aid) being looted, to a site they feel a strong sense of local and regional pride in, which they want to invest in and protect. The former school building on Ano Kouphonisi (which Colin and Michael had used some rooms of for their fieldwork laboratory in the 2006–8 campaign) is now a public museum dedicated to Keros.[57] An archaeological investigation in many ways initiated in response to the looting of an archaeological site is now contributing towards ensuring this site – and hopefully others – do not suffer similarly in the future.

But some things have changed. In 2016, in part to deal with the strong winds that whip around Keros, the team cast aside paper notes and elastic bands and went digital using iPads and GPS tracking to record every find. Digital tools are changing the way archaeology is done, allowing ever faster and more in-depth analysis of the material found. As Michael Boyd wryly noted to me during our Zoom conversation, however, there is no digital alternative for the problems of having a seventy-plus-strong team of people stuck on an uninhabited tiny steep-sided island all day. From having to bring packed lunches (sardines optional), to dealing with illness (the Prasinos' caique can leave a few feeling seasick), to the simple business of where they all go to the toilet while on Dhaskalio, this remains a human logistics operation of immense complexity – even before the team turn to the archaeology itself.[58]

Over three more seasons of excavation, from 2016 to 2018, Colin and Michael have uncovered further remarkable insights into Dhaskalio/Kavos. The first has been to flesh out the relationship between the two areas. Visitors were bringing material to the special deposits on Kavos from 2750 BCE (the beginning of 'Phase A' of the site). At this time on Dhaskalio, there were no monumental buildings and development started on a few structures; there is also plentiful evidence for food processing, heating and consumption.[59] During 'Phase B' (2550–2400 BCE), roughly the period when the Great Pyramid at Giza was being constructed in Egypt, the special deposits continued to be in use and most of the settlement buildings were constructed on Dhaskalio, where there is also evidence for much more storage and transportation of foodstuffs and other goods than before.[60] But in Phase C (2400–2300 BCE), the special deposits on Kavos were only rarely interacted with, whereas this was the time that the hall, summit enclosure and court area were built in marble on the summit of Dhaskalio; storage and transportation jars make up over 57 per cent of all the vessel finds.[61]

What this indicates is that we are looking at a shifting set of reasons for people coming to Keros. It began, around 2750 BCE, with people drawn to it as a site of ritual deposition of broken figurines and pottery. Over time, as this activity led to a sense of community and congregation, with Keros as a result increasing in importance as a 'symbolic attractor' in the region, Dhaskalio became home to a small permanent community, but was also developed to provide support, accommodation and community spaces for the larger numbers coming periodically to conduct ritual deposition at Kavos.[62] In 2008, the team investigating Dhaskalio had mapped the corner of a wall at the base of the islet just by where the team had proved the ancient causeway between Dhaskalio and Kavos to have been. When Michael and Colin returned in 2016, they discussed investigating this precise area with a full excavation trench. Michael described it to me as simply 'having a hunch'.[63] What emerged was a monumental ceremonial stairway (with a full drainage system underneath it) leading up from the causeway towards the summit of Dhaskalio, connecting Dhaskalio and Kavos. Arriving visitors, docking either north or south of the causeway depending on the wind, now had a ceremonial stairway to aid their movement between Dhaskalio and Kavos. Michael admitted to me that he has enjoyed walking the staircase himself, imagining ancient visitors doing the same roughly 4,500 years ago.[64]

When these ancient visitors moved from Dhaskalio to Kavos, it's clear they were moving between two spaces very different in use and meaning. Dhaskalio increasingly was home to a significant number of built structures. Kavos only ever had one building (the Doumas house). Dhaskalio was littered with detritus from food processing, consumption and cooking. No evidence for a fire being lit has been found in the area of the special deposits.[65] Not a single folded-arm figurine has been found on

Dhaskalio in comparison to the hundreds in the special deposits on Kavos.[66] Equally, on Dhaskalio evidence of metalworking – of casting ancient metal objects – has been found.[67] No such evidence has been found in the area of the special deposits, although in an area 120 metres north of the Special Deposit North, known as the 'Kavos promontory', there is plentiful evidence for the smelting of ancient metals (the strong winds on the promontory would have helped to achieve the very high temperatures necessary for the smelting process). The area of the promontory, like Dhaskalio, has also yielded no figurines (nor any marble artefact).[68] Given that all the ores to smelt and cast would have had to be imported to Keros, it poses the question: why go through the trouble of bringing them here? Michael Boyd thinks the answer must lie in the emerging centrality of Keros within the Aegean thanks to its use as a site of ritual deposition. Because people came to Keros to do one thing over a long period of time, the site became a good option for a location to do lots of things. On the back of its reputation as a symbolic attractor, Dhaskalio thus became potentially 'the biggest settlement in the Aegean Sea at that time' – it evolved to become not just a site of ritual deposition, but a powerful resource and manufacturing centre in its own right.[69] It is a story of 'snowball' development that mirrors the origin stories of many great urban centres of civilisations around the world. One of the metal items cast on Dhaskalio, which the team found the mould for in the 2016–18 excavations, was a spearhead.[70] It seems ironic that an island that initially attracted people to come together and build community relations by depositing broken objects at the end of their useful lives became, over time, also an island worth bringing raw materials to in order to make new things – new things that could well be used to do harm to others.

And in the end, it seems, Dhaskalio won out. Activity at the special deposits tails off in Phase C, 2400–2300 BCE. But it is to this phase that the great ceremonial buildings on the summit of Dhaskalio should be dated.[71] Dhaskalio had outgrown the need for the special deposits to draw people to Keros – now it drew them itself. In the summit enclosure, dating to Phase C, a new ritual practice of depositing a pebble seems to have started, a pebble that, analysis shows us, expressly was brought from the nearby island of Kouphonisi to Dhaskalio.[72]

But if you thought the Keros Enigma had now been completely unravelled – you would be wrong. Pebbles were not the only thing being brought to Dhaskalio across the sea; the shining marble used to build its grand monumental structures came from elsewhere too. In fact it is now estimated that the sixty buildings on Dhaskalio built in Phases B and C would have required just over 11,000 tons of marble. That marble, it has now been shown, came from south-eastern Naxos, about 10 kilometres from Keros.[73] To move that amount of marble across the sea to Keros from Naxos, given the size of boats available at that time, would have needed roughly 3,500 return trips, covering in total more than 40,000 nautical miles. All of which would have to have been achieved through man-driven oar power, as sail boats were yet to be developed.[74] Kavos on Keros may be the location of the earliest maritime sanctuary in the world, but Dhaskalio is now understood, as a recent Greek TV documentary involving Colin and Michael put it, to be at the epicentre of the 'greatest [act of] prehistoric sea transportation anywhere in the world', happening well over a thousand years before the Uluburun cargo ship set sail.[75]

Over the course of Colin's lifetime, Keros has been rehabilitated from an uninhabited, unimportant island, left as prey to looters, to a place of global importance: it's the location of the world's earliest maritime sanctuary, drawing people to it from across the Aegean to participate in rituals of congregation and community development, which developed into the biggest settlement and production centre of its time in the Aegean, thanks to the greatest act of prehistoric sea transportation anywhere in the world. This complete transformation in our understanding of the significance of Keros has only been possible due to the efforts, over more than six decades, of teams of archaeologists from different nations around the world applying the very latest in scientific techniques to analyse the finds from the sporadic excavations. Although Colin Renfrew has been a leading figure, it's taken many, many people contributing fragments of understanding to complete Keros's story. As Michael Boyd points out, he has never before been involved in an excavation of such scale and complexity.[76]

At the same time, the story of our interest in Keros, dating back to the very first finds there in the nineteenth century, underlines quite how much the discipline of archaeology has developed over that time. Not simply in techniques and technologies of excavation, but equally in response to the evolving debate over how, where and by whom discoveries should be maintained and displayed. The Keros team have, particularly in their renewed efforts since 2006, worked hand in hand with the Greek archaeological authorities as well, crucially, with the local community on nearby Ano Kouphonisi to build both an understanding of, and a current local pride in, Keros's past. That has involved not only the establishment of a local museum to display locally the key finds, but a continued process of public discussion and engagement that will hopefully ensure the community plays an active role in maintaining and protecting their past in the future. The team's commitment to engaging in not just local but much wider public discussion about the site and what it represents (through TV documentaries, talks and wider writing) is also an important symbol of how much the discipline has realised the need for it to be a continual part of the ever-evolving academic and public discourse about Keros's meaning and value.

In terms of understanding the Keros Enigma, Colin Renfrew smiles when thinking back over the way Keros has presented to him and the team 'a whole bundle of problems'.[77] 'It takes time to understand the truth,' he says simply.[78] And that quest is far from over. The team are currently working on the publications from their latest series of excavation, but then the plan is to go back to Keros once more. Colin, at the age of eighty-four, has his eye on excavating a cave up above the natural amphitheatre of Kavos, which he thinks holds yet more mysteries.[79] Michael still wants to understand better how the settlement on Dhaskalio first developed alongside the community rituals on Kavos.[80] And then there are the bigger questions, which Michael and Colin admit they may never find the answers to. In particular, why Keros?[81] Why, in 2750 BCE, did people choose Keros, compared to all the other islands, as the place to begin their community ritual deposition of broken figurines?

Keros, it seems, may always retain something of its mystery – despite all our efforts over the course of the last three centuries and the cumulative weight of the development of the discipline of archaeology during that time. For me, that is only right. Mystery is something that the past should never give up completely. It is the essence of our love affair with it: the fact that we can never know everything that is underneath our feet, or be sure we know the full story of what we hold in our hands. The past will always be one step ahead.

Epilogue

The Future of Our Past

In some ways, this book could be thought of as a recipe book – offering an insight into what exactly is required to cook up a discovery. What we have learnt as we have followed our discoverers through time and across the world, through every kind of climate and landscape, seeking out many different kinds of objects, settlements and civilisations, is that – as Indiana Jones so rightly said – X never, ever marks the spot (although the built stone burial kurgans of the Altai might be said to come pretty close!). But what has I think become clear through these eight stories of discovery is that there is a recipe for a great find.

The first crucial ingredients are the factors that influence our discoverers into looking for particular things in particular places at particular times. As argued at the very beginning of this book, we can't look for everything, so anything we do look for is the result of active choice. But that choice is shaped for us. In the early chapters of this book, we saw how discoveries like the Rosetta Stone in Egypt, Marc Aurel Stein's endless finds in the Taklamakan Desert, and those of Hiram Bingham at Machu Picchu, were set in motion because of key geopolitical shifts and foci that prompted interest and excavation in those regions at those particular times. In the case of the Rosetta Stone in Egypt, that geopolitical focus was France's desire to counterbalance British power in India by controlling Egypt (coupled with French fascination with Egyptology). In the case of Stein, it was the

251

British desire to map and counter the spread of Russian and Chinese influence on the borders of its Indian Empire in the Taklamakan, one of the last 'unknown parts of the world'. In the case of Bingham, it was North America's renewed interest in South America as a political and cultural partner of worth that invigorated archaeological interest in the civilisations of South America's past. To that list might well be added the more unusual case of the Terracotta Warriors, in which it was the changing national attitude towards the Qin dynasty that enabled not the discovery itself, but the *survival* of the discovery of those first Terracotta Warriors, and the subsequent study and excavation of the Terracotta Army. Without that shift – while the discovery may still have been made – it is likely that the finds would have remained uncelebrated and certainly not been followed up.

Through the course of the later chapters, we saw those geopolitical and national forces recede somewhat, as archaeology and anthropology developed as disciplines and matured to set their own agendas of interest with a greater degree of independence from national and international politics and warfare. But these forces were – and are – no less powerful than the geopolitical ones that proceeded them. Whether it was the intense debate about the geographical origins of early man in Africa that helped focus the endeavours of the Leakeys in Tanzania and Kenya, or the gradual acceptance of the value (and seriousness) of underwater archaeology that galvanised the team that found the Uluburun shipwreck; or the gradual rediscovery of the importance of the ancient cultures of the Steppe, which had been so long overlooked, that encouraged the investigation of their burials in the Altai; or the slow-burn need to understand more about civilisations that have left no literature behind that motivated the six-decades-long investigation of Keros in the Aegean – probably none of these discoveries would have been made if the swirling forces of academic discussion, debate and dissension had not prioritised these issues and thus prioritised finding evidence that could help illuminate them.

Yet setting the agenda is only one ingredient in the recipe for a great discovery. A discovery needs a discoverer to respond to the call. And that discoverer – or in more recent decades, most often an international team of discoverers – will often have spent their life gathering the skills, knowledge, expertise, technologies and experience to be able to bring the exact mix of information, ideas and abilities to the table to help unlock the secrets of the past, push the boundaries of their subject and challenge our accepted sense of ourselves and our past. For me, they are an extraordinary set of human beings, so often putting aside their own comforts, driving themselves to feats of human endurance and discomfort few of us would relish or entertain, in (mostly patient) pursuit of knowledge, discovery and, of course, individual (and team) glory.

We have – thankfully – seen over the course of the two hundred-plus years covered by the stories in this book the role of discoverer be increasingly taken up by women. In the last half-century, we have also seen individuals and small groups, rather than simply jetting in from their home nation and conducting the work themselves, work in partnership with experts local to the discovery. And the most recent excavations are characterised by larger international teams of men and women all bringing more and more specialist skills to bear on making a discovery. Sometimes we may feel the characteristics of these discoverers, particularly in the earlier stories of discovery we encountered, don't actually add up to producing particularly admirable characters, or ones that we would feel much in common with or indeed want to spend any time with. And certainly, as we have seen in a number of our stories of discovery, they make choices that today we do not admire and that we have more recently sought to reverse. But without them, the recipe simply does not work.

There is, however, another crucial ingredient without which the discovery process is doomed: luck and/or accident. Geopolitical forces and academic priorities have directed people with all the necessary skills and expertise to search for particular parts of the past across the globe on an ongoing basis; but they haven't made the discoveries that really challenge and deliver a step change in our sense of the past without a little bit of luck. Mary Leakey had the so-called 'Leakey Luck', which brought not only several extraordinary finds but also, on occasion, a discovery at just the right moment when a film crew was inbound to capture it. Dr Natalia Polosmak was directed to a particular kurgan fortuitously by a Russian soldier (having picked a random spot in the Altai to begin her survey and excavations). Sometimes that luck is better termed an accident, particularly given the more ambiguous outcomes of the discovery for the discoverers. Take the soldier, for instance, who found the Rosetta Stone, digging for material to rebuild a defensive wall but ending up dying in battle thousands of miles away. Or the farmers who chose to dig a well in a particular spot and came across the first Terracotta Warriors, but whose personal lives saw little improvement as a result. And of course there is the ambiguous line between well-informed guesswork, good preparation and luck. Would Mehmed, for instance, have ever spotted the 'metal biscuit with ears' while sponge diving if the underwater archaeological team had not spent so much time collaborating with sponge-diving crews informing them what to look for? In whatever shape, luck and/or accident always plays a crucial role in discovery.

If luck is the final key ingredient, there is one more thing that shapes a discovery into something that pierces and settles into the global consciousness: an X(tra) factor if you will. As Dr Natalia Polosmak put it: 'history needs personalities'. Truly era-defining discoveries, like those encountered in this book, have that extra something that makes them sensational. Sometimes that sensationalism comes through the window they provide onto an intensely human moment of our past, like the semi-preserved tattooed body of 'the Lady' surrounded by her burial objects. Sometimes it is the incredible scale of the find, like that of the Terracotta Warriors, that humbles us into entirely reimagining our sense of the power and abilities of past societies. Or perhaps, as with the Rosetta Stone, it is how one find can provide the 'key' to unlocking entire languages and thus ancient cultures. And sometimes, as in the case of Machu Picchu, that sensationalism is not necessarily generated at the time of discovery and is more a product of what the world chooses to make the discovery stand for. Machu Picchu, after all, is, we now know, only the holiday settlement of an Inca king housing no more than 750 people. And yet, through the legends woven around it as a 'lost city' and the ways in which it has become a beacon for different communities over time, it has become one of the key global symbols of human civilisation itself.

These are the key ingredients in the recipe of discovery, but for me the stories in this book have highlighted a bigger and even more intriguing question: just what does it mean to discover something? In the case of the Terracotta Warriors, the question of 'who discovered them' is much contested – between the farmers who 'found' them and the archaeologist who 'understood' what they were. Mehmed 'found' the metal biscuits with ears and sufficiently recognised their importance to report the find, but it was the archaeologist dive team who, over years, investigated, studied and published the find. Mehmed is thus often mentioned in the initial lines of excavation reports, but not necessarily credited as the discoverer. The inverse problem occurs with Machu Picchu. Machu Picchu was never lost: lots of locals knew about it, some were living by it, and earlier travellers seem to have visited it. But Bingham, directed to it by those locals who knew about it, was the one who brought it to world attention and so is often quoted as its discoverer (he certainly set himself up as such in his own writing about his 'lost' city). Yet at the site itself, he is commemorated as Machu Picchu's 'scientific discoverer' in an attempt to articulate the difference. We might even ask the question of Keros, where it was the looting of archaeological objects that first sparked significant archaeological interest and investigation into the island. Whose 'discovery' there?

At stake is just what do we mean by discovery: the initial find-ing of the object or the unlocking of its meaning and significance? The local knowledge of its existence or the global acknowledge-ment of its importance? And of course there is also the question of time. Many of the stories in this book cover decades, if not lifetimes, of investigation into the objects at the centre of their story. The Rosetta Stone was found in 1799, but its hieroglyphic code was not cracked until 1822, and, as we saw, we are still discovering nuances of the ancient text that give us new insights into the political circumstances of its creation in 196 BCE. Stein's finds from the Taklamakan in the early twentieth century are still being worked through today. It is only since the 1980s that schol-ars have really begun to study in earnest the finds removed from Machu Picchu by Bingham in the 1910s to ascertain the real nature of Machu Picchu as a king's holiday settlement. The study of 'Our Lady' in the Altai went on for decades, and that of Keros for more than six decades (so far!). Discovery is not always a moment of 'finding' or a 'eureka' moment of understanding. It can be a long, careful, patient – perhaps never-ending – process. As Colin Renfrew put it in relation to Keros: 'it takes time to understand the truth'. My favourite example of this by far is that of the skulls found by Mary Leakey. She found them, put them back together, studied them – all excellent elements of a 'discovery'. Yet there is still ongoing debate, especially in terms of the 'Dear Boy'/ *Zinjanthropus*/Nutcracker Man/*Australopithecus* skull, about what exactly *is* the skull that was discovered. From what era and stage of evolution does the discovery date? We have the find, yet can't quite agree on what it is. Discovery can sometimes be very tricky indeed.

If what actually constitutes a discovery is more of a moving target than we first thought, what I hope, above all, the stories in this book have underlined is how discovery challenges us. All the discoveries we have followed here have of course deepened immeasurably our connection with the past by making it more real and more human. But at the same time they have often done so by challenging our current wisdom and forcing us to rethink what we thought we knew. And at the same time, these discoveries have challenged us repeatedly to up our game in the tools and expertise we bring to the quest of uncovering them. From the ice-filled kurgans of the Altai to the Uluburun shipwreck 40-plus metres under water, to the careful sifting of earth and analysis of microscopic remains on Keros, the past has demanded that we develop new techniques and methods of analysis to be able to unlock its secrets.

Perhaps the greatest and most important challenge discovery brings us, though, is in forcing us to question continually how, where and by whom we think the past should be studied, discussed, maintained and displayed. Through the course of the chapters in this book we've seen how the discipline of archaeology has evolved in its approach to all of these questions, and in some cases moved to put right past actions now agreed to be wrong. But if anything, the challenge has become now even more complex. How can we ensure ongoing engagement between the evolving academic and public discussions about the meaning and significance of the discovery? How should we navigate the delicate balancing act required between honouring community views and the mainte-nance of space for ongoing research? How might we secure a future for the past when weighed against the mighty forces of geopolitical and global change, which in some cases threaten the past's very survival?

That idea of the past challenging us is something I relish, and that, I think, is the mainstay of its value to us today. Of course the past brings comfort, pride and a sense of belonging. But it should always also challenge us and keep the ground shifting beneath our feet. In some cases, finds have even presented a challenge to whether we should discover at all. Dr Natalia Polosmak asked the Lady of Altai to forgive her when she first removed the body from its resting place. The tomb of the Qin Emperor in China remains off-limits to excavation. In discovering the past, we now realise the need to first challenge ourselves about our right to do so. And if we do move forward to uncover it, then what speaks clearly in all of these stories is that the past takes on a life and meaning all of its own. From debates about their meaning and value in the past to discussions about their value, meaning and place in the present and the future, the objects and locations we have encountered in this book continue to challenge their discoverers and the wider world. These are debates in which everyone – not just those whose job it is to uncover the past – should have an interest and a voice, irrespective of how big a challenge that is to bring about. Because the past speaks to, and belongs to, us all.

Acknowledgements

My sincerest thanks go to Anna Baty at Hodder & Stoughton – who, in a wondrous twist of fate, reached out to talk to me about an idea that chimed with exactly what I wanted to talk to her about writing – for the fabulous feedback and discussions we had in the process of getting this book started. My deepest thanks go also to Rupert Lancaster and Ciara Mongey at Hodder for their support, feedback and insight in bringing the book to completion while Anna was on leave pursuing a different kind of adventure – motherhood! My warmest thanks also to the wider team at Hodder & Stoughton for their work on bringing the book to print, and particularly to Nick Fawcett for copy-editing the manuscript with such skill and good humour. As ever, throughout the journey of writing this book, I am also indebted to Patrick Walsh and the team at PEW Literary for their unceasing support and encouragement. This book has been an expedition across continents, eras and genres of archaeological investigation. It has been a privilege to share in the different journeys of discovery through the available source materials and, in relation to the more recent discoveries, to reach out and speak with those actually at the heart of them. My grateful thanks to all those who have given their time to speak to me and share your insights. Last, but certainly not least, I am grateful to my family for their never-ending encouragement to do what I love doing the most: sharing our extraordinary past with everyone I can.

Notes

Introduction: Who Cares About The Past?

1. Suetonius, *Life of Augustus*, 18.
2. Cassius Dio, *Roman History* 51.16.5. For discussion of how Augustus and subsequent Roman Emperors treated Alexander's body, see Andrew Erskine, 2002, 'Life After Death: Alexandria and the Body of Alexander', *Greece and Rome* 49(2): 163–79.
3. And don't get me – or any other academic involved with the study of the past – started on the way Indiana Jones never seems to have published his findings, marked his students' work, undertaken a variety of academic administrative tasks, or indeed had to keep to a teaching timetable! In more ways than one Indiana Jones is the antithesis of what working in archaeology, and indeed higher education more generally, is – or should be – about!
4. Arrian, *Anabasis* 1.11 and 4.9.
5. Herodotus, *Histories* 2.11–12.
6. Cf. Adrienne Mayor, 2000, *The First Fossil Hunters: Dinosaurs, Mammoths and Myth in Greek and Roman Times*, Princeton: Princeton University Press.
7. Plato, *Hippias Major* 285d. Cf. Dionysius of Halicarnassus, who wrote in Greek an *archaiologia* of Rome, the history of Rome from its earliest mythical beginnings: *Roman Antiquities* 1.8.2.
8. Pausanias, *Description of Greece* 5.20.8.
9. Virgil, *Georgics* 1.493–7.
10. Cf. John Boardman, 2002, *The Archaeology of Nostalgia: How the Greeks Re-created their Mythical Past*, London: Thames & Hudson.
11. Thucydides (*History of the Peloponnesian War* 1.10.2) famously argued that no one in the future would realise how important and powerful Sparta had been simply by looking at its physical remains,

whereas the power of Athens was likely to be much overrated from its magnificent ruins.

12. Pausanias 4.26.7–8.
13. William Faulkner, 1919, *Requiem for a Nun*, London: Chatto & Windus, Act 1, Scene 3.
14. Cf. Josephus's *Antiquities of the Jews* written in the late first century CE, which told the story of the Jewish people from the time of the world's beginning. Ironically, Josephus (like Dionysius of Halicarnassus) originally wrote in Greek, calling his work an *Archaiologia of the Jews*, but the title was translated for his Roman audience (and hence through time to us) as *Antiquities of the Jews*.
15. Cf. the formation in London of the *Society of Antiquaries* in 1717, replacing an earlier College of Antiquaries, founded around 1586, subsequently abolished by King James I.
16. Parallel to this development of antiquarianism and its subsequent (re)birth as archaeology was also the separation in academic study between those who studied the past through its surviving literary sources ('history') and those who studied it through its surviving material sources (antiquarians/archaeologists). This division is now challenged by scholars, who argue that, while there are of course particular skill sets required to work with and understand particular kinds of (either literary or physical) evidence, we also need to bring all the different kinds of evidence back together in order to produce as in-depth and fully rounded an understanding of the past as possible.
17. The Hollywood character of Indiana Jones, with his permanent call for objects to 'belong in a museum', while set up as a heroic stance helping to stop his adversaries from using them for personal gain, in many ways simply restates the colonial approach to the appropriation of excavated artefacts (alongside of course the many other ways in which the films set up an uncomfortable series of comparisons between East and West). For further discussion on the complex relationship modern archaeologists have with the character of Indiana Jones see Marilyn Johnson, 2014, *Lives in Ruins: Archaeologists and the Seductive Lure of Human Rubble*, London: HarperCollins.
18. E.g., C. and G. Scarre (eds), 2012, *The Ethics of Archaeology*, Cambridge: Cambridge University Press; G. Scarre and R. Coningham (eds), 2013, *Appropriating the Past*, Cambridge: Cambridge University Press.

Chapter 1

1. Lesley and Roy Adkins, 2000, *The Keys of Egypt: The Race to Read the Hieroglyphs*, London: HarperCollins, 35.

2. Jason Thompson, 1992, *Sir Gardner Wilkinson and His Circle*, Austin: University of Texas Press, 22 (*Courier de l'Egypte* 37 (le 29 fructidor, an VII)).

3. There is considerable divergence in the sources as to how the stone was originally found (half buried in the sand or built into an old wall that needed to be demolished to make way for new foundations for additions to the fort), and who exactly was involved in discovering the potential of the Rosetta Stone, as well as to where it initially travelled. Some reports include Lancret, others record Bouchard as reporting the find directly to General Menou (one of the key generals of the French campaign in Egypt). Some report the stone as going straight to Cairo, others record it as first being taken to Alexandria as the personal possession of Menou, only being transferred later to Cairo on the orders of Napoleon.

4. Adkins and Adkins, *The Keys of Egypt*, 2–3; Toby Wilkinson, 2020, *A World Beneath the Sands: Adventurers and Archaeologists in the Golden Age of Egyptology*, London: Picador Press, 11–13.

5. Ibid., 13–14.

6. Quoted in Charles Gillispie and Michael Dewachter (eds), 1987, *Monuments of Egypt: The Napoleonic Edition – The Complete Archaeological Plates from la Description de l'Égypte*, Princeton: Princeton Architectural Press, 3.

7. Wilkinson, *A World Beneath the Sands*, 24.

8. In taking *les savants,* no doubt Napoleon saw further potential for comparison between his expedition to Egypt and that of Alexander the Great, who had also taken intellectuals with him on his conquest of Persia: Adkins and Adkins, *Keys of Egypt*, 11.

9. Ibid., 10–11.

10. Ibid., 24.

11. Wilkinson, *World Beneath the Sands*, 25; Joyce Tyldesley, 2005, *Egypt: How a Lost Civilisation was Rediscovered*, Berkeley: University of California Press, 48.

12. It was to the Institut, for example, at its second ever meeting on 28 August 1798, that one of its members, Monsieur Monge, read a paper explaining for the first time the phenomena of the *mirage* – the false sighting of water sources in the Egyptian desert – which

had so plagued the French army on their 200-kilometre march from Alexandria to Cairo and driven many mad enough to commit suicide: Charles Coulston Gillispie, 1989, 'Aspects of the French Egyptian Expedition 1798–1801', *Proceedings of the American Philosophical Society* 133(4): 447–74.

13. Wilkinson, *World Beneath the Sands*, 27.
14. So called despite the fact that it is the southern half of Egypt. The Nile flows south to north from its sources in Uganda and South Sudan towards the Mediterranean and so this part of the country hosts the 'upper' half of the Nile.
15. Adkins and Adkins, *Keys of Egypt*, 31.
16. Ibid., 34.
17. Not to mention the two commissions of *les savants* that Napoleon ordered to head back to Upper Egypt to record in full detail all the monuments seen by the army during their march south in late 1789 and early 1799.
18. E. A. Wallis Budge, 1913, *The Rosetta Stone*, London: British Museum Press; Wilkinson, *World Beneath the Sands*, 39.
19. Adkins and Adkins, *Keys of Egypt*, 17.
20. Ibid., 37.
21. Gillispie, 'Aspects of the French Egyptian Expedition'.
22. Ibid.
23. Wilkinson, *World Beneath the Sands*, 40.
24. Matthew Raper, S. Weston et al., 'Rosetta stone, brought to England in 1802: Account of, by Matthew Raper; with three versions: Greek, English translation by S. Weston, Latin translation by Prof. Heyne; with notes by Porson, Taylor, Combe, Weston and Heyne', *Archaeologia* 16 (1812): 208–63.
25. https://blog.britishmuseum.org/everything-you-ever-wanted-to-know-about-the-rosetta-stone/.
26. http://www.bbc.co.uk/ahistoryoftheworld/objects/awwjbIoORU-aQXm9LmiTz8A.
27. The *Gentleman's Magazine*, 1802, Vol. 71, p. 1194. The story of how the Rosetta Stone had been recovered by the British from General Menou and transported to England, along with early translations of the Greek text, was also published in a special edition of the *Archaeologia* journal in 1812: Raper, Weston et al., 'Rosetta stone'.
28. https://blog.britishmuseum.org/everything-you-ever-wanted-to-know-about-the-rosetta-stone/.

29. Tyldesley, *Egypt*, 56. The twenty-nine characters were presented in an extended letter from the Swedish scholar Johan David Åkerblad to his French colleague, the Oriental scholar Silvestre de Sacy, entitled *Lettre sur l'Inscription Égyptienne de Rosette, Adressée au C.^{en} Silvestre de Sacy* (published 1802).

30. Digitised versions of the *Gentleman's Magazine* from the period 1802–3 are available to view here: https://catalog.hathitrust.org/Record/006056643.

31. You can now view a digitised version of the *Description de l'Égypte*: http://descegy.bibalex.org/.

32. Wilkinson, *World Beneath the Sands*, 52–5.

33. Ibid., 59.

34. Andrew Robinson, 2006, *The Last Man Who Knew Everything, Thomas Young, The Anonymous Polymath who Proved Newton Wrong, Explained How We See, Cured the Sick and Deciphered the Rosetta Stone, Among Other Feats of Genius*, New York: Pi Press, 1.

35. This idea too originated out of the study of Chinese, where similarly foreign names were also highlighted using cartouches. Sadly, the scholar who developed this idea, Joseph de Guignes, Professor of Syriac at the College of France in Paris, went on to argue that this may mean Chinese civilisation had started as an Egyptian colony, and thus that the Chinese language may hold the key to translating hieroglyphics! His theories were immensely popular at the time and sent many scholars on a wild goose chase attempting to translate hieroglyphics through Chinese: Adkins and Adkins, *Keys of Egypt*, 61.

36. 'Egypt' – Supplement to *Encyclopaedia Britannica* Vol. IV, Part 1, 1819.

37. On the basis that Champollion might not attribute ideas so honestly to the academics who had originally had them: Robinson, *The Last Man Who Knew Everything*, 158.

38. While this suggestion had been made by earlier scholars (in contrast to those who thought Chinese might be related to hieroglyphics), Champollion would be the one to prove the connection: Adkins and Adkins, *Keys of Egypt*, 63–5.

39. Wilkinson, *World Beneath the Sands*, 63; Andrew Robinson, 2012, *Cracking the Egyptian Code: The Revolutionary Life of Jean-François Champollion*, London: Thames & Hudson, 49.

40. Wilkinson, *World Beneath the Sands*, 64–5.

41. For further discussion of Bankes's role: Richard Parkinson, 2013, *A Little Gay History: Desire and Diversity Across the World*, New York: Columbia University Press.

42. Wilkinson, *World Beneath the Sands*, 66.

43. Ibid., 47–8, 66–7; Adkins and Adkins, *Keys of Egypt*, 1–6. See also Richard Parkinson, Whitfield Diffie, Mary Fischer and R. S. Simpson, 1999. *Cracking the Code: The Rosetta Stone and Decipherment*, Berkeley: University of California Press, 31–41.

44. Jean-François Champollion, 1822, *Lettre à M. Dacier, relative à l'alphabet des hieroglyphs phonétiques*, Paris: Firmin Didot Père et Fils. Reproduced by Hachette Livre in co-operation with the Bibliothèque de France.

45. Wilkinson, *World Beneath the Sands*, 68.

46. Letter from Thomas Young to Sir William Hamilton, 29 September 1822. Cf. Robinson, *The Last Man Who Knew Everything*, 209; Parkinson, Diffie, Fischer and Simpson, *Cracking the Code*, 36.

47. Thomas Young, 1823, *An Account of Some Recent Discoveries in Hieroglyphical Literature, and Egyptian Antiquities, Including the Author's Original Alphabet, As Extended by Mr Champollion*, London: John Murray, 43.

48. Young, *An Account of Some Recent Discoveries*, ix.

49. Robinson, *The Last Man Who Knew Everything*, 219.

50. Jean François Champollion, 1824, *Précis du système hiéroglyphique des anciens Égyptiens, ou Recherches sur les élémens premiers de cette écriture sacrée, sur leurs diverses combinaisons, et sur les rapports de ce système avec les autres méthodes graphiques égyptiennes*, Paris: Treuttel et Würtz, 327. It is testament both to how much Champollion was willing to bend with the political wind, and to how much of an extraordinary breakthrough he had made in claiming for France the ability to read Egyptian hieroglyphs, that he, a former Bonaparte supporter, now dedicated his *Précis* to the reinstated French King Louis XVIII, and that Louis received Champollion in a private audience and sent him gifts in honour of his work: Wilkinson, *World Beneath the Sands*, 72.

51. Richard Parkinson, former Curator at the British Museum: http://www.bbc.co.uk/ahistoryoftheworld/objects/awwjbIoORUaQXm9LmiTz8A.

52. A fully referenced digital version of the texts on the Rosetta Stone can be accessed here: http://rosettastone.hieroglyphic-texts.net/. To learn how to read hieroglyphics for yourself: Mark Collier and Bill

Manley, 1998, *How to Read Egyptian Hieroglyphics: A Step-by-Step Guide to Teach Yourself*, London: British Museum Press.

53. Parkinson: http://www.bbc.co.uk/ahistoryoftheworld/objects/awwjbIo ORUaQXm9LmiTz8A.
54. Ilona Regulski, Curator of Egyptian Written Culture at the British Museum: https://blog.britishmuseum.org/inheriting-the-most-iconic-object-at-the-british-museum/.
55. As the ancient writer Polybius put it, courtiers 'thought that the kingdom would gain a certain degree of firmness and a fresh impulse towards prosperity, if it were known that the king had assumed the independent direction of the government', Polybius *Histories* 18.55.3–6.
56. British Museum: *History of the World in 100 Objects: The Rosetta Stone* (podcast).
57. Regulski: https://blog.britishmuseum.org/inheriting-the-most-iconic -object-at-the-british-museum/.
58. Robinson, 2012, *Cracking the Hieroglyphic Code*, 235.
59. Bankes's role in the story of the Rosetta Stone has recently been recognised in particular by the British Museum, which has included the stone in its themed LGBTQ+ tours of the museum: https://www. theguardian.com/culture/2020/jun/25/rosetta-stone-to-be-added-to-british-museum-lgbtq-tours.

Chapter 2

1. Susan Whitfield, 2004, *Aurel Stein on the Silk Road*, Chicago: Serindia Publications, 9–10; Annabel Walker, 1995, *Aurel Stein: Pioneer of the Silk Road*, Seattle: University of Washington Press, 11.
2. Marc Aurel Stein, though from a Jewish family, was baptised into the Lutheran Church in Budapest (and given the forename Marc) as, in 1862, political and civic rights were not accorded to Jews within the Austro-Hungarian Empire. In his published works in later life, Aurel always published (and signed) his name as M. Aurel Stein. As such, he is referred to as Stein in this chapter.
3. Éva Apor, 2004, 'Sir Aurel Stein and His Hungarian background', in Helen Wang (ed.), *Sir Aurel Stein: Proceedings of the British Museum Study Day 2002*, London: British Museum Press Occasional Paper No. 142, 1–4.
4. Walker, *Aurel Stein*, 13.

5. Whitfield, *Aurel Stein on the Silk Road*, 11–13.
6. Walker, *Aurel Stein*, 13.
7. Apor, 'Sir Aurel Stein'.
8. Whitfield, *Aurel Stein on the Silk Road*, 16–18. Pinyin transcriptions of Chinese names have been used in this chapter.
9. Letter from Stein to his brother Ernst, dated 11 September 1898 (Family Correspondence of Sir Aurel Stein 1885–1925, British Academy, Boxes I and II).
10. Translations of the accounts of Xuanzang, and those of an earlier Buddhist monk, Faxian, who had travelled west in the fourth century CE, had only become available in the West after the middle of the nineteenth century: Whitfield, *Aurel Stein on the Silk Road*, 19.
11. Ibid.
12. Ferdinand von Richthofen, 1877–1912, *China, Ergebnisse eigener Reisen und darauf gegründeter Studien*, Berlin: von Dietrich Reimer (5 vols + atlas).
13. Whitfield, *Aurel Stein on the Silk Road*, 22.
14. Sven Hedin, 1898, *En färd genom Asien 1893–97* (2 vols), Stockholm: Bonniers; Fernand Grenard, 1897–8, *J.-L Dutreuil de Rhins: Mission scientifique dans la Haute Asie 1890–95* (3 vols), Paris : Lerous; Rudolf Hoernle, 1897, 'Three Further Collections of Ancient Manuscripts from Central Asia', *Journal of the Asiatic Society of Bengal* 66(4): 213–60.
15. Back in 1807, Napoleon had suggested to the Russian Tsar, Alexander I, that they should jointly invade India by land from central Asia. The threat did not materialise (not least because Napoleon ended up trying to invade Russia instead), but, following Napoleon's defeat, Russia began its own campaign of slow expansion into central Asia: Peter Hopkirk, 1990, *The Great Game: On Secret Service in High Asia*, London: John Murray, 2–4.
16. Ibid., 319.
17. Ibid., 321.
18. Ibid., 322–5. Through the 1870s and 1880s, a number of high-profile and influential books were also published in Britain and Russia analysing the motives and desired end-games of both players in central Asia: Colonel M. A. Terentiev, *Russia and England in the Struggle for the Markets of Central Asia* (this English translation of the original Russian was published in 1876 in Calcutta); Charles Marvin, 1885, *Russia's Power of Attacking India*, London: W. H.

Allen and Co.; Arminius Vambery, 1885, *The Coming Struggle for India*, London: Cassell.

19. One of these local rulers, with whom both the British and Russians had been negotiating to secure his support, was a man called Yakub Beg, who had taken control of Kashgar by force and declared himself ruler of Kashgaria in 1865: Hopkirk, *The Great Game*, 322–5.

20. Ibid., 451–71.

21. Ibid., 499.

22. Cf. Jeanette Mirsky, 1977, *Sir Aurel Stein: Archaeological Explorer*, Chicago: University of Chicago Press, 107–92.

23. Walker, *Aurel Stein*, 89.

24. M. Aurel Stein, 1903, *Sand-Buried Ruins of Khotan: Personal Narrative of a Journey of Archaeological and Geographical Exploration in Chinese Turkestan*, London: Fisher and Unwin, 112.

25. Ibid., 119.

26. Stein's achievement in winning the trust of the Chinese authorities in this period should not be underestimated, especially as his negotiations were taking place at the same time as the Boxer Rebellion against foreign influence in China was being played out in a series of major military clashes in and around Beijing to the east.

27. Stein, *Sand-Buried Ruins of Khotan*, 131.

28. Ibid., 145.

29. Ibid., 168.

30. Ibid., 292.

31. Ibid., 323.

32. Ibid., 338.

33. Ibid., 368–9.

34. Ibid., 374–7.

35. Stein, *Sand-Buried Ruins of Khotan* (1904 reprint by Hurst and Blackett, London).

36. M. Aurel Stein, 1907, *Ancient Khotan*, Oxford: Clarendon Press.

37. Cf. Mirsky, *Sir Aurel Stein*, 225–330, for Stein's second expedition.

38. Helen Wang (ed.), 2002, *Sir Aurel Stein in The Times*, London: Saffron Books, Eastern Art Publishing, 13.

39. Hopkirk, *The Great Game*, 517–19.

40. Walker, *Aurel Stein*, 139–42. Stein himself had written to the *Royal Geographic Society* in 1906 asking for equipment quickly on the basis that 'the risk of being forestalled by foreign opposition at the sites I have specially in view is considerable' (Bodleian Library MAS 297: 18–20, Stein to Keltie, Srinagar, 6 January 1906).

41. *The Times*, 8 December 1906 (Wang (ed.), *Sir Aurel Stein in The Times*, No. 7).
42. *The Times*, 25 May 1907 (Wang (ed.), *Sir Aurel Stein in The Times*, No. 8).
43. Walker, *Aurel Stein*, 91, 155. For discussion of the condensed versions for *The Times*, see Wang (ed.), 2002, *Sir Aurel Stein in The Times*, 22.
44. Lilla Russell-Smith, 2004, 'Letters, Reports and Bestsellers: Stein's Accounts of His First and Second Expeditions', in Wang (ed.), 2004, *Sir Aurel Stein*, 9–14.
45. *The Times*, 15 October 1907 (Wang (ed.), *Sir Aurel Stein in The Times*, No. 9).
46. M. Aurel Stein, 1912, *Ruins of Desert Cathay: Personal Narrative of Explorations in Central Asia and Westernmost China*, Vol. 2, London: Macmillan and Co., 159.
47. Ibid., 164.
48. Ibid., 165.
49. Ibid., 166.
50. Ibid.
51. Ibid., 167.
52. Ibid.
53. Ibid., 169.
54. Ibid., 170.
55. Ibid., 172.
56. Ibid.
57. Ibid., 174.
58. Ibid., 178.
59. Ibid., 179.
60. Ibid., 180.
61. Ibid., 181.
62. Ibid., 190.
63. Ibid., 191.
64. Ibid., 193.
65. Ibid., 194.
66. Walker, *Aurel Stein*, 175. Stein admitted that he would have offered forty horseshoes of silver/5,000 Rupees – and indeed twice that if necessary: Stein, *Ruins of Desert Cathay*, 192.
67. Whitfield, *Aurel Stein on the Silk Road*, 88.
68. Statement from the National Commission for the Preservation of Antiquities, Peking, China, quoted in Shareen Brysac, 2004, 'Sir

Aurel Stein's Fourth "American" Expedition', in Wang (ed.), 2004, *Sir Aurel Stein*, 17–22.

69. Stein, *Ruins of Desert Cathay*, 191.

70. *The Times*, 21 September 1907; 16 October 1908, 12 November 1908, 28 November 1908 (Wang (ed.), *Sir Aurel Stein in The Times*, Nos. 11–14); Walker, *Aurel Stein*, 181.

71. *The Times*, 29 January 1909 (Wang (ed.), *Sir Aurel Stein in The Times*, No. 15).

72. Whitfield, *Aurel Stein on the Silk Road*, 77. Dash II was left to early retirement with friends in England, and was sadly run over by a bus in Oxford in 1918.

73. Wang (ed.), *Sir Aurel Stein in The Times*, 16.

74. Letter from Lord Curzon to the *Royal Geographic Society* meeting, reported in *The Times*, 9 March 1909 (Wang (ed.), 2002, *Sir Aurel Stein in The Times*, No. 19).

75. Mu Soeng, 2000, *The Diamond Sutra: Transforming the Way We Perceive the World*, Boston: Wisdom Publications, 58.

76. Whitfield, 2004, *Aurel Stein on the Silk Road*, 117.

77. *The Times Literary Supplement*, 7 March 1912, 'Review of *Ruins of Desert Cathay*' by J. O. P. Bland (Wang (ed.), *Sir Aurel Stein in The Times*, No. 34).

78. Whitfield, *Aurel Stein on the Silk Road*, 88.

79. M. Aurel Stein, 1921, *Serindia*, Oxford: Clarendon Press. His full report of his third expedition was published in 1928: M. Aurel Stein, 1928, *Innermost Asia*, Oxford: Clarendon Press.

80. Whitfield, *Aurel Stein on the Silk Road*, 122.

81. The geographical surveys completed by his team of the Pamir and Karakoram mountain ranges, and of the Taklamakan, are also still in use.

Chapter 3

1. Hiram Bingham III, 1913, 'The Discovery of Machu Picchu', *Harper's Monthly* 127: 709–19; Deborah Kops, 2009, *Machu Picchu: Unearthing Ancient Worlds*, Minneapolis: Twenty-First Century Books, 21–2.

2. Lucy C. Salazar, 2004, 'Machu Picchu: Mysterious Royal Estate in the Cloud Forest', in Richard L. Burger and Lucy C. Salazar (eds), *Machu Picchu: Unveiling the Mystery of the Incas*, New Haven: Yale University Press, 21–47.

3. Hiram Bingham III, 1908, 'On the Route of Bolívar's Great March', *Geographical Journal* 32: 329–47.

4. Hiram Bingham III, 1907, 'The Possibilities of South American History and Politics as a Field for Research', Paper presented on 28 December 1907 to the American Political Science Association. The wider interest at this time in improving the relationship between North and South America (for political and economic benefit to both Americas) is underscored by the fact that Bingham's paper was immediately republished in the much-wider-circulating *Monthly Bulletin of the International Bureau of the American Republics* (Vol. 26 (February 1908): 281–99). In the Bulletin's general introduction (Vol. 26 (February 1908): 253) it was claimed that Bingham's talk was 'full of original and interesting matter of value to all students and persons concerned about that part of the world'.

5. Hiram Bingham III, 1911, *Across South America: An Account of a Journey from Buenos Aires to Lima by way of Potosí*, New York: Houghton Mifflin.

6. Hiram Bingham III, 1909, *Journal of an Expedition Across Venezuela and Columbia: An Exploration of the Route of Bolívar's Celebrated March of 1819, and of the Battlefields of Boyaca and Carabobo*, New Haven: Yale Publishing Association; Hiram Bingham III, 1911, *Across South America: An Account of a Journey from Buenos Aires to Lima by way of Potosí*, New York: Houghton Mifflin.

7. Anonymous, 1909, 'Review of A Journey Across Venezuela and Columbia', *Nature* 81: 453–4.

8. 'They tempted me to go and see what lay beyond. In the ever famous words of Rudyard Kipling there was "Something hidden! Go and find it! Go and look beyond the ranges – Something lost behind the ranges. Lost and waiting for you. Go!"' Hiram Bingham III, 2003 (1948), *Lost City of the Incas: The Story of Machu Picchu and Its Builders*, London: Weidenfeld & Nicolson, 132. The *Lost City of the Incas* has been published multiple times by multiple different presses. It was originally published in New York: Hiram Bingham III, 1948, *Lost City of the Incas: The Story of Machu Picchu and Its Builders*, New York: Duell, Sloan and Pearce. All page references, however, in this chapter to *Lost City of the Incas* refer to the 2003 paperback version published by Weidenfeld & Nicolson in London (with an introduction by Hugh Thompson).

9. Hugh Thompson, 2003, 'Introduction to *Lost City of the Incas*', in

Hiram Bingham III, *Lost City of the Incas*, London: Weidenfeld & Nicolson, xxi–xxii.

10. In a letter to *Yale Alumni Weekly* on 10 March 1911, Bingham argued that such searches could improve the quality of teaching and instruction in Latin American history back at universities like Yale: Salazar, 'Machu Picchu', 21–47.

11. Kops, *Machu Picchu*, 14.

12. Ibid., 15.

13. Cusco is the modern spelling most recognised in Peru today, with an older alternative common in many books of Cuzco.

14. Hiram Bingham III, 1909, 'Cuzco and Sacsahuaman', *Records of the Past* 8(5): 223–41.

15. Mark Rice, 2018, *Making Machu Picchu: The Politics of Tourism in Twentieth-Century Peru*, Chapel Hill: University of North Carolina Press, 12–13.

16. The Inca Empire, at its greatest extent in the early sixteenth century, was roughly equivalent in size to that of the Western Roman Empire of the late fourth century CE. Despite its significant size, however, the Inca empire was by no means the biggest empire in the world at the time – the Ming dynasty in China and the Ottoman Empire in Asia, for example, were significantly larger.

17. An alternative legend was that the first Inca ruler, Manco Cápac, had himself emerged from the lake and travelled via underground tunnels to Cusco: Nigel Davies, 1997, *The Ancient Kingdoms of Peru*, London: Penguin Books, 110–11.

18. Ibid., 136.

19. Seven hundred plates of gold were taken off the Temple of the Sun alone in Cusco by the Spanish conquistadors as part of the ransom the Inca ruler Atahualpa offered for his freedom in 1533. The total weight of gold collected from across the Inca Empire for the ransom came in at 11 tons, which was then distributed among the Spanish horsemen (who each got 40 kg) and foot soldiers (who got 20 kg): Davies, *The Ancient Kingdoms of Peru*, 189–90.

20. Ibid., 149–51.

21. Ibid., 146–7, 149–51.

22. Kops, *Machu Picchu*, 5–6.

23. Ibid., 6.

24. See, for example, the accounts of Sarmiento de Gamboa in 1572 commissioned by Viceroy Toledo (who was responsible for the capture and death of the last Inca ruler), which portray the Inca as

usurpers, versus the accounts of Garcilaso de la Vega in 1609, who portrays them as much more benevolent rulers. Cf. Davies, *The Ancient Kingdoms of Peru*, 117–18.

25. For example, the Inca road that stretches through the Atacama desert for a distance of 108 kilometres. It is 3 metres wide and has thirty-two staging posts along it. The most impressive road, however, is the Cusco–Quito highland road, which was a central artery in the Inca Empire network. This road varies between 4 metres and 14 metres wide: Davies, *The Ancient Kingdoms of Peru*, 168–70.

26. Kops, *Machu Picchu*, 8.

27. Davies, *The Ancient Kingdoms of Peru*, 127–35, 185–90.

28. Kops, *Machu Picchu*, 8–9.

29. Davies, *The Ancient Kingdoms of Peru*, 191–203.

30. Hiram Bingham III, 1912, 'The Discovery of Pre-historic Human Remains Near Cuzco, Peru', *American Journal of Science* 33: 297–305. However, when Bingham returned with a new team to Cusco in 1912, including a bone expert, George Eaton, the team, having restudied the bones and the gravel in which they were found, concluded that the bones found in 1911 weren't very old at all: Kops, *Machu Picchu*, 38–9.

31. Bingham III, 1913, 'The Discovery of Machu Picchu'.

32. Ibid.

33. Kops, *Machu Picchu*, 17–19; Rice, *Making Machu Picchu*, 21. As Bingham notes in his 1913 *Harper's Monthly* article, Giesecke's reports also tied in with the published mention of ruins in the Urubamba valley called 'Huaina Picchu or Matcho Picchu' by Wiener in his 1875 volume *Pérou et Bolivie;* Bingham III, 'The Discovery of Machu Picchu'.

34. Ibid.

35. Ibid.

36. Rice, *Making Machu Picchu*, 21.

37. Bingham III, 'The Discovery of Machu Picchu'.

38. Ibid.

39. Ibid.

40. The modern name of the site Bingham thought was Vilcabamba is Espiritu Pampa. It was confirmed as Vilcabamba by the work of US explorer Gene Savoy only in 1964. The modern name of the site Bingham identified as Vitcos is Rosaspata: Kops, *Machu Picchu*, 68.

41. Ibid., 33.

42. It's notable that all of Bingham's 1912 publications about his 1911

expedition focus on his ascent of Mount Coropuna, his discovery of early human bones in Cusco, or his discovery of the last capitals of the Inca at Vitcos and Vilcabamba. Rarely does he mention Machu Picchu: Jerry Patterson, 1957, 'Hiram Bingham, 1875–1956', *The Hispanic American Historical Review* 37(1): 131–7.

43. One of these sites – Llactapata – was only subsequently rediscovered by an international team in 2003: Kops, *Machu Picchu*, 47–51, 68.
44. Local Peruvian archaeological teams had also been working at Machu Picchu from as early as January 1912, and Peru had by this time passed legislation prohibiting the exportation of artefacts: Rice, 2018, *Making Machu Picchu*, 22.
45. Kops, *Machu Picchu*, 51.
46. Ibid., 61.
47. Hiram Bingham III, April 1913, 'In the wonderland of Peru', *National Geographic Magazine* 24(4): 388–573.
48. The 1912 expedition was sponsored by a host of US companies keen to see their goods associated with exploration and discovery (such as Kodak, but also the Winchester Repeating Arms Company), as well as by US companies working in Peru and eager to improve their reputations in both countries (for example, W. R. Grace and Co.): Rice, *Making Machu Picchu*, 22.
49. Kops, *Machu Picchu*, 61; Rice, *Making Machu Picchu*, 22. The extent to which this was a 'discovery' was challenged: on 8 September 1916, a letter was published in *The Times* (although without any documentation to support it) from German engineer Carl Haenel saying he had accompanied explorer J. M. von Hassel to the area in 1910.
50. Bingham III, 'The Discovery of Machu Picchu'.
51. Ibid.
52. Hiram Bingham III, 1922, *Inca Land: Explorations in the Highlands of Peru*, New York: Houghton Mifflin Company, Chapters 9 and 10. The book can be read online here: https://www.gutenberg.org/files/10772/10772-h/10772-h.htm.
53. Ibid., Chapters 16, 17 and 18.
54. Ibid., 338.
55. 'Review of *Inca Land: Explorations in the Highlands of Peru*', *Nature* 111(665) (1923).
56. Hiram Bingham III, 1930, *Machu Picchu: A Citadel of the Incas*, New Haven: Yale University Press.

57. J. Leslie Mitchell, 1931, 'Review of Machu Picchu: A Citadel of the Incas', *Antiquity* 5(18): 263–4. Cf. also, *New York Times*, Review, 4 May 1930, 'An Ancient City of the Incas: Dr Bingham sums up the results of the Machu Picchu Expedition' by Philip Ainsworth Means.

58. Hiram Bingham III, 2003 (1948), *Lost City of the Incas*, 270.

59. Kops, *Machu Picchu*, 61–2; Rice, *Making Machu Picchu*, 23.

60. Ibid., 24.

61. Ibid., 29, n. 83.

62. 'Cuzco Celebrates Fourth Centenary', *New York Times*, 24 March 1934.

63. Rice, *Making Machu Picchu*, 65.

64. Hiram Bingham III, 2003 (1948), *Lost City of the Incas*, 179.

65. Ibid., 185.

66. Ibid., 187.

67. The current accepted differentiation is that while others knew about and had visited Machu Picchu before Bingham, he was the 'scientific discoverer' of the site in that he recognised its importance and was the first to undertake systematic uncovering and study of it: Peter Eisner 'Who Discovered Machu Picchu?', *Smithsonian Magazine*, March 2009.

68. Quoted as 'Praise for Lost City of the Incas', in Hiram Bingham III, 2003 (1948), *Lost City of the Incas*.

69. Mary Anne Potts, 2010, 'Finding Machu Picchu: A Look at Explorer Hiram Bingham, a Real-Life Indiana Jones', *National Geographic Online* (26 May); Christopher Heaney, 2011, *Cradle of Gold: The Story of Hiram Bingham, a Real-Life Indiana Jones, and the Search for Machu Picchu*, London: Palgrave Macmillan.

70. Rice, 2018, *Making Machu Picchu*, 100.

71. Quote from *El Comercio de Lima*, 16 July 1972: Rice, *Making Machu Picchu*, 121.

72. Ibid., 137–40.

73. Ibid., 141–2; Kops, *Machu Picchu*, 62.

74. For the discovery of the documentation and the original Spanish sources: John Howland Rowe, 1987, 'Machu Picchu a la luz de los documentos del siglo XVI', *Kuntor* 4: 12–20; Bernabé Cobo, 1979 [1653], *History of the Inca Empire*, trans. R. B. Hamilton, Austin: University of Texas Press, 135–7. For further discussion: Richard L. Burger and Lucy C. Salazar, 2004, 'Introduction', in Burger and Salazar (eds), *Machu Picchu*, 2; Salazar, 'Machu Picchu'.

75. Ibid.
76. Ibid.
77. Ibid., 21–47.
78. Salazar, 'Machu Picchu'.
79. Ibid.
80. Alfredo Valencia Zegarra (trans. Richard L. Burger), 2004, 'Recent Archaeological Investigations at Machu Picchu', in Burger and Salazar (eds), *Machu Picchu*, 71–82.
81. Richard L. Burger, 2004, 'Scientific Insights into Daily Life at Machu Picchu', in Burger and Salazar (eds), *Machu Picchu*, 85–106.
82. Ibid.
83. Rice, *Making Machu Picchu*, 155.
84. Ibid.
85. Jorge A. Flores Ochoa (trans. Richard L. Burger), 'Contemporary Significance of Machu Picchu', in Burger and Salazar (eds), *Machu Picchu*, 109–23.
86. Rice, *Making Machu Picchu*, 166; Flores Ochoa, 'Contemporary Significance of Machu Picchu'.

Chapter 4

1. Mary Leakey, 1984, *Disclosing the Past: An Autobiography*, London: Doubleday, 173–4.
2. Ibid., 178.
3. Ibid., 174.
4. Ibid., 173; Mary Bowman-Kruhm, 2010, *The Leakeys: A Biography*, New York: Prometheus Books, 114.
5. Mary received four honorary doctorates during her life from universities in Africa, the USA and the UK (alongside a long list of medals and awards), but never used the title Dr in front of her name in her publications or in day-to-day life. I have maintained her preference here in this text.
6. Leakey, *Disclosing the Past*, 168–72.
7. Deborah Heiligman, 1995, *Mary Leakey: In Search of Human Beginnings*, New York: Scientific American Books, 58.
8. https://www.washingtonpost.com/archive/local/1996/12/10/eminent-archaeologist-mary-leakey-dies-at-83/d2010875-7d07-42fb-9532-c237405940d0/.
9. Mary Leakey and Richard Hay, 1982, 'The Fossil Footprints of Laetoli', *Scientific American* 246(2): 50–7; Mary Leakey and J. M.

Harris 1987, *Laetoli: A Pliocene Site in Northern Tanzania*, Oxford: Clarendon Press; Tim White and Gen Suwa, 1987, 'Hominid Footprints at Laetoli: Facts and Interpretations', *American Journal of Physical Anthropology* 72(4): 485–514.

10. Leakey, *Disclosing the Past*, 212.
11. Ibid., 23.
12. Ibid., 25.
13. Heiligman, *Mary Leakey*, 10. John Frere published his – later celebrated – article in 1798, the same year that Nelson won the Battle of the Nile again Napoleon, trapping his army in Egypt soon after they had discovered the Rosetta Stone.
14. Leakey, *Disclosing the Past*, 211.
15. Ibid., 35.
16. Ibid., 39. Dr Thompson was offered the post of Disney Professor of Archaeology at Cambridge in 1938 but refused it, and the post was subsequently offered to Dr Dorothy Garrod, who served in the post from 1939–52. Dorothy was the first female ever to hold a 'Chair' (the most prestigious professorial post) at either Oxford or Cambridge.
17. Bowman-Kruhm, *The Leakeys*, 33. At this time, many were convinced that the 'missing link' between ape and man had been found in Sussex, England, in 1912: Piltdown Man. However, this was eventually, in 1953, proved to be a hoax in which the jaw of a modern human had been linked with an orangutan's jawbone.
18. Heiligman, *Mary Leakey*, 31–5.
19. Mary Leakey, 1979, *Olduvai Gorge: My Search for Early Man*, London: Collins, 12–14.
20. Leakey, *Disclosing the Past*, 55.
21. This find became known as OH2 – Olduvai Hominid 2 (after the skeleton found by Hans Reck back in 1913 was labelled as OH1): Leakey, *Disclosing the Past*, 56.
22. Leakey, *Disclosing the Past*, 56–9; Leakey, *Olduvai Gorge*, 15–16; Bowman-Kruhm, *The Leakeys*, 53.
23. Leakey, *Disclosing the Past*, 58.
24. Leakey, *Olduvai Gorge*, 16; Heiligman, *Mary Leakey*, 36.
25. Leakey, *Disclosing the Past*, 63.
26. Heiligman, *Mary*, 39–40; Bowman-Kruhm, *The Leakeys*, 55.
27. Leakey, *Disclosing the Past*, 67.
28. Ibid., 69–80.
29. Ibid., 75; Bowman-Kruhm, *The Leakeys*, 56–61.

30. Leakey, *Disclosing the Past*, 90.
31. Bowman-Kruhm, *The Leakeys*, 70.
32. Leakey, *Disclosing the Past*, 83, 96; Bowman-Kruhm, *The Leakeys*, 66, 71.
33. Leakey, *Disclosing the Past*, 96.
34. Ibid., 102.
35. Heiligman, *Mary Leakey*, 43–4.
36. In the 1960s, some further fragments of this skull were found hiding under a tortoise shell in a box of Rusinga Island fossil finds dating back to Mary and Louis's 1947 excavation season – and these have now been added to the *Proconsul* skull: Leakey, *Disclosing the Past*, 99.
37. Ibid., 99. Indeed it was the very first skull of a Miocene-era ape to be found: ibid., 212.
38. As Mary later put it: 'Even if *Proconsul* is perhaps not a direct human ancestor, maybe our personal tribute [conceiving a child] was not wholly inappropriate': Leakey, *Disclosing the Past*, 99.
39. Ibid., 99–102; Heiligman, *Mary Leakey*, 45.
40. Ibid., 46.
41. The skull remained the property of the British Museum of Natural History until 1982, when it was proved (thanks to Mary Leakey finding the key documentation) that the Kenyan government had only let it out of the country in 1948 as a loan. It has now been returned to Kenya and can be seen in Nairobi's National Museum: Bowman-Kruhm, *The Leakeys*, 84.
42. Her work was published in Mary Leakey, 1983, *Africa's Vanishing Art*, New York: Doubleday; Leakey, *Disclosing the Past*, 105–6.
43. Ibid., 106.
44. Ibid.
45. Bowman-Kruhm, *The Leakeys*, 77.
46. Leakey, *Olduvai Gorge*, 19.
47. Ibid., 42.
48. Ibid., 43.
49. Heiligman, *Mary Leakey*, 49.
50. Bowman-Kruhm, *The Leakeys*, 79.
51. Ibid., 77.
52. Ibid., 80.
53. Leakey, *Disclosing the Past*, 120–1.
54. Cf. Sonia Cole, 1975, *Leakey's Luck: The Life of Louis Leakey 1903–1972*, London: Collins.

55. Heiligman, *Mary Leakey*, 52–3; Leakey, *Olduvai Gorge*, 75–6.

56. Dear Boy is known in the Olduvai excavation records as OH5: Olduvai Hominid No. 5).

57. Leakey, *Disclosing the Past*, 120–1.

58. Leakey, *Olduvai Gorge*, 73–4; Phillip V. Tobias, 1967, *Olduvai Gorge Volume 2: The Cranium and Maxillary Dentition of Australopithecus (Zinjanthropus) Boisei*, Cambridge: Cambridge University Press.

59. Leakey, *Olduvai Gorge*, 168–9. It is now thought that *Australopithecus boisei* represents an 'extinct side-line of hominid evolution not in the direct ancestry of man': Leakey, *Olduvai Gorge*, 17.

60. Leakey, *Disclosing the Past*, 213.

61. In 1962, Mary and Louis were awarded the gold Hubbard Award from the National Geographic Society for their work.

62. Simon's time with Mary came to an end when back in Nairobi he got drunk on a series of bottles of whiskey, sherry and Drambuie and had to be rehomed: Leakey, *Olduvai Gorge*, 29.

63. Ibid., 31. Mary had a number of other pets, including snakes and owls (for whom she kept minced rat meat in the camp refrigerator).

64. The dating of the different beds at Olduvai was further enhanced by the on-site work of geologist Richard Hay, who participated in each season from 1962 to 1974: Richard Hay, 1976, *The Geology of Olduvai Gorge*, Berkeley: University of California Press.

65. Leakey, *Disclosing the Past*, 213.

66. The *Homo habilis* remains from the lower part of Bed I were found in 1968 by one of Mary's African excavators, Peter Nzube, who found an almost complete cranium (OH24) dating to earlier than 1.75 million years ago: Leakey, *Olduvai Gorge*, 80.

67. Leakey, *Olduvai Gorge*, 73–4. For detailed discussion of the finds in the different beds see: Mary Leakey, 1971, *Olduvai Gorge Volume 3: Excavations in Beds I and II*, Cambridge: Cambridge University Press; Mary Leakey and D. Roe, 1994, *Olduvai Gorge Volume 5: Excavations in Beds III, IV and the Masek Beds (1968–1971)*, Cambridge: Cambridge University Press.

68. Mary Leakey, *Olduvai Gorge*, 14.

69. Ibid., 22.

70. Ibid., 36. It was in fact while building the museum that one of Mary's African excavators, Ndibo Mbuika, found a(nother) *Homo habilis* skull (OH13), which proved to be the latest dated specimen to be found in the stratigraphy of the gorge: Leakey, *Olduvai Gorge*, 78.

71. Leakey, *Disclosing the Past*, 157.
72. Heiligman, *Mary Leakey*, 38; Bowman-Kruhm, *The Leakeys*, 112.
73. Leakey, *Disclosing the Past*, 199.
74. From 1964 at Olduvai, she worked in accordance with the Tanzanian government's new Antiquities legislation, which required explicit government permission for excavation. Mary's subsequent permits for excavation were granted only on the condition that all finds stayed within the country (with the potential for loans abroad): Leakey, *Olduvai Gorge*, 37. As discussed in an earlier note, in the early 1980s, it was Mary who found evidence to help prove the Kenyan government's case that the export of the *Proconsul africanus* skull from Rusinga Island to the UK back in 1948–9 had been a loan, rather than a gift. As a result the skull is now back in Kenya: Leakey, *Disclosing the Past*, 101.
75. Ibid., 200.

Chapter 5

1. Pinyin transliteration is used for Chinese names and terms in this chapter, except for bibliography titles where the original transliteration has been maintained.
2. This period of time is known traditionally in Chinese history as two distinct eras: the 'Spring and Autumn period' (776–476 BCE) due to the name of an important surviving text dated to this time, and the 'Warring States period' (476–221 BCE), named for the gathering intensity of the conflict at this time, leading to Qin's eventual emergence as the sole survivor in 221 BCE. Cf. M. Scott, 2016, *Ancient Worlds: An Epic History of East and West*, London: Hutchinson, 111–214.
3. D. Bodde, 1967, *China's First Unifier: A Study of the Ch'in Dynasty as Seen in the Life of Li Ssu*, Hong Kong: Hong Kong University Press, 4–5.
4. F. Wood, 2007, *China's First Emperor and His Terracotta Warriors*, New York: St Martin's Press, 21.
5. The size of territory conquered and commanded by the Qin would not be significantly expanded by any future Chinese rulers until the eighteenth century, when the Qing emperors expanded the country northwards and westwards to resemble more what is now China. Moreover, while China has always referred to itself as *Zhongguo*, 'Central/Middle Kingdom', the modern name of

'China' is most likely a derivation of the Greek, Roman (and even Indian) transliterations of Qin: Wood, *China's First Emperor*, 27. Cf. M. E. Lewis, 2007, *The Early Chinese Empires: Qin and Han*, Cambridge, MA: Harvard University Press.

6. Due to its position on the border of the Chinese world, the Qin state was often considered to be somewhat 'barbarian', or its inhabitants, at least, to be descended from barbarians: Wood, *China's First Emperor*, 20.

7. Scott, *Ancient Worlds*, 139; W. Scheidel, 2009, 'From the "Great Convergence" to the "First Great Divergence": Roman and Qin-Han state formation and its aftermath', in W. Scheidel (ed.), *Rome and China: Comparative Perspectives on Ancient World Empires*, Oxford: Oxford University Press, 11–23.

8. Para 3 (p. 185) in Yang Shang, *The Book of Lord Shang. A Classic of the Chinese School of Law*, translated from the Chinese with Introduction and Notes by Dr J. J. L. Duyvendak, London: Arthur Probsthain, 1928.

9. Cf. the description of the state of Qin, c.400 BCE: 'Qin's character is strong, the land treacherous and the government severe. Their rewards and punishments are believed in, the people never yield but instead are all fiery and contentious': Wu Qi, *Wuzi*, Section 2, 'Evaluating the Enemy'. The full text can be read in translation in R. D. Sawyer, 2007, *The Seven Military Classics of Ancient China*, New York: Basic Books.

10. Scott, *Ancient Worlds*, 99, 161.

11. E. Burman, 2018, *Terracotta Warriors: History, Mystery and the Latest Discoveries*, London: Weidenfeld & Nicolson, 29.

12. Ibid., 32.

13. *Zhan Guo Ce (Annals of the Warring States) The Book of Qin*, Section 2, 'The Story of Su Qin', translation by J. I. Crump Jr, *Chan Kuo Ts'e*, 1970, Oxford: Clarendon Press, 55.

14. The grandfather and father of King Zheng were not half as successful as his great-grandfather and great-great grandfather. His grandfather ruled for just three days after his coronation and his father for three years.

15. Sima Qian, *Shiji*, 6, translation by B. Watson, 1993, *Records of the Grand Historian: Qin Dynasty*, New York: Columbia University Press, 38–9. The comment was made when King Zheng was twenty-two years old, nine years after coming to the throne.

16. Quoted in Burman, *Terracotta Warriors*, 41.

17. Wood, *China's First Emperor*, 26.
18. Mencius Part II, XXI, 2, translated by J. Legge, 1875, *The Chinese Classic: Volume 2 – The Life and Teaching of Mencius*, London: Trübner and Co., 335.
19. Cf. A. F. P. Hulsewe, 1985, *Remnants of Qin Law*, Leiden: Brill.
20. Sima Qian, *Shiji*, 6, translated by R. Dawson, 2007, *Sima Qian the First Emperor: Selections from the Historical Records*, Oxford: Oxford University Press, 64.
21. Jane Portal, 2007, *The Terracotta Warriors*, London: British Museum Press, 10.
22. Wood, *China's First Emperor*, 28.
23. Sima Qian, *Shiji*, 6 (trans. Dawson, *Sima Qian the First Emperor*), 64.
24. Sima Qian, *Shiji*, 6 (trans. Dawson, *Sima Qian the First Emperor*), 74.
25. Wood, *China's First Emperor*, 78–88.
26. Burman, *Terracotta Warriors*, 49–52.
27. Cf. Sima Qian, *Shiji*, 88 (trans. Dawson, *Sima Qian the First Emperor*), 53–9.
28. Scott, *Ancient Worlds*, 162–3.
29. Sima Qian, *Shiji*, 6 (trans. Dawson, *Sima Qian the First Emperor*), 81.
30. Wood, *China's First Emperor*, 115–22.
31. Sima Qian, *Shiji*, 6 (trans. Dawson, *Sima Qian the First Emperor*), 75.
32. Wood, *China's First Emperor*, 128–9.
33. Sima Qian, *Shiji*, 6 (trans. Dawson, *Sima Qian the First Emperor*), 82–3.
34. Sima Qian, *Shiji*, 6 and 7 (trans. Dawson, *Sima Qian the First Emperor*, 82–3, 103–33.
35. Burman, *Terracotta Warriors*, 93–4.
36. S. Faison, 'Clinton in China: The Antiquities – 2 Tales of Who Found the Terracotta Men', *New York Times* 25 June 1998; Wood, *China's First Emperor*, 1; Burman, *Terracotta Warriors*, xx.
37. Xudong Yang and Dahai Shao, 'The man who dug a well and found an army', 15 March 2013. Published on www.swissinfo.ch.
38. Yang and Shao, 'The man who dug a well'.
39. Yang and Shao, 'The man who dug a well'.
40. M. Ives and K. Kan, 'Zhao Kangmin, Restorer of China's Ancient Terracotta Warriors, Dies at 81', *New York Times*, 22 May 2018.

41. Ibid.

42. Yang and Shao, 'The man who dug a well'.

43. Cf. J. Glancey, 'The Army that Conquered the World', BBC Culture website, 12 April 2017.

44. Burman, *Terracotta Warriors*, xxi.

45. Wood, *China's First Emperor*, 141–59.

46. As named by French Prime Minister (at the time) Jacques Chirac in September 1987.

47. Burman, *Terracotta Warriors*, 78–84, 151–2; Wood, *China's First Emperor*, 131–2; Portal, *The Terracotta Warriors*, 11.

48. Ibid., 41.

49. Burman, *Terracotta Warriors*, 87, 95–7; Portal, *The Terracotta Warriors*, 17.

50. Ibid., 92.

51. Burman, *Terracotta Warriors*, 98–9, 136–7, 178; Portal, *The Terracotta Warriors*, 16.

52. Ibid., 6.

53. *Lüshi Chunqiu* (Annals of Lü Buwei) 10/3.1, translated by J. Knoblock and J. Riegel, 2001, *Annals of Lü Buwei*, Stanford: Stanford University Press, 230.

54. Sima Qian, *Shiji*, 6 (trans. Dawson, *Sima Qian the First Emperor*), 83.

55. Similar scenes of destruction have been found at other Qin-era tombs, like that of the First Emperor's grandmother, the Queen Dowager Xia: Burman, 2018, *Terracotta Warriors*, 142–3; Wood, *China's First Emperor*, 132.

56. Ibid., 132; Portal, *The First Emperor*, 207.

57. For discussion: L. Ledderose, 2000, 'A Magic Army for the Emperor', in L. Ledderose (ed.), *Ten Thousand Things: Module and Mass Production in Chinese Art*, Princeton: Princeton University Press, 51–74. Many of the figures are stamped with characters to indicate their maker and/or provenance – suggesting a very well-organised factory-like process for their production: Burman, *Terracotta Warriors*, 168.

58. Ibid., 111; H. Wu, 2005, 'On Tomb Figurines: The Beginning of a Visual Tradition', in H. Wu and K. R. Tsiang (eds), *Body and Face in Chinese Visual Culture*, Cambridge, MA: Harvard University Press, 13–47.

59. Wood, *China's First Emperor*, 134; Ledderose, 'A Magic Army for the Emperor'.

60. Burman, *Terracotta Warriors*, 151.
61. Ibid., 90–1. Lots of bronze weaponry is missing from the warriors and it is suspected that because they were such good usable weapons, they were taken by the rebels ransacking the tomb complex at the time of the collapse of the Qin Empire: Wood, *China's First Emperor*, 135.
62. Burman, *Terracotta Warriors*, 169.
63. Ibid., 112–13.
64. Sima Qian, *Shiji*, 123, translated by B. Watson, 1993, *Records of the Grand Historian: Han Dynasty Volume II*, New York: Columbia University Press, 233–6.
65. Burman, *Terracotta Warriors*, 152–66; L. Nickel, 2013, 'The First Emperor and Sculpture in China', *Bulletin of the School of Oriental and African Studies* 76(3): 413–47.
66. Portal, *The Terracotta Warriors*, 16, 66–8.
67. The Terracotta Warrior exhibition at the British Museum, September 2007–April 2008, broke records for advance ticket sales and was the second most popular exhibition in the museum's entire history.
68. https://jingdaily.com/chinas-terracotta-warriors-storm-sydney/.
69. http://global.chinadaily.com.cn/a/202101/05/WS5ff3d11aa31024ad0baa0834.html.
70. Yang and Shao, 'The man who dug a well'.
71. Ives and Kan 'Zhao Kangmin'. The rivalry continues at the tourist site itself, with different sellers claiming to have found the warriors: Faison, 'Clinton in China'.
72. E.g. www.travelchinaguide.com: https://www.travelchinaguide.com/attraction/shaanxi/xian/terra_cotta_army/face_3.htm.
73. Faison, 'Clinton in China'.
74. Zhao Xu, 'Yang Zhifa, 76, soldiers on amid terracotta warriors', *New York Times*, 9 December 2014.
75. Glancey, 'The Army that Conquered the World'.
76. 'That's life. Even if there is a lot of injustice in society, there's no point in getting angry about it': Yang and Shao, 'The man who dug a well'.
77. Reported (in 2017) as comments made back in 2007 to the *South China Morning Post*, in Glancey, 'The Army that Conquered the World'.

Chapter 6

1. My thanks to Mehmed Çakir, now sixty-three years old, for responding to my request for an interview. In response to my questions, he provided written answers in Turkish. My thanks also go to my Turkish friends and colleagues Munir Akdogan, Dr Kerim Altug and Dr Bahadir Berkaya for helping to secure the interview with Mehmed and for translating his responses alongside, in the case of Dr Berkaya, for telling me the story of his own involvement in the discovery.
2. G. F. Bass, P. Throckmorton, J. Du Plat Taylor, J. B. Hennessy, A. R. Shulman and H.-G. Buchholz, 1967, 'Cape Gelidonya: A Bronze Age Shipwreck', *Transactions of the American Philosophical Society* 57(8): 1–177.
3. 'He' is used throughout here, as sponge-diving has always been considered in Turkey a male-only profession.
4. Bass, Throckmorton, et al., 'Cape Gelidonya'.
5. G. F. Bass, 2005, 'Introduction', in G. F. Bass (ed.), *Beneath the Seven Seas: Adventures with the Institute of Nautical Archaeology*, London: Thames & Hudson, 10–27.
6. My thanks to Dr Bahadir Berkaya for giving his time for a telephone interview in autumn 2020.
7. Bahadir Berkaya, personal communication, October 2020.
8. Cemal is now the Frederick R. Mayer Faculty Professor of Nautical Archaeology at Texas A&M University.
9. G. F. Bass, 1986, 'A Bronze Age Shipwreck at Ulu Burun (Kas): 1984 Campaign', *American Journal of Archaeology* 90(3): 269–96.
10. C. Pulak, 2005, 'Discovering a Royal Ship from the Age of King Tut: Ulu Burun Turkey', in G. Bass (ed.), *Beneath the Seven Seas: Adventures with the Institute of Nautical Archaeology*, London: Thames and Hudson, 34–47.
11. C. Pulak, 1988, 'The Bronze Age Shipwreck at Ulu Burun, Turkey: 1985 Campaign', *American Journal of Archaeology* 92(1): 1–37.
12. Most early publications spell Ulu Burun as two words, but Uluburun is a better rendition of the traditional Turkish spelling and is used in most recent publications. I have thus used it throughout this chapter.
13. Bass, Throckmorton, et al., 'Cape Gelidonya'.
14. K. Meckelroy (ed.), 1980, *Archaeology Under Water: An Atlas of the World's Submerged Sites*, Berkshire: McGraw Hill.
15. Bass, 'A Bronze Age Shipwreck'.

16. Bass, 'Introduction'.
17. C. Pulak, 1998, 'The Uluburun Shipwreck: An Overview', *International Journal of Nautical Archaeology* 27(3): 188–224.
18. C. Pulak, 2012, 'Uluburun Shipwreck', in E. H. Cline (ed.), *The Oxford Handbook of the Bronze Age Aegean*, Oxford: Oxford University Press, 863–79.
19. Bass, 'A Bronze Age Shipwreck'.
20. Ibid.
21. Ibid.
22. Bass, Throckmorton, et al., 'Cape Gelidonya'.
23. Cf. Monroe, 2010, 'Sunk Costs at Late Bronze Age Uluburun', *Bulletin of the American Schools of Oriental Research* 357: 19–33.
24. A. Hauptmann, R. Maddin and M. Prange, 2002, 'On the Structure and Composition of Copper and Tin Ingots Excavated from the Shipwreck of Uluburun', *Bulletin of the American Schools of Oriental Research* 328: 1–30.
25. Pulak, 'The Uluburun Shipwreck'; Hauptmann, Maddin and Prange, 'On the Structure and Composition of Copper and Tin Ingots'.
26. Pulak, 'The Uluburun Shipwreck'.
27. Hauptmann, Maddin and Prange, 'On the Structure and Composition of Copper and Tin Ingots'.
28. J. D. Muhly, 1985, 'Sources of Tin and the Beginnings of Bronze Metallurgy', *American Journal of Archaeology* 89: 275–91; Hauptmann, Maddin and Prange, 'On the Structure and Composition of Copper and Tin Ingots'.
29. Pulak, 'Discovering a Royal Ship'.
30. C. Haldane, 1993, 'Evidence for Organic Cargoes in the Late Bronze Age', *World Archaeology* 24(3): 348–60; Pulak, 'Uluburun Shipwreck'.
31. Ibid.
32. A. Anastassiades and L. Ellis, 2008, 'The Conservation of Glass Ingots from the Bronze Age Uluburun Shipwreck', *Studies in Conservation* 53(4): 225–37.
33. Pulak, 'Uluburun Shipwreck'.
34. G. F. Bass, C. Pulak, D. Collon and J. Weinstein, 1989, 'The Bronze Age Shipwreck at Ulu Burun: 1986 Campaign', *American Journal of Archaeology* 93(1): 1–29.
35. It is in fact the largest single deposit of olive stones from the Late Bronze Age Mediterranean: Haldane, 'Evidence for Organic Cargoes'.

36. C. Ward, 2003, 'Pomegranates in Eastern Mediterranean Contexts during the Late Bronze Age', *World Archaeology* 34(3): 529–41.

37. Pulak, 'Uluburun Shipwreck'.

38. T. Cucchi, 2008, 'Uluburun Shipwreck Stowaway House Mouse: Molar Shape Analysis and Indirect Clues about the Vessel's Last Journey', *Journal of Archaeological Science* 35: 2953–59.

39. F. W. Welter-Schultes, 2008, 'Bronze Age Shipwreck Snails from Turkey: First Direct Evidence for Oversea Carriage of Land Snails in Antiquity', *Journal of Molluscan Studies* 74(1): 79–87.

40. Pulak, 'Uluburun Shipwreck'.

41. J. Vidal, 2006, 'Ugarit and the Southern Levantine Ports', *Journal of the Economic and Social History of the Orient* 49(3): 269–79; A. and S. Sherratt, 1991, 'From Luxuries to Commodities: The Nature of Mediterranean Bronze Age Trading Systems', in N. Gale (ed.), *Bronze Age Trade in the Mediterranean*, Jonsered: Paul Aströms Förlag, 351–86.

42. Pulak, 'Uluburun Shipwreck'.

43. C. Bachhuber, 2006, 'Aegean Interest on the Uluburun Ship', *American Journal of Archaeology* 110(3): 345–63.

44. Güzden Varinlioglu, 2020, 'Assessing a Decade of Kas Underwater Archaeopark', *International Journal of Nautical Archaeology* 49(1): 74–86.

Chapter 7

1. My sincerest thanks to Dr Natalia Polosmak, the discoverer of the Princess of Altai, who kindly agreed to be interviewed for this chapter, and responded to my questions via email in May 2021.

2. *Moscow Times*, 16 April 2020.

3. *Siberian Times*, 21 August 2014; G. Plets, N. Konstantinov, V. Soenov and E. Robinson, 2013, 'Repatriation, Doxa and Contested Heritages: The Return of an Altai Princess in an International Perspective', *Anthropology and Archaeology of Eurasia* 52(2): 73–100. For the Altai epic of Ochi-Bala: V. M. Gatsak (ed.), 1997, *The Altaic Heroic Narratives of 'Ochi-Bala' and 'Khan-Altyn'*, Vol. 15 of *Folklore Monuments of the Peoples of Siberia and the Far East*, published by the Russian Academy of Sciences.

4. *Siberian Times*, 14 August 2012; Plets, Konstantinov, Soenov and Robinson, 'Repatriation, Doxa and Contested Heritages'. Some of the excavation team even claimed they had been visited by

nightmares at the time of excavation, as if the 'place was testing our will to be there': PBS documentary, *Ice Mummies: Siberian Ice Maiden*, aired 24 November 1998.

5. *Siberian Times*, 14 August 2012; the *Observer*, 3 October 2017; *Moscow Times*, 16 April 2020.

6. Dr Natalia Polosmak, interview, 13 May 2021; *Siberian Times*, 14 August 2012; Plets, Konstantinov, Soenov and Robinson, 'Repatriation, Doxa and Contested Heritages'.

7. TASS Russian News Agency, 26 September 2012.

8. *Siberian Times*, 21 August 2014.

9. Ibid.

10. Ibid.; campaigners note that a similar ancient preserved body, the 'Saka King', was re-buried in Kazakhstan in July 2013 after a decade of indigenous activism: Plets, Konstantinov, Soenov and Robinson, 'Repatriation, Doxa and Contested Heritages'.

11. *Siberian Times*, 21 August 2014.

12. *Moscow Times*, 16 April 2020.

13. N. Polosmak, 'A Mummy Unearthed from the Pastures of Heaven', *National Geographic* 186(4): 80–103; PBS documentary, *Ice Mummies*. It was not without irony that the Republic of Altai, when banning any further excavation on the Plateau after the removal of the princess's remains in 1993, declared the Ukok 'a Quiet Zone'.

14. Polosmak, 'A Mummy Unearthed'.

15. Herodotus, *Histories* 4.71–2.

16. B. Cunliffe, 2015, *By Steppe, Ocean and Desert: The Birth of Eurasia*, Oxford: Oxford University Press, 234–5.

17. Sima Qian, *Shiji*, Chapter 110 (translated in B. Watson 1993 *Sima Qian: Records of the Grand Historian* Volume 2 New Yorks: Columbia University Press, 129–62).

18. Cunliffe, *By Steppe, Ocean and Desert*, 226–36.

19. F. Van Noten and N. Polosmak, 1995, 'The Frozen Tombs of the Scythians', *Endeavour* 19(2): 76–82.

20. S. I. Rudenko, 1953, *The Cultures of the Altai Mountains Population in Scythian Times*, Moscow (Leningrad: in Russian). Cunliffe, *By Steppe, Ocean and Desert*, 236–42; Van Noten and Polosmak, 'The Frozen Tombs of the Scythians'; Polosmak, 'Twenty Years After', *Science First Hand* 37(N1): 6–23; Polosmak, 'On the Path to Celestial Pastures', *Science First Hand* 39(N3): 6–17.

21. Cunliffe, *By Steppe, Ocean and Desert*, 236–42; Van Noten and

Polosmak, 'The Frozen Tombs of the Scythians'; Polosmak, 'Twenty Years After'; Polosmak, 'On the Path to Celestial Pastures'. The preserved corpses are now on display, alongside many of the surviving objects from these tombs, in the Hermitage Museum in St Petersburg.

22. Van Noten and Polosmak, 'The Frozen Tombs of the Scythians'; N. Polosmak, 2015, 'A Different Archaeology: Pazyryk Culture, A Snapshot', *Science First Hand* 42(N3): 78–103.

23. Polosmak, 'A Mummy Unearthed'.

24. Ibid.

25. Ibid.

26. N. Polosmak, 1995, 'The Ak-Alakh "Frozen Grave" Barrow', *Ancient Civilisations from Scythia to Siberia* 1(3): 346–54.

27. Ibid.; A. Pilipenko, R. Trapezov and N. Polosmak, 2015, 'A Paleogenetic Study of Pazyryk People Buried at Ak-Alakha-1, the Altai Mountains', *Archaeology, Ethnology and Anthropology of Eurasia* 43(4): 144–50.

28. Polosmak, 'The Ak-Alakh "Frozen Grave" Barrow'.

29. Ibid.

30. Polosmak, 'A Mummy Unearthed'.

31. Ibid.; PBS documentary, *Ice Mummies*.

32. Polosmak, 'The Burial of a Noble Pazyryk Woman'.

33. N. Polosmak, 2017 (ed.), 'The Ukok Diary', *Science First Hand* 47(N2/3): 138–44.

34. Ibid.

35. Ibid.

36. Ibid.

37. Ibid.

38. Ibid.

39. Polosmak, 'The Burial of a Noble Pazyryk Woman'.

40. Ibid.; Polosmak, 'A Mummy Unearthed'.

41. Ibid.; PBS documentary, *Ice Mummies*.

42. Polosmak, 'The Burial of a Noble Pazyryk Woman'; Polosmak, 'A Mummy Unearthed'; PBS documentary, *Ice Mummies*.

43. Polosmak, 'The Burial of a Noble Pazyryk Woman'.

44. Ibid.; Polosmak, 'A Mummy Unearthed'; Polosmak (ed.), 'The Ukok Diary'.

45. Polosmak, 'A Mummy Unearthed'; Polosmak (ed.), 'The Ukok Diary'.

46. Polosmak, 'A Mummy Unearthed'.

47. Ibid.; Polosmak (ed.), 'The Ukok Diary'.

48. Polosmak, 'A Mummy Unearthed'.

49. Ibid.; Polosmak (ed.), 'The Ukok Diary'; Polosmak, 'The Burial of a Noble Pazyryk Woman'.

50. Polosmak, 'A Mummy Unearthed'; Polosmak (ed.), 'The Ukok Diary'.

51. That science was applied to preserving her body, which, now out of the ice, began to decay, in part thanks to faulty freezers at the Institute in Novosibirsk. The Lady was dispatched to specialists based at the Lenin Mausoleum, who exposed her to a bath of chemicals, just like they had done Lenin's body, and successfully arrested and reversed the deterioration: Polosmak, 'Twenty Years After'.

52. V. Molodin and N. Polosmak, 2016, 'A Multidisciplinary Approach to the Study of Archaeological Complexes with Mummified Objects', *Herald of the Russian Academy of Sciences* 86(2): 111–17.

53. Polosmak, 'A Mummy Unearthed'; Polosmak, 'The Burial of a Noble Pazyryk Woman'; Polosmak, 'Twenty Years After'; PBS documentary, *Ice Mummies*.

54. Polosmak, 'A Mummy Unearthed'; Polosmak, 'The Burial of a Noble Pazyryk Woman'; Polosmak, 'Twenty Years After'.

55. N. Polosmak, 2015, 'A Different Archaeology: Pazyryk Culture, a Snapshot', *Science First Hand* 42(N3): 78–103.

56. Polosmak, 'On the Path to Celestial Pastures'.

57. N. Polosmak, 2005, 'Purple and Gold over Thousands of Years', *Science First Hand* 4(N1): 32–55; Molodin and Polosmak, 'A Multidisciplinary Approach'; N. Polosmak, 2019, 'The Kashmir Diary', *Science First Hand* 51(1): 44–65.

58. Polosmak, 'Twenty Years After'; Polosmak, 'On the Path to Celestial Pastures'; T. Chikisheva, N. Polosmak and A. Zubova, 2015, 'The Burial at Ak-Alakh-3 Mound 1, Gorny Altai, New Findings', *Archaeology, Ethnology and Anthropology of Eurasia* 43(1): 144–54; A. Pilipenko, R. Trapezov and N. Polosmak, 2015, 'A Genetic Analysis of Human Remains from Ak-Alakh-3 Burial Mound 1, Gorny Altai', *Archaeology, Ethnology and Anthropology of Eurasia* 43(2): 138–45.

59. Polosmak, 'The Burial of a Noble Pazyryk Woman'.

60. Polosmak, 'A Mummy Unearthed'; Polosmak, 'The Burial of a Noble Pazyryk Woman'.

61. A. Letyagin, A. Savelov and N. Polosmak, 2014, 'High Field Magnetic Resonance Imaging of a Mummy from Ak-Alakh-3

Mound 1, Ukok Plateau, Gorny Altai: Findings and Interpretations', *Archaeology, Ethnology and Anthropology of Eurasia* 42(4): 83–91; Polosmak, 'On the Path to Celestial Pastures'; Molodin and Polosmak, 'A Multidisciplinary Approach'.

62. Polosmak, 'On the Path to Celestial Pastures'; Molodin and Polosmak, 'A Multidisciplinary Approach'.
63. V. Trunova and N. Polosmak, 2015, 'Secrets of Copper Hair', *Science First Hand* 42(N3): 22–3; Polosmak, 'A Different Archaeology'. Such hemp/copper inhalation has been shown to be a very common trait among the Pazyryk people: V. Trunova and N. Polosmak, 2006, 'Mortal Delight: SR Finds the Murderer', *Science First Hand* 7(N2): 38–49.
64. Chikisheva, Polosmak and Zubova, 'The Burial at Ak-Alakh-3 Mound 1'.
65. Polosmak, 'On the Path to Celestial Pastures'.
66. M. Eliade, 1964, *Shamanism: Archaic Techniques of Ecstasy*. London: Routledge.
67. Chikisheva, Polosmak and Zubova, 'The Burial at Ak-Alakh-3 Mound 1'.
68. Polosmak, 'A Different Archaeology'.
69. Polosmak, 'The Ukok Diary'.
70. Dr Natalia Polosmak, interview.
71. Ibid.
72. TASS Russian News Agency; Plets, Konstantinov, Soenov and Robinson, 'Repatriation, Doxa and Contested Heritages'.
73. Molodin and Polosmak, 'A Multidisciplinary Approach'.
74. https://www.gazprom.com/projects/power-of-siberia/.
75. J. Bourgeois, A. de Wulf, R. Goossens and W. Gheyle, 2007, 'Saving the Frozen Scythian Tombs of the Altai Mountains (Central Asia)', *World Archaeology* 39(3): 458–74.
76. Polosmak, interview.
77. Polosmak, 'A Mummy Unearthed'.
78. Polosmak, 'The Ukok Diary'.
79. Both Russia and the Altai have tried to claim the Lady as 'their' ancestor. Against the identification of the Lady by local communities as Ochi-Bala of Altai heroic epic, forensic studies by the Moscow police and the Russian Federal Security Bureau 'showed' that the Lady was 100 per cent Caucasian without Mongolian features, 'proving' there was no connection between this ancient Altai resident and the current inhabitants. Similarly, genetic studies concluded

that she had no relationship to the Altai's current inhabitants. These arguments based on facial features and genetics were dismissed by many in the Altai, who pointed out that, whatever her features or genetics, she had been found in the Altai and was part of Altai heritage. Cf. Plets, Konstantinov, Soenov and Robinson, 'Repatriation, Doxa and Contested Heritages'.

80. Polosmak, 'The Ukok Diary'.
81. Polosmak, 'The Kashmir Diary'; Polosmak, interview.

Chapter 8

1. My thanks to Professor Lord Colin Renfrew and Dr Michael Boyd for agreeing to give a lengthy interview over Zoom on the topic of Keros to me on 26 February 2021, which is referenced throughout this chapter.
2. C. Renfrew, O. Philaniotou, N. Brodie, G. Gavalas and M. Boyd (eds), 2018, *The Marble Finds from Kavos and the Archaeology of Ritual*, Vol. 3, Cambridge: McDonald Institute for Archaeological Research, 38.
3. *Inscriptiones Graecae* I 37.21 (425–0 BCE).
4. Colin Renfrew, interview, 26 February 2021.
5. Renfrew, interview; Colin Renfrew's Balzan Prize Acceptance Speech, 18 November 2004: https://www.balzan.org/en/prizewinners/colin-renfrew/rome-18-11-2004-renfrew.
6. Renfrew, interview.
7. C. Renfrew, O. Philaniotou, N. Brodie, G. Gavalas and M . Boyd (eds), 2013, *The Settlement at Dhaskalio: The Sanctuary on Keros and the Origins of Aegean Ritual Practice – the Excavations of 2006–8*, Vol. 1, Cambridge: McDonald Institute for Archaeological Research, 10–11.
8. C. Renfrew, O. Philaniotou, N. Brodie, G. Gavalas and M. Boyd (eds), 2015, *Kavos and the Special Deposits: The Sanctuary on Keros and the Origins of Aegean Ritual Practice – the Excavations of 2006–8*, Vol. 2, Cambridge: McDonald Institute for Archaeological Research, 402.
9. Ano Kouphonisi has a sister island, Kato Kouphonisi, which is uninhabited. Together the two islands are often collectively known as Kouphonisia.
10. ERT documentary broadcast, 20 July 2020, *The Enigma of Keros*: https://www.youtube.com/watch?v=ZdQpvPnnFqo. For further

discussion about what local inhabitants may have known: G. Papamichelakis and C. Renfrew, 2010, 'Hearsay about the "Keros Hoard"', *American Journal of Archaeology* 114: 181–5.

11. Renfrew, interview.

12. Ibid.

13. Renfrew, Philaniotou, Brodie, Gavalas and Boyd (eds), *The Settlement at Dhaskalio*, 13.

14. Ibid., 188.

15. Renfrew, interview.

16. ERT documentary, *The Enigma of Keros*. It was only discovered years later that Doumas had actually ended up visiting just before Renfrew that summer of 1963, on 13 June, having been able to secure a lift direct to Keros on the Goulandris's private yacht: Renfrew, Philaniotou, Brodie, Gavalas and Boyd (eds), *The Settlement at Dhaskalio*, 79.

17. C. Renfrew, C. Doumas, L. Marangou and G. Gavalas (eds), 2007, *Keros, Dhaskalio Kavos: The Investigations of 1987–88*, Cambridge: McDonald Institute for Archaeological Research, 20; Renfrew, Philaniotou, Brodie, Gavalas and Boyd (eds), *The Settlement at Dhaskalio*, 188.

18. Renfrew, Doumas, Marangou and Gavalas (eds), *Keros, Dhaskalio Kavos*, 29.

19. Ibid., 32–6, 116.

20. Ibid., 5.

21. This is the same post that was offered to Dr Gertrude Caton Thompson (mentor of Mary Leakey) in 1938, who turned it down; it was subsequently offered to Dr Dorothy Garrod in 1939, who became the first female holder of a Chair (the most illustrious professorial position) in the history of Oxford and Cambridge.

22. Renfrew, interview.

23. ERT documentary, *The Enigma of Keros*.

24. Renfrew, Doumas, Marangou and Gavalas (eds), *Keros, Dhaskalio Kavos*, 6.

25. Ibid., 116, 178.

26. Ibid., 36.

27. Ibid., 61, 73, 159–60, 185; C. Broodbank, 2000, *An Island Archaeology of the Early Cyclades*, Cambridge: Cambridge University Press, 267–72.

28. Renfrew, Doumas, Marangou and Gavalas (eds), *Keros, Dhaskalio*

Kavos, 284, 287, 297, 413; C. Renfrew, 1991, *The Cycladic Spirit: Masterpieces from the Nicholas P. Goulandris Collection*, New York: Harry Abrams, 59, 99–101.

29. Renfrew, interview.
30. Ibid.
31. Renfrew, Doumas, Marangou and Gavalas (eds), *Keros, Dhaskalio Kavos*, 73.
32. Renfrew, Philaniotou, Brodie, Gavalas and Boyd (eds), *Kavos and the Special Deposits*, 9.
33. Colin Renfrew and Michael Boyd, interview.
34. Renfrew, Philaniotou, Brodie, Gavalas and Boyd (eds), *The Settlement at Dhaskalio*, 1, 15.
35. Renfrew, interview.
36. Renfrew, Philaniotou, Brodie, Gavalas and Boyd (eds), *Kavos and the Special Deposits*, 9, 382.
37. Ibid., 353. It is 'the largest assemblage of Early Cycladic sculpture and vessels ever recovered in a controlled excavation': Renfrew, Philaniotou, Brodie, Gavalas and Boyd (eds), *The Marble Finds from Kavos*, xxi.
38. Renfrew, Philaniotou, Brodie, Gavalas and Boyd (eds), *Kavos and the Special Deposits*, 3, 209.
39. Ibid., 382–3.
40. Ibid., 209.
41. Michael Boyd, interview.
42. Renfrew, Philaniotou, Brodie, Gavalas and Boyd (eds), *The Settlement at Dhaskalio*, 309, 323, 377.
43. C. Renfrew, M. Boyd and C. Bronk Ramsey, 2012, 'The Oldest Maritime Sanctuary? Dating the Sanctuary at Keros and the Cycladic Early Bronze Age', *Antiquity* 86: 144–60.
44. Ibid.; C. Renfrew, 2013, 'The Sanctuary at Keros: Questions of Materiality and Monumentality', *Journal of the British Academy* 1: 187–212; Renfrew, Philaniotou, Brodie, Gavalas and Boyd (eds), *Kavos and the Special Deposits*, 555.
45. Renfrew, Philaniotou, Brodie, Gavalas and Boyd (eds), *The Settlement at Dhaskalio*, 51–3.
46. Renfrew, Philaniotou, Brodie, Gavalas and Boyd (eds), *Kavos and the Special Deposits*, 385.
47. Renfrew, 'The Sanctuary at Keros'; Renfrew, Philaniotou, Brodie, Gavalas and Boyd (eds), *Kavos and the Special Deposits*, 555–60.

48. Renfrew, 'The Sanctuary at Keros'; Renfrew, Philaniotou, Brodie, Gavalas and Boyd (eds), *Kavos and the Special Deposits*, 389; ERT documentary, *The Enigma of Keros*.
49. Ibid.
50. Renfrew, Philaniotou, Brodie, Gavalas and Boyd (eds), *The Settlement at Dhaskalio*, 720; Renfrew, Philaniotou, Brodie, Gavalas and Boyd (eds), *Kavos and the Special Deposits*, 388.
51. Renfrew, 'The Sanctuary at Keros'; Renfrew, Philaniotou, Brodie, Gavalas and Boyd (eds), *Kavos and the Special Deposits*, 560.
52. Renfrew, Philaniotou, Brodie, Gavalas and Boyd (eds), *The Marble Finds from Kavos*, 19.
53. Renfrew, 'The Sanctuary at Keros'; ERT documentary, *The Enigma of Keros*.
54. Ibid.; Renfrew, Philaniotou, Brodie, Gavalas and Boyd (eds), *Kavos and the Special Deposits*, 387.
55. ERT documentary, *The Enigma of Keros*.
56. Renfrew and Boyd, interview.
57. Ibid.
58. Ibid.
59. Renfrew, Philaniotou, Brodie, Gavalas and Boyd (eds), *The Marble Finds from Kavos*, 435.
60. Ibid.
61. Ibid.
62. The organic remains on Dhaskalio suggest this could not have been a place of permanent occupation for a large population: Renfrew, Philaniotou, Brodie, Gavalas, Boyd (eds), *The Settlement at Dhaskalio*, 709; Renfrew, Philaniotou, Brodie, Gavalas and Boyd (eds), *The Marble Finds from Kavos*, 442.
63. Renfrew and Boyd, interview; ERT documentary, *The Enigma of Keros*.
64. Renfrew and Boyd, interview.
65. Renfrew, Philaniotou, Brodie, Gavalas and Boyd (eds), *The Marble Finds from Kavos*, 540.
66. Renfrew, Philaniotou, Brodie, Gavalas and Boyd (eds), *The Settlement at Dhaskalio*, 713; Renfrew, Philaniotou, Brodie, Gavalas and Boyd (eds), *The Marble Finds from Kavos*, 40, 533.
67. Ibid., 711.
68. Renfrew, Philaniotou, Brodie, Gavalas and Boyd (eds), *Kavos and the Special Deposits*, 510, 516, 549–60.
69. ERT documentary, *The Enigma of Keros*; https://www.arch.cam.

ac.uk/research/projects/current-projects/keros-project/2015-2018-keros-naxos-seaways (accessed 19 March 2021).

70. Found in Trench H on Dhaskalio: ERT documentary, *The Enigma of Keros*.

71. Renfrew, Philaniotou, Brodie, Gavalas, Boyd (eds), *The Settlement at Dhaskalio*, 706, 715.

72. Ibid., 713; Renfrew, Philaniotou, Brodie, Gavalas and Boyd (eds), *The Marble Finds from Kavos*, 539.

73. Renfrew, Philaniotou, Brodie, Gavalas and Boyd (eds), *The Settlement at Dhaskalio*, 323.

74. Renfrew, Philaniotou, Brodie, Gavalas and Boyd (eds), *The Marble Finds from Kavos*, 556.

75. ERT documentary, *The Enigma of Keros*.

76. Renfrew and Boyd, interview.

77. Ibid.

78. ERT documentary, *The Enigma of Keros*.

79. Renfrew and Boyd, interview.

80. Ibid.

81. Renfrew, Philaniotou, Brodie, Gavalas and Boyd (eds), *The Marble Finds from Kavos*, 557.

Picture Acknowledgements

Terracotta Army, view of Pit 1, 2015. Wikipedia Creative Commons 3.0 License / Jmhullot.

Cleaning of amphora INA slide KW7309 Ref 632 © Institute of Nautical Archaeology.

On Shore Excavation Camp, INA Ref 643 © Institute of Nautical Archaeology.

Uluburun replica shipwreck, Kas, Lykia, Turkey, 2010. Alamy 2J2BGEF © Helmut Corneli / Alamy Stock Photo.

Photograph of the kurgan of the Altai Princess, from N. Polosmak, 2014, 'Twenty Years After', SCIENCE First Hand (N1)37. 6-23. Photographer: Georg Gerster.

Photograph of Natalia Polosmak, from N. Polosmak, 2014, 'Twenty Years After', SCIENCE First Hand (N1)37. 6-23. Photographer unknown.

Princess Ukok/Princess of the Altai. Alamy 2BJM12C © agefotostock / Alamy Stock Photo.

A collection of the many purposefully broken Cycladic figurines found in excavations on Keros. Permission given by Michael Boyd. The rights to the monuments depicted belong to the Ministry of Culture and Sports (Law 4858/2021). The archaeological sites of Keros and Dhaskalio are under the jurisdiction of the Ephorate of Antiquities of Cyclades. Hellenic Ministry of Culture and Sports/ Cultural Resources Management and Development Agency.

Image taken at Trench F, looking east towards Kavos. A team of archaeologists at the archaeological site on the islet of Dhaskalio during the filming of the documentary *Keros: The Mystery of the Broken Figurines*, a National Geographic and Cosmote TV co-production. The rights to the monuments depicted belong to the Ministry of Culture and Sports (Law 4858/2021). The archaeological sites of Keros and Dhaskalio are under the jurisdiction of the Ephorate of Antiquities of Cyclades. Hellenic Ministry of Culture and Sports/ Cultural Resources Management and Development Agency.

Index

Index